I0168114

The Good The Bad

&

The Truth

The Good The Bad

& The Truth

Copyright © Niven Dallas 2011 V5

All Rights Reserved

No part of this publication may be reproduced, stored in a retrieval system, or transmitted in any form by any means. Including (electronic, mechanical, photocopying, recording or otherwise,) without the prior written permission of the publisher. Nor be otherwise circulated in any form of electronic storage, binding, or cover other than that in which it is published and without a similar condition, including this condition being imposed on the subsequent purchaser.

Cover design and artwork by Niven Dallas

The front cover photo shows the authors 1960 Ford Zephyr at the Northern Territory/West Australian State boarder in the big wet of early February 1969. Back cover photo by Shutterstock.

Amazon Create Space Edition 28th January 2015

Author website: http://www.nivendallas.com

Paperback ISBN: 978-0-9875833-1-4

E-book ISBN: 978-0-9875833-0-7

The Good The Bad

&

The Truth

By Niven Dallas
Book two in the four book series
Dallas short stories

Authors Note

This collection of short stories, are but a few reproduced from true events in the author's life. Be aware, the stories are not in any exact chronological order of events. However, I have attempted to set them in a sort of order, only to be reminded of an earlier tale too good to leave out of this book.

These tales are carefully reproduced for readers, who appreciate interesting stories, at interesting times in outback Australia. Stories told from a new Australian's point of view in a new country, with a dash of humour.

The author has written these stories as close as can be remembered, drawing on the memories of those involved. Some of the characters names and the exact period regretfully changed at the request of the persons involved. To avoid, well who would know what.

Nevertheless, these were great times. Providing a number of great stories, created by many memorable people and friends. Thank you all for allowing me to share these stories.

Table of Contents

Other Titles by Niven Dallas

DALLAS SHORT STORY COLLECTIONS

REALISTIC FICTION NOVELS

Prologue

What makes a good Aboriginal tracker, or should it be said who; then again, "Are all black trackers black?" These critical questions are truthfully answered in a very amusing story that explains everything you would ever want to know about Aboriginal bush trackers. More importantly, this story explains how a real black tracker works; in addition, how these people are eventually chosen for this important job.

**

Sad but true, I have discovered that refined warnings or good advice is useless on dumb people, and not much in the way of constructive help with smart people. I must admit, at times I could have been one of those dumb people, read these stories, I will let you be the judge.

**

I will start this collection of true stories with a story about Royalty, "The Royal Picnic." It is a sad fact that Royal events are rare in the Australia, and rarer still for a young businessman in the new outback town of Kununurra. Then again, I did have something the powerful bureaucratic minds of this small West Australian government town wanted, and it was not me.

**

This was a beautiful boat; I did not hesitate for a second the day an opportunity presented to buy the Vendal III. She cost us all of our savings, most of the business overdraft and almost our marriage… Then again, she did save my sanity, and the boat name… have I spelt it wrong. Nope, it is just the middle of my name... niVENDALlas…

I will recall a boating experience that will always remain imbedded in my mind. This memorable event beginning with a simple, innocent phone call. Then in less than a week this small boating favour, almost developed into a frightening incident of the greatest political and international proportions for Australia.

***

The phone was ringing; however, I was daydreaming of what I must do first. Open the mail laying on my desk thereby ruining this day reading my overdue bills, or answer the phone.

Part One: They want my boat

Chapter One:

The Top Secret Royal Visit

My decision that morning was easy; I would answer this annoying phone.

It was just after seven in the morning, I was on my third black coffee, being one hour into a new tropical working day, when that phone rang. The noise intruding on my valued few minutes of solitude and peace.

Robyn the ever-tactful nineteen-year-old office girl, hire-car hostess had just arrived, eagerly grabbing the phone first and then yelling through the half-closed office door.

'Boss it's for you, some bloke called Colin Tremby, are you in or bloody out?'

Now Colin is a very important man in Kununurra, in fact he is the boss of the PWD (Public Works Department) and not a man to keep waiting on the phone. Thinking this call may be about some new government work… then again, maybe not as he could have simply instructed one of his supervisors to call.

Thinking then again, who knows, it could be another shattering service complaint, like the other day when a PWD vehicle lost its front-wheel in the middle of the town. The vehicle had only just left our workshops after having completed a first service. Well I guess there is only one-way to find out.

'You can put Colin through Robyn.' thinking it better to get in first.

'Hi Colin, about that Suzuki wheel problem the other day, I am very sorry about that, you see my new mechanic couldn't find the split-pin box to lock the big Jesus nut that holds the wheel on and...

I was abruptly interrupted by Colin's smooth, faultless interjection.

'Good morning Niven, this call is not about that particular stupid and unprofessional catastrophe. However, I am happy to note that you are fully aware of the disgraceful incident.'

I sensed we were not starting off well, still cringing at his deep stab at our poor work quality and service performance, wondered what will be text. 'Niven, I have called to ask if you would consider doing me a small personal favour.'

Personal favour, was this correct, did Colin say personal favour. I was shortly caught off guard, and at the same time extremely suspicious at this proposed request. Why would Colin Tremby, being one of the righteous tin gods of this town want a favour from Niven Dallas... considered as a lowlife of this town? After all, we were not on his tight list of socialising brown-nosed power climbers.

Colin would not even return a polite acknowledgement nod of hello in the local pub. We were well down in the pecking order of his casual acquaintances. You see, this was Kununurra, and very much a Government run and managed town.

***

The Town of Kununurra was originally created to provide the dual-purpose of a service infrastructure centre for the Ord River Irrigation Scheme, and as the most northerly West Australian Government administration centre. This new town was a Town Planning special design concept, built with all new ideas from the ground up, (so the government town planning architects say.) Kununurra is I believe, still the only purpose-built "Government town" created in Australia in the last fifty years.

Having said this, you can now imagine the large number of Government employees living, and working in this town. Kununurra at that time was a sort of satellite West Australian Government administration home for the remote North-West.

The new town of Kununurra, positioned as the last northern town still within Western Australia, being only forty-two kilometres from the Northern Territory state border. This town is the home to not only the PWD, but the MRD (Main Roads Department), and the Agriculture Department. Kununurra was also the regional home to the Crown Law Department, Department of Land and Surveys, Office of the North-West, State Housing, Regional Hospital Service, the Post Office, and many others.

These government people socialised in very tight groups, especially if they held a management position of some sort, which could be anything above that of a lowly supervisor. After all this was 1976, in the reign of Sir Charles Court the affirmative ruling Premier of Western Australia, the very father of the Ord River Irrigation Scheme. Sir Charles was a man with remarkable vision, a man who against huge opposition had built the Kununurra diversion dam across the Ord River.

This special dam was the first bold step in taming the mighty Ord. Built with the planned purpose for providing an irrigation canal system, to irrigate the vast surrounding rich fertile lands.

At that time, the strategy and plan being to create the founding of a new cotton growing industry in North Western Australia. An industry that was unfortunately doomed from the start through lack of basic research, and a large quantity of arrogant government ignorance.

***

Sir Charles went on to build another dam up-stream. This time the huge, but simple earth and rock-filled Argyle dam creating one of the world's largest man-made freshwater lakes. This Lake Argyle is huge, covering an area of some 980 square kilometres.

The next significant group within the town was obviously the farming community. Many of whom came from all parts of the world. There were a number of farmers from America,

3

Mexico, Germany, from South Africa and Rhodesia, from Canada, and even a few Australians.

These cotton farmers were all very experienced no nonsense type of people, who had little time for the local Australian Government social snobbery. They, the farmers were after all the very reason for the establishment of this new Kimberley town, and apparently, the required large contingent of short-term itinerant Government personnel stationed in this new town.

Another point worth mentioning here was that these new farmers did have a lot of money, well… they did when they first started out farming on the Ord. Alas the government land contract demanded that the only crop to be developed, and grown on the Ord, would be cotton. Unfortunately, many good Ord farmers went bankrupt trying hard to comply with their limited and strict government land contract.

These once cashed-up pioneer cotton farmers were ultimately forced to rely on the poor and unreliable Australian Government area-research data.

After a long Government enforced seven years of bad luck, a penalty suffered by the Ord cotton farming industry, the Government finally acknowledged they were wrong.

This government back-down decision was not given lightly, but drawn out over many years of painful effort by the farmers. Ultimately, the farmers proved that KRS, (Kimberley Research Station) after some sixty-seven years of Ord area research, was a total and useless waste of taxpayer's money. In addition, this now included the unfortunate, early cotton farmer's development money.

We soon found out that these modern farming pioneers most certainly did know how to farm successfully, and before long, found it was not by growing cotton.

***

The Government employed personnel were encouraged to socialise and get to know the farmers. However, the farmers were not so responsive, and had their own social group of Kununurra like-minded and, well… permanent friends.

The third group, or "caste" of Kununurra dwellers were the small business service providers. Retailers, fuel suppliers, and farm machinery service and so on. This was our lowly group or caste. Then of course, there was the lowest caste of all, the seasonal itinerate farm workers, nowadays we would call them backpackers.

***

All my thoughts had gone astray as I came back to reality and gingerly enquired.

'Favour eh, can I ask you what this is all about Colin?'

There was a pause as Colin took a deep breath and guessed he had a lot to say. Well at least it was going to be about something other than cutting off any further vehicle servicing, and not about the wayward Suzuki wheel disaster… so far so good.

'Niven I assume you have read the newspapers, and are aware the West Australian Government is currently hosting His Highness the Crown Prince of Thailand for a short stay. The Prince is at this time training with our armed forces in Western Australia.

The Prince has just completed an SAS military-field course in the Broome area. He now wishes to make an unscheduled private visit to the Ord River Scheme on his way back to Thailand via Darwin. Are you following me on this matter so far?'

***

Typical of government bureaucrats, Colin thinks us low castes are also dumb, but he did raise a point. Since there was no local radio station, only long wave ABC radio and no TV, also the newspapers were always around three days old. I might not have known what was going on out there in the big world beyond the Kimberley.

As luck would have it, Trevor Tough who owned the menswear shop in town was also an enthusiastic soldier in the AAR (Australian Army Reserve). Trevor had just returned from AAR duty in Broome and told me all about his latest army mission, which included playing soldiers with the Crown Prince of Thailand.

'Yeah I'm with you so far. I do know that the Crown Prince of Thailand is now in Broome playing soldiers with our army reserves. So what's up then, do you want me to leave town for a few days to reduce any possible embarrassment to the local Kununurra Government and senior public servants?'

(Government people do not like, and utterly detest the title Public Servants.)

There was a short pause and a snort of distaste, replying with a smug...

'No, that will not be necessary this time Niven. I am in fact calling you on behalf of the newly appointed Regional Administrator of the North-West Roger Gayton.'

I had heard about this bloke on the town mumble-vine. This bloke was another expensive well-paid, titled, fat bureaucrat, now stationed up here to host tea parties for the visiting senior government departmental heads.

These visitors were deserving government people that find it necessary to flee the cold months down in Perth. A sort of paid holiday and a reward for the all complying brown-nose public servants.

Colin continued...

'The new Administrator, who has only been in Kununurra for a few weeks, has been given an important task by Sir Charles Court to show the Crown Prince around the Ord. By the way, this royal visit is not public knowledge; as such, this conversation must remain secret.

The Prince will only have one night and one day in Kununurra, and has expressed a desire to see the Ord River. Roger Gayton suggested we should take the Prince for a short cruise up the Ord River Diversion Dam.

Since you have the biggest and nicest boat around, I have been asked to give you a call to see if you would let us use your boat for the Crown Prince visit.'

This was an unusual turn of events. The Kununurra Government officials want to borrow my pride-and-joy the Vendal III. They want my beautiful Penguin twenty-four foot, three and a half ton cabin cruiser, to take a Prince on a bloody joy ride up the Ord River Dam... without me... Hang on; I had to confirm if this was indeed the case, maybe I am deaf as well as dumb.

'Colin, just who did you have in mind to drive my, expensive family boat on this very auspicious and special Royal occasion?'

Colin was quick with an answer.

'Well we only have one choice; we are going to ask Gregory McQuie (the white knight.) Gregory knows this area well, and its history from conception. Greg is also well spoken, and does look superb in his navel whites.'

I was now starting to fume at the idea... the bloody cheek of this government bloke. Thinking, they should use Greg's boat. After all, the boat is a massive seventy-foot long tourist catamaran with plenty of space for all the government officials. It also has two full size toilets on-board for all the government crap.

'Sorry to say Colin, but the answer is no. You should be using Greg's large tourist boat.'

There was a long hanging moment of silence at the other end of the phone. Immediately sensing that a rejection was entirely unexpected. This requested boat-borrowing favour, and my quick rejection, was not going down well at all.

Admittedly, I almost agreed since my future business life in Kununurra without any government work would have been very grim indeed, Colin would know this. He would also know that I am a stubborn person, with firm principles on things, especially where my boat was concerned.

With this unexpected rejection in mind, Colin like a true bureaucrat tried again, but this time from another angle.

'Greg's boat is much too big and far too slow for this trip. The Prince only has one day to see the Ord. He will arrive the previous day on the midday jet, and much of that time already accounted for in attending civic functions.

This courtesy to the Crown Prince would go down well for you and the town of Kununurra. We are willing to pay for all the fuel, food, and drinks.'

I thought about this for a microsecond, noting that no mention of payment for service being offered. Was he expecting the use of my boat without cost... free? I then announced in a steady firm voice.

'I'm sorry Colin, the answer is still no.'

Again, a period of silence, this time Colin attempted to cover the phone with his hand, but I clearly heard his frustrated comment.

'The little shithead bastard has knocked us back, what will we do now. The bloody Prince has been told by that new bloody idiot of an Administrator he's going on a fast luxury boat-trip up the Ord River?' There was a gentle rustling then Colin came smoothly back.

'Niven, I would suggest you may wish to reconsider this matter. If I were you, it might pay to think this situation over before you reject it. In the meantime, I will get the new Administrator Mr Gayton to talk to you directly. You can expect his phone call shortly to sort things out.'

This was the typical government solution to any bad news, pass the problem on to someone else, and keep your hands clean. Then again, in my suspicious mind that last comment sounded much like a veiled threat.

***

I quietly hung up the phone thinking what bad things will happen next. Just then, the lovely Robyn burst into my office. She was fuming and had obviously been listening to my conversation, quite the normal thing in our small business office.

'Well boss, that all went down like a lead balloon, from now on you can kiss fucking goodbye to any future work from the government. I mean you would take anybody else up the river on a whim to get out of the office and on the piss for the day... for nothing. What's so different this time and they're paying for everything?'

Robyn was of course perfectly correct, she knew me well. However, this was all about the government tin gods jockeying and improving their own governmental image and social standing. There would be no glory in lending my boat for this trip: for me, or my business.

***

The next day I was very surprised by a visit from the local Police, none other than the most senior officer, Police Sergeant Tom Corker. He was waiting in the outer office when Robyn whispered into the phone...

'What the hell have you done this time boss; the Police Sergeant is here in person to see you. They normally just send over a regular cop to tell you off. It must be something pretty bad... and he won't say what it's all about?'

Robyn had a point; this must indeed be a serious matter...

'I really don't know what it's about Robyn, and I don't recollect doing anything wrong lately so I'm as much in the dark as you are. Just send in the Sergeant, and listen at the door as usual.'

The door opened and in stepped Sergeant Corker, a big man with a big but serious smile. He removed his hat, which was always a good sign; thinking this may not be as bad as I had first thought. I gestured for Tom to sit down opposite my desk, and he obliged... another good sign but before doing so he said in his very broad English accent,

'Do ya mind if I close the office door Niven. What I ave ta say is highly classified information, for your ears only, if you know what I mean.'

I thought closing the office door is going to really piss Robyn off "highly classified information," she would have heard that comment from Tom.

The adjoining office door was covered both sides in a thick padded vinyl material, brass-tack studied to give a sort of boy's club effect and was, well... quite soundproof.

The padded effect followed through to the front of the built-in, fully stocked bar in one corner of the office, complete with mirror backing and glass shelving. I liked my office it was my sanctuary, my business control centre.

Both of the upstairs offices; being the outer reception office, and my office were directly over the top of the existing electronics service workshop. This formed a sort of mezzanine office, which overlooked the main mechanical service workshop area. Apart from the low hum of the air-conditioning, all was quiet in a cocooned silence. This was a well-insulated and peaceful place.to preserve all sanity... and enjoy a nice drink with friends.

Next to the office-entry door was the gun-rack. Firmly mounted to the wall displaying a nice collection of four high-powered guns.

In the wall behind my desk was another identical padded door leading to... well nowhere. This other door had been included in the original building design for future extensions to adding some toilets.

The only thing was I had ran out of building money, so this part of the office development never happened. As such, the door led to a four-metre drop into the open, dirt backyard.

On more than a number of occasions, while being distracted, my visiting office guests, having overindulged in the delights of the well-stocked office bar. Then looking for the toilets, had unwittingly exited via this door. Hence, the local rumours of a visit to the Niven Dallas office can be an unforgetful experience.

This was Sergeant Tom's first exposure to my rather special office or should I say the Dallas den. He was slowly turning his head, scanning his eyes over this spectacle taking in every detail as only any good copper would.

Tom then leaned closer; closed one eye and raised one bushy eyebrow, then spoke in his broad cockney accent.

'I bet you 'av' some right old doos in 'er. This place reminds me orf the padded cells in the Perth central lock-up, cep't they don't av a wet bar, an a bloody goon rack.'

Tom chuckled at his own little joke while he continued to checkout my office with his roving eyes.

***

Sergeant Tom Corker was a well-liked copper in the Town; he was very much old school, a sort of Dixon of Dock Green type British bobby style with a very dry sense of humour. I would bet he was over sixty, over six feet tall and a bit on the heavy side by about twenty kilos. He had an English ruddy face and sharp inquisitive eyes that missed nothing.

Tom was busy reading upside down, my stack of mail, placed in front of me, when I then decided to make my opening move.

'Well, what's all this secret stuff about then Tom; do you want me for some dangerous undercover Police work or something?'

Tom stopped reading my mail, leant further forward, looked me in the eye, and speaking in a hushed voice...

'I'm serious about the secret bit Niven, I 'av' been told by my superiors ta get your assurance that anything I discuss with you will remain in confidence, within these 'ear, four... walls.' Tom looked around the timber and padded walls, 'so w'at ya say?'

Tom's eyes slowly scanned the office walls yet again. I thought to myself all this silly secrecy stuff, this surely couldn't be about the Crown Prince of Thailand's visit here, well I guess there's only one way to find out...

'Tom, this is not about the Crown Prince of Thailand's one day visit to the Ord River is it?'

Both of the Sergeant's bushy eyebrows shot up in surprise. He looked behind him as if someone might be near enough to hear then leaned forward again. I followed his lead. We were almost nose-to-nose when the Sergeant stated his concern in a low guarded voice.

'Now how in the 'ell did you just know all about that me lad. The Crown Prince's visit 'ear, and 'is movements aren't advertised cos there worried some nutter might try ta bump 'em orff?'

Still in our protracted position, I replied in a slow but steady voice.

'Because a mister Colin Tremby called me yesterday and asked me if he could borrow my bloody boat to take the Prince for a spin up the Ord River.

And another thing Tom, I was also told all about the Royal visit by Trevor Tough who is an officer in the Australian Army Reserve, and just back from playing war games with the Crown Prince in Broome.'

Tom flopped back into the chair, threw his arms in the air with a look of utter amazement on his face, and replied with a sigh of defeat in his voice.

'Well it's all bloody well out there then ain't it, every bastard knows all about the Crown Prince o' Thailand coming ta Kununurra. We'll have all the media and every bleeding nutcase from miles around turn up ta 'av' a go at the Prince... so much for keeping 'is bleeding visit a secret.'

Tom was visibly upset; he was after all a true professional cop. This was not the correct way to handle such important things about the security of a visiting member of Royalty.

It was now obvious that as the most senior ranking Police officer in this area. Sergeant Tom Corker would have had a very large part to play in ensuring the safety of the Crown Prince while on his patch.

Then a thought hit me, why in hell was the Sergeant here, talking to me about the Crown Prince?

'Tom, where do I fit into all this Royal secrecy stuff?'

Tom was still visibly upset, with hunched shoulders shaking his head in disbelief, then in a look of professional disgust continued.

'Well I've been sent 'ear by the new Administrator o' the North-West Roger Gayton ta ask if ya would provide yer boat and yer time to run the Crown Prince up the river next Thursday. If ya say it's okay he wants a meeting pronto in his office.'

By the sound of things, Tom obviously did not know the new Administrator had already asked Colin Tremby to try to negotiate the very same boat deal. It now appeared that Tom was being somewhat manipulated into getting me to provide my boat, and that I was now being compromised by the use of the local law enforcement.

The Sergeant, being a well-liked and respected no nonsense copper, this was not Tom's style; but whose style was it?

I had never met the new Administrator of the North-West but he sounded like a very interesting person, by all accounts a true and well-practised manipulative bureaucrat.

I then explained to Tom that I was expecting a call from the new Administrator on this very same matter, as advised by the boss of the Public Works Department Colin Tremby.

Tom's eyes narrowed at the realisation that he was being used; used in his position as the top cop in Kununurra to pressure a small businessperson into providing his boat for a Government purpose. I could tell by the grim look on Tom's face that he did not like being the tool of manipulation. I thought I might try to de-fuse the issue a little.

'Serge you have to understand, I don't really object to the Prince using my boat for a spin up the Ord River. But it would have to be on my terms with me as the captain, and not the bloody "White Knight," Greg McQuie as the captain.'

Tom levered himself out of the chair to his full height, then placed his hat firmly on his head adjusting the peak-angle for a maximum Police effect… adding with a smile.

'Well then, that's all sorted, we can all meet up with the Administrator Roger tomorrow and go over the details of this 'ear Royal voyage.' Chuckling at his own joke again adding, 'we best have the meeting in 'is office Niven, this one might give him the idea he was short changed with his new bleeding Kununurra Government office.'

***

Robyn pounced on me two seconds after Sergeant Tom had left the office; the door had only just closed behind him.

'What's going on, why is the Police Sergeant coming here, they normally ring up, and you go running into the police station to sort out any of your bigger stuff up cop problems?'

'Sorry Robyn I can't say as I've been sworn to secrecy. Bound by the official secrecy act and all that stuff, given my word as a gentleman...' Sweet little Robyn interrupted my full swing explanation story.

'Official secrets act my arse. I bet it's all about the Crown Prince of Thailand coming here next week. Colin Tremby couldn't get your boat for the Prince's fishing trip up the Ord, so they sent in the law to lean on you a bit... and my bet is that you bloody-well caved in.'

If only Robyn knew how correct she was. However, now sworn to secrecy on this Royal matter, I must adopt a very bureaucratic reply to Robyn's direct and nosy questions.

'Robyn I am sorry, I am not at liberty to discuss these matters with anyone, and I'm not in a position to either confirm or deny your theory on any royal visits. You will just have to listen at keyholes as usual for your information. Haven't you got something more important to do like polishing your nails or something?'

Swooning out of the office with my nose in the air, I faintly heard the word "Asshole" as I closed the door behind me.

***

The meeting with the Administrator of the North-West was scheduled for an early start, ten thirty sharp in the morning as advised by Robyn (my hire car hostess, sort of secretary,) and later confirmed again by Sergeant Tom.

This time of ten thirty, being considered a very sensible hour for a high-ranking city government official, a time almost halfway through my normal working day.

I arrived at my usual time of ten minutes late, nevertheless Sergeant Tom was already there waiting in the Administrators waiting room. Tom nodded but said nothing. I looked around and then sat down on the nice new cheap plastic chair.

My eyes scanned the waiting room. I noticed they had completely changed the place since I was last in this building. They had obviously spent a lot of tax money on the place.

Tom was engrossed in reading an important looking manila file. He did not look very happy at all, but he did look immaculate in his freshly pressed tropical khaki Police uniform. A quick glance, his large black police issue shoes, amazed me. They both radiated a shine to a level I never thought possible. He still had on his police hat so I assumed this was indeed going to be a very important meeting.

In contrast, I looked down at my attire. I was wearing the standard Kimberley businessperson's suit, a well-worn and washed King-Gee khaki workers short-sleeved shirt, with a matching pair of short pants. This casual tropical style was set off with thick white bobby socks and scuffed dirty brown hushpuppies.

I was starting to feel a little underdressed for the occasion when suddenly a door opened and a thin matron looking woman in her late sixties appeared, displaying a thin worn smile. She was wearing a pair of reading glasses perched on the end of her button nose; she paused, and then clasping her hands as if in prayer...

'Gentlemen,' she announced in a crisp clear voice, 'I am terribly sorry for this unfortunate delay however the Administrator will be free shortly.'

The woman then scurried back out through the door. Tom was not amused; he stood up then slapped the manila file on his thigh and started pacing the room. I could sense the anger, he paused, and then Tom then let loose in his broad British accent.

'I've been 'ear' ha'rf an hour now; I got a bloody Police station ta run. These bleeding government blokes must be on a nu'ver planet or sumfink.'

I was thinking, Tom was also a government bloke, when just then, the door to the Administrators office opened and I cast my first look upon the new Administrator for the North-West.

He was a splendid example of a well-fed middle-aged man, with a pleasant, but well-practised government smile, looking for all the world as if he were passing wind. Roger the Administrator was about six foot two in the old scale, maybe sixty with a wobbling double chin, visibly overweight with an un-mistakable air of self-importance. He sported a well-developed potbelly and judging by his pale complexion, he was very much an in-door man.

The Administrator was dressed in a well-used, full city-style business suit. With a crisp white business shirt and bright yellow tie, set off with nice gold cufflinks. The long black pants ended at highly polished black shoes that rivalled the Sergeants for shine. Even with the excellent air-conditioning, the Administrator was still having problems holding back the sweat gathering on his beading brow and chins, then with a practiced artificial bow.

'Sorry about the short wait gentlemen, please do come in.' waving us both through the door of his office with another slight dignified bow.

At the door, the Administrator briefly stopped me and turned expertly to rush through the new-bloke greeting formality. We shook hands in the usual civil manner.

To me Rogers's handshake was limp and quick, being soft like a little girl. He made no eye contact in a sort of (get it over and done with) attitude. On the other hand, he greeted Sergeant

Tom like a long lost friend with a clasped handshake and eye contact. Tom and I then followed Roger into his new office.

Glancing around I thought to myself, hell they must have the same bloke set-up all the government offices since they all looked just the same.

This office was quite large, with the entire back wall fitted-out with cheap wood-laminated cupboards and bookshelves. Every inch was loaded with old books and files that were only there for show and never read.

In the centre of the room was a standard issue government timber laminated cheap desk with a government blotter and three pens placed neatly above.

A picture of Sir Charles Court sternly beamed down from one wall, and a picture of the Queen stared grimly back across at Sir Charles from the opposite wall. No drinks bar or gun racks to be seen in this sterilised and unfriendly office.

Sitting in one of the four large leather chairs placed opposite the standard cheap government desk was a slight built man of Asian origin. He was wearing a neat looking well-cut safari suit. I immediately thought I must ask him where I might buy one... but then I thought, not now. Roger performed the introduction, as I was the closest...

'Mr Dallas, this is Mr Chati Neeroopatonasa aide to His Royal Highness the Crown Prince of Thailand, I present Mr Niven Dallas, local town business proprietor.'

Well I must say my title sounded good to me... The man extended his arm while still sitting in his chair offering a limp wet-fish handshake only marginally better than that of the Administrators. Then looking me in the eye he spoke in impeccable Queen's English, quietly advising me.

'My name is Chati Niratpattanasai,' then turning to stare vehemently at Roger the Administrator. 'It would seem Australian officials are not able to get their tongue around the simple pronunciation of my name,' then looking directly at me again. 'I will however make the small effort to remember your name Mister Niven Dallas.'

My jaw dropped a bit, as this was obviously a covert and subdued warning that went firmly into my thick head... get this man's name right.

Now it was Tom's turn. Chati could speak better English than the Sergeant. This would be very interesting. Roger the Administrator did his intro thing, again displaying a weak smile as if he was passing more wind.

'Sergeant Corker, allow me to introduce Mr Chatty Neerooparramatta aide to His Royal Highness the Crown Prince of Thailand. May I present Senior Sergeant Tomas Corker second-class, principal and most senior Police Officer in this vast region of Western Australia.'

This time the edict was remarkably different. Chati rose from his comfortable leather chair, with hand extended to meet Tom's hesitant hand. Then with a well-practised smile, and in polite crisp Queen's English...

'How do you do, I am pleased to meet you Sergeant Corker,' then with a swift breath, breaking into a pattern of light conversation.

'You know Sergeant; it has always interested me as to why the Australian Police do not carry side-arms. Would this be because of a cost factor, or is there some other reason? By the way, my name is pronounced Chati Niratpattanasai.'

Both Roger and I were smiling away, casually trying to blend into the background un-noticed, when suddenly verbal catastrophe struck. Tom cheerfully responded to the Royal aids polite introduction banter.

'Am pleased ta meet yer sir, 'av' yer enjoyed yo'r stay in Australia. A must say Sir I like yo'r safari suit. Oh, and we don't carry goons, 'caus we don't need 'em 'ear. Yer see sir, there ain't nobody around ear to shoot.'

Chati shifted his mouth to an odd angle, and then innocently replied in his crisp English. You know something Sergeant; I didn't understand a fucking word you said old chap.'

The shocked look on the Sergeants face only matched that of the Administrators. As for me, well I just knew I was going to like this little Thai-Lander. Tom, with a special effort just had to reply to that native Australian description of his British accent.

'Don't yer worry sir, most Australians can't understand me either?

With that, we all erupted into raucous laughter. Thinking this Royal boating thing was going to be fun... In the days ahead I found out, just how wrong a man can be.

***

I was soon to learn that Chati was a very smart and well-travelled man. He had a degree in law from Oxford University (no doubt where he learnt the art of swearing in perfect English) and an MBA from Harvard University. His job as part of the Thai Royal House was to sort out and plan the Crown Princes complicated travel itinerary, security and all the other special expected Royal protocol requirements.

This particular meeting was to advise us on how we were to address the Crown Prince, and how we should act in the presence of Thai Royalty. The first such lesson was to be conducted in the same office tomorrow, a Tuesday. This time at what they considered an early hour of eight in the morning.

The Crown Prince would arrive on the Wednesday midday jet from Broome, and the Ord River Diversion Dam boat trip scheduled for an early start on Thursday morning. The Crown Prince was then due to depart on the same day for Darwin on the Kununurra one o'clock jet to meet the Royal Thai Airways flight back to Bangkok.

Timing would be very tight, however; we all agreed we could achieve this plan, as such was acceptable.

This simple plan later proved to be a normal government bungled gross understatement.

Chapter Two:

How not to talk to a Prince

Our meeting the next day started badly, we suffered yet another half-hour long wait in Rogers little waiting room. This had Tom smoking at the ears again with a grim look on his face.

At my wife's suggestion, I had decided to wear my last new shirt, and attempted to clean my shoes. I did feel a little better in that I had made some sort of effort.

Just then, the Administrators office door swung open and we were both ushered into Rogers's office. Handshaking out the way we soon got down to the serious business of learning Thai Royal protocol.

Our first lesson started with a brief history on Thailand's rich culture, strong economy and the present constitutional monarchy King Rama IX of the Chakri Dynasty. I had been to Thailand only two years previously on my honeymoon, and was in awe at the great beauty and wealth of King Bhumibol Adulyadej, Rama IX Grand Palace.

It was about then that I made my first of many uninformed mistakes. I was soon to find out that a political disaster was only one unguarded word away.

This catastrophe easily began by casually mentioning to Chati that I had always thought the previous name of "Siam" was a beautiful name for their country, why the change. The very polite Chati quickly put my nice innocent enquiring thought into firm perspective.

Clasping his hands firmly behind his back and pacing the floor like a Gestapo SS officer, he stopped and then swiftly turned to glare at the three dumb ignorant Australians. We were all standing in a row like frightened schoolboys awaiting their punishment.

'Gentlemen, I must caution you on what you can and cannot say about Thailand while in the presence of His Highness the Crown Prince.'

Chati then scanned our faces to confirm he had our total attention and that his words had sunk in. He then continued.

'My country's name was changed from Siam to Thailand in 1939 with the advent of an elected democratic Government.

You should also be aware that my country has never been "Colonised" by westerners as many of our neighbours have, as indeed Australasia still is.' (Glancing at Tom and the Administrator I was quite sure that this timely, sniping remark about the British occupying Australia was lost on both, and had sailed right over their smiling heads.) Chati then went on with his lecture.

'History however, shows that a military coup in 1932 led by a group of western educated Thai military officers took control of the capital Bangkok while His Majesty the King was on holiday. These officers called themselves the Peoples Party.

As a first change; this new party renamed Siam to Thailand, meaning Land of the Free. I hope you can now understand the great sensitivity around this matter of our nation's name. I can assure you all, it is far better that you refrain from saying anything at all while in the presence of His Highness the Crown Prince of Thailand.'

We were all listening so intently to this remarkable period of Thai history and important Royal advice, that none of us had noticed that Chati had stopped talking. Then Chati pursed his lips scanning our faces for some sort of intelligent reaction, and then resumed his instruction patter.

'His Highness will be accompanied by two personal guards; both are very high-ranking military personnel. Both are (Phon Tri) Major Generals, both speak excellent English, and fully armed at all times. Is this understood?' spinning his head around in our direction, scanning our faces for any hint of objection.

We all nodded our heads in silence like three little boys to an angry headmaster.

'None of you should ever address the Crown Prince directly. Only the Administrator as the senior Australian government representative may talk directly to the Prince, even so, that will only be via one of His Highnesses personal guards.'

Chati stepped up close to Sergeant Tom, looking up at him in the eye. Tom remained silent, staring out over the Royal aids head with a slight hint of a smile. A flicker of challenge crossed the Royal Aids face. Then changing his mind, returned to the matter at hand.

'You must remember; never make direct eye contact with the Prince, never turn your back or attempt touch the Prince. Do not point your fingers or arms, or talk loudly in the presence of the Prince. In our advanced and well-developed culture, these primitive crude actions are considered as rude and most offensive.

If the Crown Prince walks toward you, you must step aside, head slightly bowed. If by some chance you are addressed directly by the Prince, you must respond "Your Highness" and do remember that we are mainly a Buddhist Nation by some ninety-five percent. His Highness is a strict vegetarian and does not smoke or take alcohol... any questions so far?'

My hand shot up like a little schoolboy plying for attention to speak... the crisp response was an unexpected change of softened demeanour.

'Yes Mr Dallas.'

Chati quickly acknowledgment the request with a finger pointing in my direction; apparently, Thai protocol did not apply to ignorant low-caste Australians.

'A number of things come to mind Sir,' (I thought I would copy Tom with a "Sir" as I, just as everybody else, could not pronounce the Royal aide's surname.)

'As Captain of the boat I have the responsibility for the total safety of the vessel and all who sail on her. Just boarding the boat may prove a little tricky without a helping hand. In addition, the boat has to accelerate hard to gain cruise speed, to get the thing up on to plane, and then decelerate to stop the vessel. All these movements can be quite sudden, or savage, requiring some assistance to the passengers.

I would normally advise everyone to sit and to hang-on like hell while this was going on. When we do get up and going, we will be cruising at around twenty-eight knots.' Then giving this some further thought. 'I suppose we will also be stopping every now and again to take in the local sights, so all this action will be repeated a number of times.'

Chati the aide came back to me swiftly with an answer to all my concerned questions, and more.

'Be advised Mister Dallas, His Highness is in prime fit condition having just completed an exhausting Australian SAS military training course. The Prince's personal guard, indeed if at all required, will provide any needed help to the Prince.

Should you find it necessary to make any sudden moves with the vessel you should tell the Administrator, who will then advise one of the Prince's guards, who will in turn discreetly advise His Highness.' Then cocking his head in Rogers's direction. 'The Administrator has already provided me with a number of excellent suggestions on how the boat trip will be conducted.'

This was all news to me, and a ludicrous system of communication. I could not believe my ears... was this person for real. The Crown Prince would be over the back transom of the boat in a second and in the water before we got to second base on this system of delayed "pass the parcel" or Chinese whispers style of communication.

My surprised look must have put Chati on high idiot alert. He was a man used to being in charge and would not accept any contradictions to his instructions or for that matter tolerate fools.

As I took a deep breath for the reply to Chati's unworkable chain of instructions, the Administrator quickly cut me off with an open raised hand of stop. He had been listening to my list of possible boating problems, and with a very confident; I am in command expression. Turned to Chati confirming in an authoritative voice total acknowledgement to all the arrangements on my behalf.

'All is fully and well understood Mr Neerooparraminto.' A groaning sigh left Chati's lips at this further attempt by Roger to pronounce his name. 'We will all comply to the letter with your instructions, so now all there is left to do is to set the time-frame for tomorrows grand Royal river voyage, ho ho ha ha ha.'

This was I think, a Senior Public Servant level three joke, a joke made in a failed attempt to lighten up the already tight and tense atmosphere that now filled the office. Chati was not at all amused at the Administrators feeble attempt at humour.

Anything to do with his Crown Prince was a very serious matter indeed. Tom had sat in silence all of this time sternly staring out from under the peak of his Police hat. He then broke into a not so well thought out, and unfortunately unrehearsed cockney accent Police speech.

'Well I fink we should all get away early on Thursday morn' as it'll take us over an hour ta get up the river and another ta get back. Then say another hour-in a 'arf at the big fig tree that'll bring us back by around midday just in time to shove 'im back on the one o'clock plane ta Darwin.'

***

I could tell from the Sergeants rushed summary of the proposed event; he just wanted this meeting to finish. Tom obviously needed to get back to his busy Police station. Then again, the grim look on Chati's face, and the tightly clenched fists told me that Mr Chati Niratpattanasai was not at all happy with our grasp of the Thai Royal protocol, or the proposed plan… This was not a good start.

The ever polite, Chati was well in control of his inner feelings, again turning to look up at Tom. Staring directly into his eyes, he then in a low controlled voice slowly replied.

'Sergeant Tomas Corker, second-class, I assume that your reference to "shove im back on the plane" is your description of the Crown Prince of Thailand's formal departure by aircraft from Kununurra?'

Tom was not-at-all fussed at this pick-up on his less than elegant description of the Prince's departure schedule. Tom was after all a busy cop and this was all just a waste of his valuable time. Tom raised his bushy eyebrows in a look of indifference and replied with the hint of a smile.

'I'm sorry sir I don't mean no disrespect for the Crown Prince. It's just the way it comes out with me London pommy accent. Now there was no 'arm done or intended sir.'

To which Chati enthusiastically replied, clasping his hands firmly behind his back again, and jutting out his chin for further affect.

'This gentlemen is the very reason why we are having this meeting, to avoid any such derogatory or thoughtless comments being uttered in the presence of His Highness.'

Chati looked worried now, in a sort of defeated way. He obviously thought he was not getting the protocol message across to these three dumb bush Australians, and imagined the worst may happen. He had no idea at that time how right he was.

On the other hand, it all sounded very innocent to me in a sort of "Dixon of Dock Green" type comment, and as Tom had said, "No 'arm was done or intended." However, the terrified look on the Administrators face told another story.

Roger the Administrator was jaw dropped speechless at the terrible way the meeting was going, displaying obvious demise at the lack of any genuine progress.

The situation was now becoming clear to me; only now did I realised that this was an important political and Government appointment for Roger. In addition, this was I suppose, really his first formal function in his new role as the Administrator of the North-West.

Yes, this was indeed a very serious and important appointment. Knowing that this new government position was especially created for him by no other than Sir Charles Court the Premier of Western Australia.

Now it appeared that not all was going well... at all. Like a true well-oiled bureaucrat and senior public servant, Roger again took command of the rapidly deteriorating situation. Taking a deep breath, he then launched into verbal action.

'Mr Nerraparramatta'

Chati's eyebrows shot up followed with a thunderous look of disgust at Rogers's continuing attempt at pronouncing his name.

'Let me assure you sir that our Government will extend every courtesy and consideration to your Crown Prince. As Administrator for the North-West of Western Australia, being the most senior Australian Government representative in this area. We look forward to, and honoured to host the Crown Prince of Thailand during his short visit to Kununurra and the Ord River Irrigation Scheme.

Chati listened politely. I could see by the look on his face that he was not impressed, or convinced with Administrator Roger's poor attempt at assuring him everything was going to be as planned.

He knew all too well that this was just more of the same civil servant Government hot-air huff and puff crap that he had heard many times before from around the world. He was still not convinced that we bush Australians could pull off an incident free Royal visit.

Chati scanned our faces once more then sadly looked out the window next to his chair and said softly...

'Gentlemen, I must leave you now to prepare for the Crown Prince's arrival tomorrow, there is still much to do. I will give you some time to develop a final plan for the Prince's Ord River boat cruise.

Please advise me in plenty of time so I may consider the itinerary, and can inspect and ultimately approve of the plan. I must also remind you all, that at no time should you take any photos or recordings of any part of this Royal event.'

Turning to Roger, Chati the Royal aide looked up at him, and made his last parting comment, in a not-so-well concealed snarl...

'Mr Administrator... Sir, you are again advised that my surname is Niratpattanasai spelt N-I-R-A-T-P-A-T-T-A-N-A-S-A-I.'

***

A glum looking Chati then slowly looked around at each of us and left the office without a further word. Roger looked a

bit miffed at Chati's lack of confidence in his grand speech...
Tom had much more to say.

'Why the bleeding fuck don't ya just call 'em "Sir" like me
and Niven. You bloody well insulted the little bloke by trying
ta get his friggin name right... fucking it up six or seven
bleeding times.'

Roger jumped in to defend himself, as only a well-
experienced bureaucrat would do at such a vehement attack on
his polished administration performance.

'Tom we are expected for diplomacy reasons to use our
foreign guest's names when addressing them; it is part of my
job and long training.'

Tom blasted back before Roger had time to continue.

'Not if ya keep-on stuffing is bleeding name up, time and
again.'

It was time I stepped between these two civil servants
before they became less than civil, and resorted to
bureaucratic blows.

'Now, now you blokes, we have more important things to
discuss. The Administrator can practice Chati's surname and
get it right later, but right now, we need to form a cunning
workable plan. One that will pass the Royal aide's detailed
scrutiny.

Now did my ears hear right, Sergeant Tom mentioned
something earlier about the fig tree up the Ord river?'

The Administrator reclaimed a little of his somewhat
dented composure, then attempting to convince me answering
my worrying question with a hint of official pride.

'Well yes, my wife heard about this place when talking to
the other ladies in Town. Apparently, it's a great spot on the
riverbank for a picnic and a swim. It was suggested to, and
accepted by the Crown Prince as the place he wants to visit.'

Tom had noticed my growing concern and quickly
claimed all innocence to this dim-witted boating plan. With a
worried look waving his head and hands in denial, then added
his bit.

'I don't know nufink about it Niven. I thought you already
knew all about the fig tree picnic bit?'

This all came as a complete surprise, so I then added my view on this picnic area choice.

'You guys must be stark-raving fucking bonkers. This fig-tree place is very remote; it is on a large sweeping bend some twenty miles up the Ord River. The only interesting thing about this place is a large fig tree growing out over the water, which is nice and handy for shade.

This massive old fig tree is on a high mud bank; along one side of the bank is a small creek running into the river. This creek is flowing in full flood at this time, which is a big problem on its own, but worse, it is full of mean crocodiles, big hairy spiders, and poisonous snakes. Nobody goes up to the fig tree at this time of the year.

Another thing you should remember is the temperature will be up around forty-two degree Celsius and very humid, and my boat is not air-conditioned.'

None of these obvious dangers or discomforts bothered city slicker Roger. Nor did it deter him from forging ahead with his mighty master plan. Roger continued in total ignorance of the obvious danger he presented to his Royal guest, continuing to defend his wife's suggested poor choice of a picnic spot.

He then offered what he thought was further support for his silly choice.

'I was told that you and a few of the other boats go up there quite a lot for a bar-b-cue, and it's one of the best places on the river. I also understand that you have all the cooking equipment and ground covers and such left at the site?'

'Yes Roger we do have some on site equipment, the gear is wrapped in a large old truck tarp, tied to a low hanging branch of the fig tree. The standard procedure is, as we approach the fig tree mud bank. We wake up all the dozing crocs with a few gunshots to scare them off, but they do not go far, so we have to keep an eye on them. Then we beat the hell out of the old truck tarp with sticks while still roped to the branch to frighten all the snakes out.

The next part is we then spray the tarp as we unfold it on the ground to kill all the hairy spiders that refuse to go.

The so-called bar-b-cue is a hole in the ground covered with a steel plate sitting on four well-charred rocks. Now I do not entertain Royalty very often. But I would guess His Royal Highness the Crown Prince of Thailand will be expecting something a little more up-market than what I have just described to you both?'

Tom was looking up at the ceiling, no doubt seeking a divine diversion from this difficult problem. While Roger was stroking his chin in deep thought considering a new defence approach to support his great plan; frankly, I do not think he had heard a word I had just said. He raised a finger calling for ultimate attention, then took a deep breath, and opened up his mind.

'As I see things, the Crown Prince has already been experiencing the rough side of Australia. In the last few months, he has been with the SAS jumping out of planes and on field manoeuvres, tomorrow will be his last day in Australia as the Prince flies back to Thailand on a connecting Thai-air flight from Darwin. I don't think any of this will bother the Prince.' Roger continued his line of thought.

'I'm sure I can get the Hotel to put together a very nice cold lunch for us all, so no cooking required, that will also take care of the vegetarian problem.

We can have a selection of food and soft drinks quickly pre-approved by the Prince's aide. Niven I assume you have some sort of refrigeration on your boat?'

'I sure do Roger it is called an Esky, a very large cooler-box Esky so we will also need a lot of ice. I do think your idea and solution for the picnic food is great one, and you are probably right about the Prince being aware of the rough side of Australia. However my concern is, and add it should also be yours, is for the safety of the Crown Prince Thailand while he is in our care.

I insist that we should reconsider this picnic location. We should find a better safer picnic spot for the Crown Prince to stretch his legs.'

Sergeant Tom had the look of a very worried cop after hearing my views and detailed objections on the picnic site, (or so I had thought) and then added his most important observation yet to the conversation, and the ultimate picnic plan.

'My concern is these blokes are all bleeding teetotallers… what the 'ell are we going to drink tomorrow? It's gonna be a bloody long 'ot day out there on that bloody river fir four bleeding hours without a decent drink.'

***

Much as I tried, I could not convince the Administrator to change his mind on the fig tree picnic destination. I was amazed to discover that the fig tree picnic location was not negotiable.

Roger then advised in his well-practised administrative tone that there would be no changes to this plan. Reason being the Prince was expecting to go to that scenic spot, adding the matter now closed to all and any further discussion.

***

The departure point would be from the old water-irrigation pump station, just upstream from the diversion dam wall. This position resolved two things, a safe place to park the three required cars, no doubt guarded by one of Toms Policemen.

In addition, a more important reason being; this was the only easy way to get the Royal party on and off the boat, as there was a proper boat-dock and short boardwalk.

For some unknown reason, a time of eight in the morning was set for the departure. The time decided by the Administrator Roger Gayton as a proper and most civil time for a Royal Prince to embark on his river cruise.

This late start was a worry. It would then give us a time-window of only some four hours to complete our picnic and sightseeing trip. Acceptable, assuming we got the Crown Prince back to the Pump Station at around twelve-midday.

If everything went to plan, we should then have a full hour for the Prince to get ready for his one o'clock jet departure from Kununurra to Darwin.

According to Roger the Administrator, everything for the Royal Ord River voyage, had been expertly planned and fully accounted for. Chati the Thai Royal aide had finally approved

29

the sailing plan, including all the drinks, and the food suggestions.

***

My business day (at my desk) normally starts around five thirty in the morning so an eight o'clock boating departure time was for me no problem. For the others this (so-called) early departure proved to be a little more of a challenge.

The Administrator and the Sergeant had already experienced a busy long day. Both expected to be on duty at the airport to welcome the Crown Prince to Kununurra. I had also heard on the gossip mumble-vine that the Crown Prince would on arrival, be taken for a short tour of the town and local scenic sights.

The Prince would then end his first day with a formal dinner at KRS. (Kimberley Research Station) being a small Government agriculture research centre on the banks of the Ord River, which was established way back in 1945, and is just six kilometres from the town of Kununurra.

As expected, all of the many important town dignitaries were invited along to this rather unique Royal event. No doubt, Roger and Tom will have had a very tiresome day, and a very late night performing their civil duties.

As was normal and expected, low caste Kununurra people such as I, were not invited to this taxpayer-funded party.

***

It was nearly ten-thirty; the morning had been and gone as I headed back to the office. Robyn pounced on me as I entered the door trying in all manner of ways to extract any morsel of information in a rapid staccato of probing questions.

I casually advised Robyn that I would be at home for the rest of the day getting the boat ready for an early start tomorrow. Robyn, wide-eyed gave a very satisfied, 'aah haa, I thought so, and now you've caved in and agreed to take the Prince boating.'

Much to Robyn's displeasure, I ignored her further probing questions, deciding to spend the rest of my afternoon cleaning and polishing the Vendal III. I must admit my boat presented far better than me.

The on-board flush toilet being cleaned to perfection and looked like new, the fuel tanks were topped up and the batteries were put on a trickle charge just in case. Then full attention given to the all-important on-board minibar, this being carefully checked, and stocked with adequate supplies prior to going on such a long, and who knows, dangerous voyage up the Ord River.

The Vendal III was probably the only decent cabin cruiser style boat available on the Ord River at that time fitted with a private flush toilet and hand basin. It was also the only boat around fitted with a long-range HF radio communication system, as I owned a small radio sales and service company Kimberley Electronics. This HF marine radio being fitted-out with Marine, Aircraft, Royal Flying Doctor, and my private company channels.

Slow as I may be, it later occurred to me that this was most likely the main reason why the Vendal III was the preferred boat to take the Prince up the Ord River. This powerful on-board HF radio transmitter later proved to be invaluable, and saved the Australian Government much embarrassment.

Chapter Three:

The Royal Voyage

At 5:15 am on Thursday morning, it was still an ink black night with very little moon as I went about launching the heavy boat at the ski club ramp. This ski club built facility being just a little downstream from the Pump Station dock.

As expected, my powerful torch exposed a number of red-eyed locals watching my every move. I splashed the water a few times and threw some large rocks at the nosy inquisitive crocodiles.

This was after all their bit of the river, with me being the intruder. The crocs scurried away to a safe distance and settled down to watch, barking at me just to let me know that they were there, declaring they wanted their riverbank back.

Most of the local crocodiles that live above the Diversion dam were the freshwater Johnson. They have similar instincts to a cat being more inquisitive than dangerous; however, the males will fiercely defend their territory, especially during the mating season.

The females will ferociously defend their nests and eggs if you are too dumb to heed their warnings.

Then again, we were after all only some three hundred metres away from the Kununurra diversion dam wall, this being the only divider between the mighty Ord River and access to the Cambridge Gulf and the sea.

Many large salt-water crocodiles live in the Ord River at the base of this dam, at the lower side of this diversion dam wall. In recent times, a number of them had been spotted lazing around in the upper areas of the diversion dam so they obviously do not mind a bit of cross-country travel now and again.

Both species of croc do look quite similar but have very different natures. A hungry salt-water croc will attack unprovoked and will patiently hunt and stalk any pray. Not many people know that a croc can out-run a man in a short burst, and they can also climb trees with very little effort... so much for the silly Tarzan stories.

Then there are the many poisonous snakes that live in and around the Ord River who are also very good swimmers, I have learnt always to respect reptiles and their habitats. It's always best to be very, very cautious, especially since it was impossible to establish a salt from a fresh water croc in the dark, or see a swimming snake... especially while splashing around a muddy river bank on a dark morning like this.

With all this in mind, I had long since perfected the art of launching and retrieving my heavy boat single-handed without ever stepping a foot in the water.

I decided on this occasion to use my well-tried (ramp-run) launch method, mainly because I had nobody around to help me with the boat-launching task.

The standard procedure for this type of launch is to remove all the trailer boat lockdowns. Insert all the drain plugs, raise the stern-drive leg to the maximum position, fold up the rear boarding ladder, and then tie a fifty foot long rope from the bow rope ring to the trailer winch handle.

The plan is to then reverse rapidly back down the launch ramp into the water, and then apply the brakes sharply. This allows all three and a half ton of boat to slide with ease back off the trailer into the water. The tethered rope should then stop the boat at its length, and then used to pull the boat back to the shore... so easy... a piece of cake.

In all my years in the Kimberley, I have found the tropical Ord mosquito's start to terrorise people at dusk and have their last feed at dawn... about this very time.

I had sprayed myself in anticipation of an all-out attack, but my attraction was so overwhelming to them they ignored my protection, and successfully attacked me in squadrons. It was still very dark and the mosquito attack had completely distracted me to the point that I had failed to secure the fifty-foot bow rope to the trailer winch handle.

I slowly rolled out of the Toyota Landcruiser cab after what I had thought to be another successful boat launch. This confident mode soon dispelled, as I did not feel the expected jolt of the extended rope stopping the boat.

I looked back in utter astonishment in the dim light of my vehicle trailer lights, briefly to capture the view of my rapidly disappearing pride and joy the Vendal III. She was making her own way out into the river, backwards amongst the waiting crocodiles. My immediate conclusion was this is not a good start to this special Royal occasion on this hopefully fine tropical day.

Was this yet another Dallas tragedy unfolding before me? I made the instant decision to perform a hero act and dived headlong into the river swimming as fast as my thrashing arms would drive me after the unseen, rapidly departing trailing rope.

By some act of luck, one of my thrashing arms caught the invisible semi-submerged nylon rope. With the rope wrapped tightly around my left hand, I held on like grim death refusing ever to let go while at the same time being dragged along, mostly under the water by the heavy retreating boat.

The boat eventually slowed down as I managed to haul in the slack rope then swam quickly to the transom, still holding tightly onto the rope. In the dark, I bobbed up to reach the folded stainless boarding ladder hitting my head hard on the up-tilted stern-drive leg, splitting my head open on the leg fin. While nursing this cranial damage with blood flowing everywhere, I had this distinct feeling that I was not alone.

With one arm over the stern-drive leg (I knew where it was now,) I made a panic pull up the high stern. Fumbling in the dark, I reached for the folded boarding ladder, un-latching it with the speed and strength of a superman. With lightning speed, I was safely up and on to the boat rear deck.

I turned around to look over the transom at the water, in the low breaking morning light I could clearly observed two large crocodiles in the very place I was four seconds ago, they were both loudly advised to go get their breakfast somewhere else.

With the stern-drive lowered, and the start button pushed the engine burst into life, frightening the disappointed crocs away. I then quickly retrieved the fifty foot of launching rope and stowed it before gently motoring out into the main Ord River toward the M1 pump-station dock.

***

All was now going well, having the Vendal III firmly tied up to the pump-station dock by six am. A deep red sun was just coming up over Lilly Creek and the Town of Kununurra.

The air was still and warm promising to be a beautiful tropical morning on the Ord River. Now all I needed to do was check out the extent of damage to my throbbing head.

With the help of a shaving mirror, and the toilet door mirror I had a good view of my head damage, I must admit it hurt a great deal more than it looked. I then bathed the large gash on my head with stinging iodine from the medical kit and decided it was best to cover-up this mess, as the sight of my bloody head may offend the Crown Prince. As I was studying this mess, a brilliant idea came to my painful mind; I would wear my old Captains hat to hide my bleeding head.

I rummaged around in the storage locker and eventually found the old thing. It was looking a bit sad from dunking in the river many times but still had the gold braid firmly attached. However, when I tried it on it was much too small.

Ether my head had swollen due to the recent bump or the hat had shrunk no doubt because of the many times in the water. Nevertheless, it was still the perfect answer to hide my damaged head and then I had another great idea.

I cut a slit up the back of the cap to increase the band size and tried it on... perfect. From the front nobody would ever know about my small hat and damaged head, this I reasoned since protocol would not allow me to turn my back to the Prince. Even so, I was still very wet from my scary boat-launching episode.

While rummaging in the lockers for the Captains hat I had also came across a pair of white footy shorts and a white tee shirt. I quickly changed into my new uniform, then opened the toilet door to inspect my creation in the full-length mirror.

Eat your heart out Mr Gregory McQuie (known as the white knight,) now I was just as equally well attired to suit this auspicious Royal occasion. Although I might leave the cap off for a while, and let some air, get around the now large and growing bump on my head.

Two Panadol later to help my throbbing head I then settled down to wait for my Royal passengers, it was now coming up to six o'clock, and time for a well-earned cup of coffee and a blissful two hours wait to the Royal voyage.

***

This is the most beautiful time of the day in the tropics, and one of the main reasons why I like to start my day an hour or so before sunrise. The last of the fruit bats were screeching overhead in their thousands, making their way so accurately back to their roost to hang upside-down in the trees that line the banks of the Ord River.

They would have had a busy night feeding on all the beautiful mangos and other delicious fruits grown to perfection by our very capable Ord farmers. At the same time, I saw the first dense flocks of white cockatoos (Cacatua sanguinea.)

The little bastards were calling out to all their mates, 'Come-on you guy's, its daylight again, let's go eat.' They were leaving their roosting trees by the thousands along the riverbank. Making a thick white flight path, direct to the main farm irrigation area where they will feed on an abundance of beautifully grown seed crops, sunflower, sorghum, and many other carefully grown delights.

When they have taken on their fill, just like juvenile delinquents, they will continue to damage anything that takes there fancy to relieve their obvious boredom. Then as the sun goes down, they will stagger back full, barely able to fly in the fading light to their tree roost by the Ord, crapping on everything along the way. Both of these flying crop destroyers are untouchables, as they are now both a protected Australian species.

The flying crop carnage and damage goes on day and night every day of the year. Watching this noisy aerial scene, I was thinking a few years ago we just used to blast a few hundred out of the sky with shotguns.

These smart birds soon got the message and stayed away, their breeding numbers were fewer, and the Ord farmers were no longer feeding or supporting the cockatoos... However, this pest culling was not acceptable by our Government do-gooders. Mainly taxpayer funded university environmental graduates, and so-called indispensable flora & fauna advisers.

Who would want to be an Ord River farmer with tax funded weirdos like this who would report any bird culling, and have you fined by the law for simply protecting your crop. Strangely, these tax paid weirdos only arrived in Kununurra when it was cold down south... another paid government holiday.

Sipping my coffee I began reflecting on what was left on my, to do list, before the Royal passengers arrived. Thinking to myself, things may well have turned out worse. I could have lost the boat, or had my bum nipped by an angry croc or, hit my head on the sharp propeller instead of the blunt stern-leg fin... Just then, I had a sudden heart wrenching thought.

The boat propeller, hell now I remember. About two weeks ago, I had struck a submerged rock in the river, changing over to my spare prop. The propeller now fitted to the boat was a cruise prop, designed to give best fuel consumption and lower engine revs.

The only problem was, with this prop it will take one hell of a while, and a big shift of the passenger weight to get this heavy boat up onto fast plane. Apparently, we are going to be carrying a full-weight payload, this weight matter was now critical.

According to my slick mathematics that would consist of six heavy men on-board, two of them very large, and we were now also carrying a full fuel load... plus not forgetting a large, heavy Esky of ice, food and drinks.

My brain was starting to have depressive thoughts of an early Royal picnic disaster. Maybe Chati was right after all; maybe we were just a lot of ignorant Australian bush idiots.

One thing was for certain, if we do not get this boat up on to the fast plane, we will only make at-best a water speed of some twelve knots. At that low speed, it will take us over two hours to get as far as the fig tree picnic spot. Thinking to myself in depressive thoughts… this was bad.

More thinking did not improve the situation, surely things could not get any worse; however, a few hours later that day proved that thought wrong… incredibly wrong.

***

The calm weather had me suspicious, in the fast gaining light; the surface mist was rapidly clearing over the water to expose a flat millpond without a hint of a breeze. I chuckled to myself; with no wind, just as well we are not a sailing boat. Then looking over the side of the boat at the still water, to see my own reflection on the eerily flat and quiet water. The birds had gone and it was now ghostly quiet.

Looking up at the sky it was a perfect golden glow in this early morning light. This I knew will soon become a bright tropical blue sky, and then I looked to the north and my heart sank.

The distant clouds were distinctively anvil clouds of cumulonimbus, the nasty ones that most shipping and aircraft avoid at all costs. These cloud build up's were still way-out over the Cambridge Gulf but I knew they were heading our way.

We were obviously in a low-pressure cell; tapping the barometer with my finger the needle sprung backwards from around 1012mb to 1000mb, the preverbal calm before the storm. It was after all still early March and at the end of the wet season, this type of weather was not that unusual for this time of the year... although, please not today.

Switching on the HF radio I then selected the Kununurra airport ATIS (Air Traffic Information Service) which only provided information that I already knew. Wind Nil, Cloud CAVOK, (Ceiling and Visibility Okay) temperature 29°C, and a QNH of 1000mb. This weather may well be acceptable for

39

local flying, but what was the four-hour area forecast going to be?

Selecting the Marine weather channel told me a different story, there was a late cyclone building up off the northern coast in the Cambridge Gulf. It was currently a category two and stationary, the synopsis was that it would make its way into the Gulf by mid-afternoon.

I thought that will be okay as we will be back long before this weather system builds up to any size that might concern us.

My watch caught my attention it had already gone eight fifteen and nobody had arrived yet. I was starting to panic when I spotted a small dust trail rising on the levee-bank entry road. Shortly after a lone Police car pulled up in front of the Pump House building, a young copper jumped out and came directly to me at a run yelling out.

'They're on their way, quick, give me a hand with this big Esky its bloody heavy,' then noticing my bloody head bump, 'what the hell happened to your head mate?'

I told him it's a long story, and jumped off the boat to help him load all the food and drinks on-board the Vendal III. Then I quickly cleaned up my coffee cup and gently replaced my Captains hat to cover my sore head.

It was now a beautiful full tropical morning, already hot and muggy. At least the mosquitoes had gone to bed for the day, and then I absent-mindedly wondered... what this distinctive day would bring.

I was still practising my standing to attention at the boat helm when two-of-the flashiest looking cars in town (no doubt borrowed for the occasion) pulled up right in front of the pump-station walkway. Then two casually, but immaculately dressed Thai military officers jumped out of the first car and opened the rear door wide.

I watched with expectant interest but no one came out, meanwhile the second car which had just pulled up threw open all the doors. Out spilt Roger the Administrator and Tom the Police Sergeant. They walked hurriedly towards the boat, stopped at right angle to the boarding step, and stood side by side solemnly to attention, chest out and arms by their sides like tin soldiers.

While watching this unusual and grand spectacle, I did not notice the Crown Prince had already alighted from the other car and had formed a short detachment. One Thai guard at the rear, the Crown Prince and Chati side by side and the other Thai guard in the front. They then proceeded to slow march the short distance down the pump station boardwalk towards Tom and Roger standing stiffly to attention by my boat.

Fear gripped me; surely, Chati is not coming along too. The boat was already well overloaded. He did say that he was going on ahead to Darwin to arrange Royal things there.

The slow procession arrived at the boarding step and the first Thai officer stepped nimbly on to the boat and stood sideways. The second Thai officer remained on the dock and took up a position opposite Tom the Police Sergeant. The Crown Prince stopped just short of the step and Chati smartly stepped sideways to stand alongside the second Thai officer.

There was a moment of uncomfortable silence as the Crown Prince stood to Royal attention between the four forming a guard of honour. I watched all of this ceremony in utter amazement while standing boldly to attention at my boat helm seat.

***

The Crown Prince was nothing like I had imagined. He was about 22, quite tall for a Thai with a slim athletic build, dressed in a very smart khaki long pants and matching short sleeve shirt. As expected the Prince and his Royal guards were dressed in Thai military uniform, but casually to suit the hot climate, open neck shirts... no tie or hats.

Both Thai officers were armed with large military issue 1911 Colt 45 automatic pistols, connected by a very smart gold braided lanyard clipped under their right-hand epaulette. Chati the Royal aide was now standing to attention eyes fixed straight ahead, and then he spoke breaking the long silence in a clear but steady voice.

'We present His Royal Highness Prince Maha Vajiralongkorn, the second son of their Majesties King

41

Bhumibol Adulyadej and Queen Sirikit of Thailand, conferred by the King as The Crown Prince of Thailand Somdech Phra Borama Orasadahiraj Chao Fah Maha Vajiralongkorn Sayam.'

The Crown Prince then stepped on-board the Vendal III. I did my thing and bowed my head, just as well I had my Captains hat on otherwise my blooded head would have ceremoniously welcomed the Crown Prince on-board the Vendal III. I thought at the time maybe I should have piped the Crown Prince aboard as I did have a bosons whistle in the locker somewhere, never mind too late now... maybe for next time.

With a regal glance, the Prince briefly looked around then sat down on the co-helm seat opposite me and stared straight ahead out of the spotlessly clean front screen. The two Thai officers took upstanding positions, at ease behind the two raised co-helm and Captains seats, hands clasped behind their backs, one behind the Prince, and one behind me. Tom and Roger followed them on-board and sat down on the rear transom deck, one each side of the engine hatch.

Chati stood to attention stern faced at the boarding step, and to my relief remained on the dock. The young copper released both the front and rear docking ropes, and with a gentle kick, we drifted serenely away from the Pump Station dock on the very calm water. I was thinking, what this would have looked like to any early morning observer or a tourist. I fired up the engine and gently motored out to the middle of the river in the unusually calm water.

Roger and Tom had taken up positions sitting on the wide transom either side of the large Esky that now sat neatly over the engine hatch. We were fortunate as this boat had a good size flat entertaining floor area behind the Captains and co-helm seats. This large open deck area is shaded from the hot tropical sun, by a full-length white canvas canopy offering excellent protection.

This large shade-canopy firmly attached to the boat by two stout aluminium poles to which both Tom and Roger were now grimly holding. I was delighted to see that they had remembered my warning about hanging on to something.

However, both looked like they had missed many hours sleep, but now was not the time for either of them to be nodding off.

Everything looked fine except for one thing. I knew we could never get this now heavy, overloaded boat up on fast plane. The mobile weight urgently required redistribution, now was the time to try out the Chati system of on-board communications. I was thinking this protocol thing should be fun. I must now attempt to have a wee chat with Roger in his shell-like ear about this pending important matter.

***

As we reached the middle of the river, I set the helm to dead ahead and the engine revs to a fast idle tracking a straight line at about nine knots, then wandered back for my chat with Roger. I had noticed that Roger was again in a full business suit complete with jacket and tie and Tom was also wearing a nice matching tie to his Police uniform complete with flat hat, yet the Crown Prince and his two military Royal guard officers were dressed informally in neat open necked shirts. In a low voice, I explained the immediate and grim boating situation.

'Roger, we have a small problem; it basically comes down to a lot of weight in this boat being in the wrong place at this time.' Tom was now leaning forward listening intently.

'If I were to open up the throttles on this boat right now in an attempt to get the bugger up onto fast plane, you, and Tom would disappear over the back of the transom into the river. (Tom took a quick glance over the back at the churning water.) As for those two very serious looking well-armed Thai officers, with their hands clasped behind their backs. They would end up taking several involuntary steps backwards and finish up crushed against the transom about where you and Tom are sitting right now.'

Looking at their faces, I could tell they both had no idea what I was talking about and so decided to continue with a little more detail and urgency...

'I think we would all agree that this imminent disaster would present as a catastrophe of the highest order, and one that should be avoided at all costs... agreed?'

Both Tom and Roger nodded their heads vigorously. I could tell that I now had their full attention by using the all-powerful word "catastrophe." Roger with a frown whispered.

'Why the hell would all that happen, what should we do?'

Tom whispered the answer into Rogers's ear loud enough for all on board to hear.

'Easy ta understand Roger; it's like being on the tube train, ya know, the London underground; if ya doesn't 'ang on to a strap when the tube starts moving you'll end up two carriages down the bleeding train.'

I thought how neat an explanation was that, an excellent description. Then speaking in a low voice.

'Precisely Tom, spot on.' I was starting to feel happy that they may have actually both grasped the problem well, and as a reward and some encouragement added, 'an excellent analogy Tom, I could not have put it a better way myself.'

Roger then replied sheepishly.

'I have never been on the London underground.'

Tom and I looked at each other in utter amazed silence. Tom removed his hat, shook his head, and rolled his eyes in disbelief. This was not reaching Roger at all... I decided on the more direct approach.

'Roger we need to get all the mobile weight on this boat up to the front of the boat, and we will have to advise everybody to hang on while I open the throttles to get this bloody boat up onto fast plane. If we don't get this thing up onto plane, we will never get to the bloody fig tree and back by midday.'

Roger looked very hot and frustrated in his nice striped business suit. He then put on his best firm smile, saying with confidence, he would advise the Thai officers of this boat problem. I thought to myself, well this should be interesting.

Roger then whispered my weight distribution instructions to the Royal guard standing behind the Prince. With little or no expression, the officer then turned and relayed the instructions to the Prince.

Now, I do not know exactly word-for-word what Roger said to the Royal guard. However, I do know how Chinese whispers work. How a simple instruction can be totally misunderstood, bastardised and lost when passing on just a few words in a chain to others.

Roger nodded they were ready. I then opened the throttle a little as a signal. The boat squatted down at the rear and the bow rose sharply in the water. Everybody was now aware of the situation, and could see what was required.

Quick as a flash the Crown Prince leapt sprightly up on-to the side deck of the cabin walk, and ran up to the front bow deck. He then clutched on to the stainless steel bow rail with both hands. The two Royal guards quickly followed him on to the deck, one on each side of the cabin taking a kneeling position behind the Crown Prince, as if operating a 25-pounder field gun.

I was standing up at the raised helm position looking on through the windscreen utterly amazed and terrified at this sudden spectacle. A quick glimpse back told me the two heavies were busy talking, facing each other, still sitting on the rear transom completely oblivious to what was happening up on the front deck. They could-not see what was going on up-front because of the now high angle of the bow and the rear sun awning. The engine noise level almost drowned my raised shout of urgency.

'You two, had better get up to the front of the boat right now or we will be in this half-plane position forever.'

To my utter amazement both Roger and Tom started to climb out onto the side-deck to join the other three on the bow. In their haste, they had not noticed the Royal party were missing. I grabbed a hold of them and yelled into their ears.

'Get up to the front of the cabin you stupid fuckers, and be quick. Through that bloody door there,' pointing to the entrance of the cabin between the helm seats. They stumbled around and found their way through to the front vee-bunk section. I opened up the throttles to full power and the Vendal III rose slowly up in the water on step to a perfect level plane.

She skimmed across the Dam at a neat thirty knots, bringing the power back provided a nice cruise of twenty-six knots and the sound level fell dramatically to a low quiet hum.

I stuck my head into the closed curtain shaded cabin and advised Roger and Tom they could come back up on deck now. They both emerged with big smiles and a visible look of relief on their faces. They obviously thought everything was okay now. As they emerged from the cabin, they looked around for the Prince, and then following my eyes looking through the front screen… at what I was looking at.

The Crown Prince was now standing to attention on the bow, leaning hard into the wind like a snow skier with his two Royal guards, one each side of him still in the twenty-five pound kneeling position. Shirts and hair billowing in the twenty-six knot wind. Rogers's eyes widened like saucers and his hand went to cover his mouth as he uttered aloud.

'O' my God what the fuck are they all doing out there?'

I replied somewhat casually, in an attempt to reduce the brutal impact of a possible Australian international incident and a catastrophic political disaster.

'It's not as bad as it looks Roger; I've done that on a number of occasions when I was drunk and out of my mind. The trick is to get back into the boat without falling off the bloody thing. Listen, as I can't talk to them from here.' Nodding my head at the Royal party, 'so you must. And be quick about it before we hit a wave or a log or a bloody crocodile and loose the damn Prince overboard.'

Tom nodded his head rapidly in agreement. Roger looked terrified at the thought of crawling out on to the deck of this fast moving boat to attract the attention of one of the forward-looking Royal guards.

Mustering up his courage, the Administrator, complete in his full city slicker suit pulled himself halfway out on to the side deck into the full blast of the twenty-six knot slipstream. Tom looked on in relief grateful that it was not him. I tapped Roger on his rather large arse, motioned him to come back into the safety of the cabin, and whispered into his ear...

'Roger old boy, why don't you just go through the fucking cabin and open the forward hatch which is directly behind the Crown Prince and between the two Royal guards, it's much easier and safer? Oh and leave the damn hatch open to let the breeze through.'

Roger was not amused at my laid-back style of bush humour, giving me a look that would have killed any normal healthy civil servant, he then dashed off to save the Prince. Tom burst out in fits laughter.

'Well Niven you certainly know 'ow ta stir up the bleeding Administrator, 'e won't be asking you fe'r any more boating favours.'

I replied with an evil smile.

'That was my very point Tom. I can do without all this drama in my life. I would be quite happy to be on Rogers ignore Dallas list.'

***

The Crown Prince and his two Royal guards nimbly jumped down the hatch into the cabin and resumed their previous positions on the helm deck without any fuss or a word spoken. All appeared normal and safe again, as Tom would say. "No 'arm done then." I must admit I have never seen the Ord River so calm, some would say like a millpond, but having never seen a millpond I could not compare. Let us just say the water was like a sheet of glass as I trimmed out the Vendal III to its best performance.

She now sat on the water completely flat without any hint of vertical movement while skimming along at just under twenty-seven knots. At this speed, the noise levels on the Vendal III were very subdued, just a low hum, conversation on-board was easy with the loudest noise being that of the water hissing past the hull. You could not have asked for a better, or more perfect boating experience.

Everybody on-board had sensed the same feeling as the on-board mood had become very relaxed. From the corner of my eye, I noticed that even the Crown Prince had a smile on his face. He was genuinely enjoying this relaxing boating experience.

***

With the boat trimmed and tracking straight, we were still a long way from the fig tree picnic spot and still short on time, it was now a quarter past nine. With the boat trimmed and the steering locked in the straight-ahead position, I wandered down the back to have a chat with Roger and Tom; they were both smiling again and chatting. I smilingly interrupted their happy conversation.

'Roger it's a very hot day, might I suggest that you tend to your guests refreshment needs. I've never been on the Vendal III for this long without a drink, and I can't have a drink until our guests have been sorted out first.'

Roger was visibly jolted back into duty reality.

'Christ Niven thanks for reminding me, I will go talk to a Royal guard,' then with an enquiring firm look at me Roger then asked...

'By the way, would you have really let me crawl out onto the side of the boat to bring the Prince back?'

Realising that Roger was still quite miffed at being the target of my brand of humour.

'No of course not, I thought you had noticed the forward hatch when you and Tom were up the front earlier.'

To divert the conversation away from this touchy matter I added.

'You're looking a bit hot Roger, why don't you formally ask the Prince's permission to remove your jacket and tie? As I understand that would be the correct gentleman's protocol in such circumstances'

Roger did not look convinced at my explanation; however, he did take-up my suggestion as he later removed his suit jacket and tie. Tom removed his hat before he lost it in the slipstream and then loosened his tie.

Everyone on board was now de-stressed and cheerful, and had a drink. The Crown Prince, and his Royal guard had some nice fruit juice, and the Administrator had a can of beer suitably camouflaged by a plain cooler. Tom's eyes lit up like fairy lights after the first sip of his can of coke as I had lashed it with liberal amounts of O.P. Rum.

To my utter surprise, the Prince turned to me and asked in perfect crisp English if I had any music on-board and that he liked the Beatles. I replied that I most certainly did and produced a cassette collection for the Prince to browse and select his music choice.

The Prince made his choice of music and soon the Vendal III was whizzing along the Ord River. Blasting out a loud rendering of good Beatles music, frightening all the bats trying to get some sleep hanging in the trees. The loud noise annoying all the crocodiles, sunning themselves on the banks of the Ord River, sending them scurrying back into the river until the noise passed.

I could see the Crown Prince was enjoying himself and liked good modern music, and fast boats. He was completely at ease on a remote Australian tropical river infested by crocodiles and other nasties. This must have been a good relaxing day for the Prince being away from the stiff Royal protocol he had to endure every day. I now understood why the Crown Prince and his Royal guard were dressed so casual; this was after all one of his few Royal days off from his demanding Princely duties.

***

We had made up a bit of lost time, mainly because of the higher speed we could average on the very smooth river, and we were now fast approaching our fig tree destination. I had informed Roger and Tom of the small cyclone forming off the Cambridge Gulf, this being the cause of all this exceptional and very calm weather we were now experiencing. They both had great difficulty in understanding why a small cyclone over a hundred kilometres away had anything to do with the calm weather here.

Another pressing matter was soon fast approaching, that being the need to explain to our royal guests the method used to berth, or tie-up the Vendal III at the fig tree picnic spot. This time I had to make sure that all on-board correctly understood my boat handling intentions, and the procedure used. I could not risk any similar type of disaster like the one in getting the boat onto fast plane fiasco, so I devised a shrewd Dallas plan.

***

The Vendal III is only twenty-four feet long however, she is quite heavy for her size. This was mainly due to the large three quarter length cabin design, high freeboard, and a wide beam. She is by no means a big boat, but heavy.

I figured out that the best way to advise all on-board about the soon to happen docking procedure, was to call Roger and Tom over to me at the helm position. In this way, I could explain the procedure to Roger at the same time our Royal guests would hear all of what I had to say. This I hoped would avoid any risk of a possible Chinese whispers distortion that had caused the last drama. It was now time to implement my well-thought-out cunning plan.

I caught Rogers's attention and motioned to him, to come over to me, Tom followed. Both Roger and Tom leant in close, drinks in hand to hear what I had to say, thus ensuring that my words would reach Crown Prince and his Royal guard.

'We will be at the fig tree location in about eight minutes time. The big fig tree will be on our right-hand side, on the high side of a sweeping left turn in the river. You will notice a high vertical mud bank cut out by the flow of the river.' A quick glance at the Royal guests confirmed that my plan was working perfectly, as all were listening most intently...

'The mud bank is usually about the same height as the bow rail of the boat. As such, I normally just drive the boat up hard against the bank, directly in front of the fig tree. I then jump on to the riverbank and quickly run the anchor rope around the fig tree. Then I jump back on the boat and pull the boat up hard against the bank, tying off the rope on the front bollard. This way provides a very nice-and-easy simple step off the boat on to the riverbank. Just make sure that our very important guests are aware we will be hitting the river bank quite hard for this easy disembarking system.'

Roger nodded and went about telling the Royal guard next to him who had as planned, already heard all my instructions. I looked ahead just as the fig tree was coming into view. I could make out four large freshwater crocodiles sunning themselves on the fig tree bank as we sped towards them. They raised their heads on hearing the boat and in disgust at being disturbed dived down into the water, right in front of where we would be docking the boat.

Freshwater Johnson crocodiles are mostly timid reptiles being more curious than vicious, nevertheless, still remembering that this was the breeding season. The males will defend their patch of the riverbank, and their harem of females against seduction by other good-looking rogue males. Female crocs will always defend their nest and any eggs or young, and can be quite convincing... and this was still the mating season.

I must always keep a sharp lookout for those crocs, as they never go very far from their declared part of the river.

The moment of action was now upon us. I turned and nodded at Roger and Tom, and noted that everybody was holding on to something tightly. I was thinking, this docking should be a breeze; but just how wrong can a man be... Well I was soon to find out.

***

My riverbank ramming was a precise and perfect success. The bow ran firmly up over the soft mud bank, with the bow now set firmly against the riverbank. I quickly pulled the boat transmission back into neutral and ran along the side deck of the boat, grabbing the anchor and rope on the way.

I then leaped off the stainless steel bow rail up onto the firm riverbank; then for some reason... who knows why, one of the Royal guards had decided to follow me onto the riverbank. I had the rope around the trunk of the big fig tree and was back on-board in a flash. With the rope looped around the front bollard, I was now ready to pull the heavy boat up hard to the bank, and then it all went terribly, terribly wrong....

***

Leaping off the bow-rail has the opposite affect by pushing the boat backwards off the mud bank and back into the river. The Thai Royal guard who had decided to follow me ashore did not help much either by further increasing this backward action of the boat.

This Thai guard had immediately started to check the picnic area for any nasties that might reside on shore, as such he could not see what was about to happen next.

The boat then started to rapidly slide back down the mud bank opening up the gap between the bow of the boat and the high riverbank.

While I was, busy, head down with my docking procedure, which I had done many times before. The Crown Prince for some reason thought that I had completed the docking job, and at a run followed his onshore guard by launching His Highness off the bow rail to land on the riverbank.

By this time, the boat had continued to move still further backwards away from the bank, considerably widening the gap. The Crown Prince jumped up from the bow-rail missing his footing on the firm riverbank by quite a long way, and landing on the very edge of the vertical slippy riverbank. We all looked on in absolute terrifying horror as the Crown Prince misjudged the gap distance, falling chest first hard against the high riverbank. Fingers clawing at the soft riverbank grass in a losing battle with gravity. Slipping slowly, but surely back down the steep sloop into the muddy river almost two metres below.

Immediately I stopped pulling the boat into the riverbank for fear of running over the Crown Prince. The Prince was now out of my line of sight, trapped under the front of the boat between the steep muddy riverbank and the high bow of the boat. I could hear his shouts for help, and much splashing about in panic. The Prince was now up to his armpits in the muddy croc infested river below.

Roger, Tom, and I all gazed on in horror, suddenly frozen in shattering disbelief at the magnitude of this Royal spectacle. No doubt, Roger and Tom were visualising their rapidly diminishing careers. Both were now witness to an unfolding disaster compounded with all its possible political consequences.

Just then in a total surprise to us all, the Royal guard on the riverbank jumped into the river alongside the Crown Prince. As I started to move to the bow-rail to offer some help, the second Royal guard took an almighty running leap off the deck into the river joining the others. In horror, we watched on as now all three of Royal Thai party were splashing about in the croc-infested Ord River, directly under the bow of my boat.

I quickly tied off the boat to halt any further slide backwards and grabbed a coil of rope. I then took a run along the deck and launched myself off the bow rail in a mighty leap on to the riverbank. Stumbling on the edge of the soft riverbank and almost joining the Royal mud bath below. I then tied the rope around the fig tree and threw the line down to the three splashing and thrashing men below now completely covered in thick Ord River mud, to be honest I could not tell who was who.

First up the rope was the Crown Prince, he had little difficulty in nimbly climbing the wet and slippy rope assisted by his guards, then quickly followed by the two Royal guards.

All of them were obviously very fit men however all three looked a very sad sight indeed, standing in a line on the riverbank covered from head to foot with thick black sticky Ord River mud. The tallest mud blob was obviously the Crown Prince. They looked like movie zombies, except for their smiling white teeth. I just had to turn away for fear that the Royal party would see my un-restrained composure and decided to look away down into the muddy water.

Not a single inquisitive crocodile seen either on land or in the water, up or down the riverbanks. The Royal Ord River diving and yelling had frightened the lot away with all their mad thrashing about in the water, most probably these grossly threatened, and terrified crocs will never visit this area again.

By this time, Roger and Tom had found their way up onto the front deck and were now watching this remarkable Royal sight across the small gap to the riverbank. They both looked on in terror at this unbelievable spectacle of the three Royal mud blobs. Tom was the first to speak, eyes wide in utter disbelief mouthing words of rumbling defeated acceptance to the final out-come.

'Well that's it then, 'eir goes my fucking Police pension for bleeding sure, a fine bleeding way to end my career.'

Roger was obviously in utter bureaucratic pain, as he had both hands clamped firmly to the front of his head in some sort of attempt to block out this vision of this catastrophic unimaginable disaster.

'God, oh my God, this can't be happening, I won't have a job after this, and my career has gone for sure, what will the Premier say?'

Picking up the anchor rope, I continued to pull the boat up to the shore, the two Royal guards quickly figured out what I was doing and helped. We soon had the Vendal III tied up and docked properly.

Roger the Administrator and the Police Sergeant Tom now made the simple and easy disembarking step (as planned) stepping up from the bow of the boat onto the fig tree riverbank.

I could hear Roger and Tom apologising profusely to the Crown Prince via the Thai officers who both seemed indifferent at their attempts to make things right. Then again, it was extremely difficult to judge the Crown Prince's reaction as his face remained completely covered in thick black Ord mud.

The whole attempt at an apology looked rather silly with Roger apologising first to the Royal Thai guards while the Prince just stood calmly to one side covered in thick mud. I did not know what to do in such a situation.

I was having serious enough problems of my own, in trying not to burst out laughing at the funny side of this whole drama. Then I thought I had better be careful, as I do not want to end-up shot by a Thai Royal guard... I decided I should carry on as if nothing had happened, after all that is what the Crown Prince himself and the Royal guard were doing.

Both the Royal guards then started scooping the mud of the Crown Prince with their hands. Then remembering I carry two four litre plastic containers of emergency freshwater, I jumped down the hatch grabbed them both and a towel, delivering them quickly to the Royal guards. The Crown Prince and the Thai officers then went about cleaning the river mud from their faces and hands as best they could, as there was only just enough water to complete this small task.

Roger and Tom were standing to one side sort of huddled together like naughty schoolchildren. They were obviously still in deep shock, no doubt contemplating their bleak future, and the end of their known working life. I then asked Roger what I should do now.

Would he prefer that I take the Crown Prince back to Kununurra, or do we carry on with the picnic? Tom suggested that Roger ought to ask the Crown Prince that question; after all, it was his call.

Roger was hesitant at the thought of saying anything to the Prince (via the Royal guard) for fear he may make matters even worse. The long lonely seconds stretched out, Roger was taking his time considering Tom's suggestion.

It was obvious to all that Roger was pale and shaken, no doubt caused by this disastrous experience. Roger looked more like a pending heart attack victim with his bottom lip trembling out of control. He then mustered up some Administer courage, took a long deep breath and walked over to the closest Thai officer.

Tom and I strained to hear what Roger was saying to the officer. However, the distance was a little too far, and the conversation was in a low voice. Tom agreed with me that he could not make out anything they said so we both just waited in silent expectation.

Like a chocolate soldier the Royal guard, covered in black mud briskly marched over to the Crown Prince, no doubt to ask what his decision may be. The Thai officer then returned and briefly spoke to Roger. Even at this distance, I could see Rogers's eyebrows shoot-up and his jaw drop with the look of total surprise on his face…

What was the decision going to be? The officer still had his gun holstered so we were all going to live for a while longer. Then again before he could fire the damn thing, he would need to clean all the Ord River mud out of it first… a must do job before he could shoot us all dead.

Walking back to Tom, I could clearly see that Roger still had a very worried look on his face. I expected it was going to be something awful so I braced myself to hear the worst. This was going to be bad, very bad… at best we would all end up shot dead. Rogers's voice was a crying plea of dis-belief…

'He wants to stay. The Crown Prince wants to have his bloody picnic, this was my direct order from the Crown Prince, no ifs, or butts, and he firmly told me to bloody well "get on with it."

My thoughts were again with the young Crown Prince and what he might be feeling on this his rare day off from his boring Royal business. This was after all his day out, and from what I could see, nothing was going to spoil it, not even a dunk in the muddy Ord River. The Crown Prince of Thailand shall have his personal play day… whatever.

It was now ten thirty, I wished that I had ignored Chati and brought my camera along. Nobody in years to come will ever believe this story... On the other hand, this day was a long way from over... in fact far from it.

As I walked over to the fig tree, the two Royal guards came over to help me take down the large rolled up canvas tarp, firmly roped to a chest-high branch. I bashed the canvas with a stick, while still roped to the tree branch; only one small skinny king brown snake came out of the roll. Then armed with my can of powerful spider spray, the two muddy Royal guards and I un-rolled the canvas tarp on the ground and a scurry of large hairy spiders ran out heading at full speed for the bush.

Without a word spoken, the two Royal guards then manhandled the large Esky chest cooler off the boat, and placed it in the middle of the flat tarp. They then went about setting out the table and chair positions, unfolding five of the six light canvas chairs always kept at the base of the big fig tree.

Two chairs were placed together at one end of the large Esky facing one chair at the other end, with a further two chairs placed together, but set well behind the single chair. I studied this chair layout and concluded that Roger and Tom would most probably face the Crown Prince across my large Esky with the two Royal guards sitting at a respectable distance behind the Prince.

It was now obvious to me that I was not included, or required to attend this Royal picnic. After all, I was only the boat captain... was I correct. We were soon to find out. With the table layout complete, we were now ready for this Royal picnic to begin.

Chapter Four:

The Royal Picnic

A new level of calm had settled over our mud covered Royal Thai guests. I had also noted that Roger and Tom were showing some signs of returning to a normal decorum with a slightly less terrified look on their faces. Nevertheless, the Royal picnic lunch must proceed in the correct Royal manner observing position and rank. As such, we busily went about setting up the picnic Esky table as best we could.

When complete, they all took-up their positions at the picnic Esky; my chair layout guess proved correct with the expected protocol. The Crown Prince sat at the head of the large Esky and the two Royal guards seated directly behind him. Roger and Tom sat at the other end of the Esky facing the Prince.

As expected, I on the other hand being just the lowly boat crew required to remain on the boat, so my assumption was correct. This suited me fine, as I much preferred watching in wonderment at this rather strange mud-covered display of Royal Thai picnic protocol from the comfortable helm position of the Vendal III.

I must say, the picnic lunch generously prepared by the Hotel Kununurra, being best described as a magnificent Australian bush effort. The only thing was, the Crown Prince was not very hungry; and as such, the Royal guards did not get much to eat. Apparently, by Royal etiquette they could only eat after the Prince, and by about the same amount.

This did not deter Roger and Tom, who obviously had not noticed this Thai Royal protocol, and were soon tucking into the excellent Royal picnic feast. Tom, ever thoughtful, brought some food over to me on a large plastic plate and I met him at the bow rail to take delivery of this feast. Thanking him for thinking of me and sarcastically advising that my tail was waging madly.

Tom said it was no fun over there either, as nobody spoke a damn word and that as a lowly cop he was going to try join me on the ship for lunch. I pointed out that such a move from the Royal table (the Esky,) might be in some way regarded as an insult to the Crown Prince, and that he had better stay with the picnic party. Tom let out a low groan and returned to the Royal guests.

The Royal picnic continued on in total silence as talking in the presence of the Prince without prior permission was not the accepted protocol. To break the awkward silence I decided to turn up the volume of the Beatles this had little effect on the mood or composure of all who were sitting at the picnic table. I could see that nobody was enjoying their picnic lunch or having a good time.

***

Just as I was enjoying my lunch, I noticed a slight breeze. Shortly after a shadow formed across my lunch plate, which caused me to immediately look up and to the north. The whole of the northern sky was forming with thick black heavy cumulonimbus cloud, complete with the classic anvil heads, and was heading this way.

Time for a weather update, I switched on the HF radio again. Kununurra airport ATIS reported a temperature of 44°C, surface wind 18 knots from the north and the trend rising with a QNH down to 992mb. Therefore, the wind was picking up, and the atmospheric pressure was falling... not a good sign.

Darwin marine HF gave a far better area weather picture. There was an all station alert, a category three cyclone was gathering strength in the Cambridge Gulf, now on the move heading towards Wyndham and the northern coast.

I was about to report this worrying declining weather synopsis to Roger and looked up to see yet another amazing, and utterly unbelievable sight. The Thai Crown Prince for some bizarre reason was swinging on the low fig-tree branch. His Highness had decided to add some action to the dull and dismal picnic proceedings.

This action achieved by taking a run and jumping onto the low hanging fig-tree branch. (The very same branch that the rolled up ground tarp had previously been tied to) This tree-branch was about chest high off the ground. I say was, as the low fig tree branch promptly broke; under the weight of the Crown Prince's second, or was it his third swing. The matter completed with a resounding sharp crack and a yelp of surprise.

His Royal Highness the Prince was promptly sent tumbling to the ground with the heavy tree branch landing with a mighty thump just above the Prince's Royal head. The tree-branch just missing the Prince's head was the lucky part. However, the unlucky part was that the ground at this particular point just happens to fall away quite rapidly, falling steeply into a muddy running creek bed, which then enters the Ord River alongside the fig tree.

Unceremoniously the Crown Prince rolled down the steep slope into the shallow flowing creek bed, picking up many dead fig-tree leaves and messy figs on the way down. All of which stuck quite firmly to the sticky black mud with which the Crown Prince was already amply covered. From my raised position at the helm of the Vendal III, I witnessed the start of this unbelievable tragedy unfolding before my very eyes like a slow-motion comedy movie.

When the branch suddenly broke, the Prince had rolled down the steep bank into the creek bed, and was now out of my line of sight; I feared that the worst might have happened. My stunned, frozen body, launched into action like a costumed hero. I ran with all urgency to this odd accident scene, on my way, picking up the very same coil of rope that I used in the previous riverbank rescue.

Just as I reached the top of the steep slope both Royal guards who were first to the scene did an unbelievable and utterly ridicules thing. They both jumped down the very steep slope. Purposely rolling head over heels, just as the Prince would have done, down to the bottom of the creek bed to the patiently waiting Crown Prince below. What a catastrophe, all three of the Royal Thai party were now thoroughly covered in thick black Ord River mud, dried leaves, and rotten figs. The sort of look that came to mind was like the saying... they were well tarred and feathered.

I was later to learn that this sort of following reaction was a normal Thai gesture of saving face for the Crown Prince.

The Crown Prince attempted to climb out of the steep creek bed with both Thai guards pushing him from behind, however the Prince kept falling over and sliding back down to the bottom again. After three or four frustrating attempts, they gave up. All three just stood still and looked up at me, arms by their sides covered in thick mud and leaves. Waiting while I tied the rope to the fig tree again and quickly sent the rope down to them.

They all climbed back out of the creek bed with little effort, the Prince being first, they all looked a mess; gone were the smartly pressed uniforms and gold braid. With their hands, the Royal guards then started in an attempt to remove the thick mud and leaves from the Crown Prince again.

This scene was asking for some help. I then forgot my lowly service place, breaking the non-talking protocol by suggesting to one of the Thai officers that since I do not have any more clean water. The best I could do was a bucket on a rope over the back transom of the Vendal III. Very politely, the Thai officer accepted my offer then we all trooped off in a long line down to the back of the boat with the Beatles music blaring away... *"Yesterday, all my troubles seemed so far away, now it looks as though they're here to stay, oh I believe in yesterday."*

Roger and Tom were standing behind me. Heads bowed, silently looking the other way so as not to witness this tragic event, again contemplating the cause and the end to their long careers. Meanwhile in front of me, the Royal guards went about tipping buckets of brown Ord River water over the Crown Prince standing on the boats wide transom.

Out of respect for the Prince, I also turned away and motioned Roger and Tom to follow me over to the helm. Roger, with his now permanent very worried look etched on his face considered this the worst day in his whole memorable life.

He seriously thought he might soon have a heart attack coming on. Tom totally agreed with Roger that a heart attack might just be the best answer in this tragic situation. Adding such an event would be quite in order considering the past events, but with a somewhat restrained smile on his face.

I think that Tom in his career would have witnessed some very sad sights during his long Police service. On the other hand, this day was still far from over, and who knows, the rapidly changing weather may well be the cause of our next disaster.

I turned the Beatles music off and the HF two-way radio volume up so all could hear the current weather forecast, and then explained the weather situation in a raised voice so all could hear. I then went about trying to convince Roger this picnic should end.

'Roger this is not a good weather forecast as this cyclone system is building up very quickly and heading our way, just look at the blackening sky,' pointing to the north. 'We should get going right now at full speed back to Kununurra away from that lot.'

Roger said he would go and suggest this plan to the Crown Prince that we should leave for Kununurra soon. This was a perfect example of bureaucratic madness, to which I firmly responded.

'Roger we are long beyond the asking phase... you have got to "tell" the Crown Prince we are going back to Kununurra now, do not ask him. You have a responsibility to keep the Crown Prince of Thailand from any danger, and this is a present danger. I have seen these tropical weather patterns too many times before. They can be on us quicker than you think, can't you understand, it is not safe to stay here anymore.'

Just then, I noticed that the cell-call light was flashing on the front of the HF radio, this light flashes when my office is trying to get in touch with me. I flicked over to the company channel and immediately Robyn my sort-of hire-car hostess come secretary blasted through in her normal vocal manner.

'Where the fucking hell have you lot been? I've been trying to get you all bloody morning, haven't you heard the weather forecast. There's a bloody category three cyclone building up off the coast, can't you stupid bastards see it from there?'

If the Crown Prince of Thailand had no knowledge of English swearing, then this would have been an excellent first lesson from Robyn. However, a glance in the Crown Prince's direction confirmed that he had heard every word. He was now laughing loudly at Robyn's dramatic radio call between buckets of water cascading over him. I pushed the talk button.

'Yes Robyn, I know the weather is starting to turn bad. We are preparing to go back to Kununurra soon,' then glancing at my watch. 'It's now eleven fifteen so we should get the Crown Prince back to the Pump Station at about twelve thirty give, or take a few minutes.' Robyn clicked back,

'Well if you get back at that time you'll be thirty minutes too fucking late for the Darwin flight. The bloody jet is on the ground right now and its leaving at twelve midday sharp not one o'clock. They are all very concerned about this cyclone build-up on the flight up to Darwin. Just in case, you didn't get the urgency boss, that's in just thirty minutes time... from right now, can't you get here any earlier, maybe go faster or something?'

My brain went numb, there was no way we could cover the twenty-odd miles back to Kununurra in forty-five minutes, and we had yet to load everything back onto the boat... Think of something... shit I must think of something, and quickly.

Chapter Five:

Saved by Goldfinger

The wind was starting to blow hot and steady, this being the first early signs of an incoming bad weather front, thinking that at least the wind would be behind us now. I then launched myself into yet another action man, turning to Roger and Tom.

'Right you guys let's get this bloody boat loaded and underway. We have to get out from under this looming storm and make like a bat out of hell back to Kununurra to catch that Darwin jet.'

The radio was very loud and everybody had heard Robyn, and her usual full on swearing, all understanding the entire weather and jet departure situation. When I turned around to check on the Royal progress all three were having a good laugh, now it was the Crown Prince's turn to see the funny side of this situation. It was more than obvious to him that panic was setting in and that the pressure was now very much on us.

The Crown Prince took up his usual position at the co-helm and everybody quickly got into loading up the boat. Then I had this brilliant idea, and got back onto the radio and clicked the mike button,

'Robyn, are you still there? I've had this great idea.' Robyn got back... in a dry sort of response.

'Oh yea, and just what's that gonna be this time boss?'

Robyn had her usual sound of doubt in her voice as she had witnessed many of my not-so-great ideas in the past.

'Call John Caratti on the phone, tell him about our problem, we need him to get Goldfinger into the water and up here fast. This is the only way I can think of to get the Prince back in time to catch the jet to Darwin. Get back to me if you can get him to do this for me?'

John Caratti owned the fastest boat on the Ord River that had five seats. Goldfinger could cruise at sixty-five knots and stretch out to just under seventy knots; she was a very fast ski boat, and sexy looking with a metallic flake gold sparkle paint finish.

The boats name came from the James Bond movie Goldfinger, I wondered what His Highness the Crown Prince of Thailand would make of all this. The radio came to life interrupting my thoughts. Robyn blasted out,

'Caratti and Goldfinger are on their way, we were lucky and caught up with him at the ski beach with his boat and some new bloody barmaid in town. He knows the urgency so watch out for him.'

***

All aboard and ready to go, the engine fired up on the second turn I then put the Vendal III into reverse and opened the throttle however we went nowhere. The bow was stuck firmly into the muddy bank. Full throttle only caused the river to turn a deeper red with silt and black mud. Roger was standing next to me. I thought he might have his promised heart attack as he looked like hell.

This was a most trying day for the man. He was all out of politics and bossy overpowering administrating, or so I had thought. Just then he lapsed quite suddenly back into administrating again with a brilliant public servant idea. He suggested he would push the boat free from the riverbank; he did not seem to understand that this action would leave him stranded on the bloody riverbank. I must admit I did give this idea some serious consideration when out of the corner of my eye I could see the look on the Crown Prince's face. He had also thought of this same great master plan. I had to act quickly, announcing in a confident Captains voice...

'No need to worry gentlemen, this is just a normal boating problem and I have an easy fix.' Turning to Roger and Tom, 'if you two heavy gents would kindly just go down to the back of the boat, and sit in your positions on the transom.'

Roger and Tom both gave me glaring look at the suggestion of their generous body weight situation.

'Now gentlemen, when I gun the throttle in reverse just start rocking the boat from side to side, this will release the suction on the bow... trust me it works every time.'

I took a quick glance at the Crown Prince to confirm he was staying put this time, and then sighed in relief as the Vendal III gently slid back into the river. We were soon moving at a fast idle tracking down the centre of the river towards Kununurra. I did my usual thing in setting the helm, and then had a quiet chat with Roger and Tom still sitting on the transom.

'We must get this boat up onto fast plane for the trip back, but this time gentlemen everybody must go into the cabin,' pointing to the cabin door,

'And please gentlemen, no windsurfing on the bow this time. Roger would you get everyone to move into the cabin now and don't forget to hang on to something, when we get up on plane you can all head back to your normal positions.

This time it was a simple easy manoeuvre, we were soon cruising down the Ord River at full throttle, at twenty-eight plus knots. The Crown Prince selected a Rolling Stones tape and he cranked up the volume, everybody looked a bit more relaxed. *"I ain't got no satisfaction,"* blared out across the Ord River. Roger and Tom were not convinced this music choice was a good idea, they thought it was another of my jokes. I told them it was the Prince who selected that song not me.

***

My watch said it was now fifteen minutes to twelve, and we still had a long way to go. All the clouds to the north were gathering momentum and I could see the occasional flash of lightning. We had only been cruising for about seven or eight minutes when I caught sight of Goldfinger darting towards us.

By the time I throttled down the Vendal III and backed the boat off the plane, John was quickly alongside with his golden beauty. I could see the Crown Prince was most impressed at the sight of this beautiful boat. Then I remembered Thai's like golden things, this golden boat was very much a thing of beauty however not quite in the same way as the magnificent golden temples of Thailand.

As I tied off Goldfinger to the Vendal III, I noticed the odd startled look on Johns face. He could obviously see that the Royal party were in a mighty mess, wet from head to toe and covered in mud, yet we were all perfectly dry. I could also see that John had some very urgent questions brewing in his mind. I put my finger to my lips in a gesture of say nothing; luckily, John caught on and remained silent. Jumping into his boat, I got close enough to whisper to John.

'You have just under twenty minutes chum to get this Royal party on that bloody Darwin bound jet, if you don't we will have an almighty Australian, Royal Thai international incident on our hands.'

John looked at me with a wide grin and replied in his slight Italian accent,

'By the looks of the Thai Royal party my friend I think you blokes have already caused an international incident eh. Anyway, just think about all the worldwide press coverage that Kununurra and Australia will get, we will all be famous no. Can you see the newspaper headlines; "Australian businessman Niven Dallas tries to drown the visiting Thai Royal Party," sounds good no?'

I stared at John trying to figure out if he was serious or not, as I was about to reply he said....

'Only joking, don't panic my friend, I will get them all on the Darwin jet for you, then quietly in a Mafia sort-of-way he said... "Remember you owe me now."

The Royal party quickly transferred to the waiting ski boat. Just as I was about to cast off the bow line a Royal guard leaned forward and whispered in my ear, 'Captain, a gift from His Royal Highness' pressing a muddy coin into my hand.

***

My last view of the Crown Prince of Thailand and his Royal guard was the three of them, sitting bolt upright military style in the rear seat of Goldfinger, all still covered in Ord

River slime and mud. The Prince was sitting between his two Royal guards, which was probably just as well.

Suddenly, John snapped open the throttles of Goldfinger, which had the effect of launching this powerful ski boat forward in a mighty leap almost out of the water causing the mud covered Prince and the Royal guards to seek a quick hold onto something.

The Thai officers were lucky as the ski boat had large stainless steel grab handle-holds on the side deck next to the rear seats, but the centre position had nothing to hold onto. This mighty thrust of acceleration caused the slippery mud-covered Crown Prince, who was sitting in the middle seat to be catapulted backwards out of his seat.

This aggressive action was quickly arrested and saved only by the Prince's arms wrapping around the stout stainless-steel ski pole situated directly behind him. The extremely quick-acting Thai officers then made a grab for the Crown Prince's rapidly disappearing legs with their free hands, and slowly pulled him back on-board Goldfinger.

Yet another Royal tragedy avoided, but only by the very quick reaction of the Royal guard in saving their Crown Prince from disappearing over the back of Goldfinger. From my point of view, it was a close thing indeed. The Royal party almost ended up in the Ord River yet again. With the loud noise of the engine and the thrill of acceleration, John had never thought to look back. He was completely oblivious to this dramatic unfolding Royal dilemma happening right behind him.

Roger and Tom were watching all of this happen with mournful cries from Roger of, "I just can't believe it" and clutching his chest. "Oh God not again" Sergeant Tom the ever-practical police officer had the very answer to this entire high stress situation.

'Captain 'ave you got anything to drink on this fucking boat, I really do need a bleeding drink, and I like the way you serve your coke-a-cola.'

***

As Goldfinger speed off into the distance, being now only a dot on the water I cranked up the Vendal III and set the engine to a relaxing smart idle cruise of twelve knots. There was no hurry to get back now. It was just starting to rain, a cool welcome rain, and I felt the stress wash out of me, grateful this day was almost over.

***

Now was the ideal time to inspect my Royal gift.

Looking down at my opened palm, all my suspicions were now confirmed. The Prince had tipped me twenty cents, a bloody twenty cent coin. After removing the mud, a further inspection revealed that the coin was a shiny new nickel-plated twenty Baht, with a head on one side and an elephant on the other. Slipping the coin into my pocket to join the others, I decided that I too deserved a drink.

Tom was lamenting about his lost Police pension; how he and his wife would be poor in retirement without it. Roger was rehearsing his detailed explanation for his boss Sir Charles Court and his (It was not my fault) speech while we leisurely motored back to the Pump Station dock. As we approached the Pump Station I was in one of my daydreaming moods going over the days memorable events when the radio blasted me back into reality, it was the delightful young Robyn calling...

'Well you buggers are bloody lucky; I've just been told that they all got on the plane. They held the bloody jet up another half-hour for the Prince and his Royal party, all wet through and covered in mud. What the fuck have you guys done to the Prince? People in powerful positions are asking tough questions, I'm pretty sure you're all in real deep shit this time.'

***

Roger and Tom had heard every word of this radio call, and were wincing at the thought of what was to come from their superiors. Roger looked like he was about to cry, and Tom mumbled something about he only had a few more years to go to his retirement. This was not sounding good, I thought I had a boat Captains responsibility to cheer them both up a bit.

'Listen you guys, don't get all upset over Robyn's ranting views on our right Royal situation, she is after all only my 19-year old hire car hostess'.... Roger butted in.

'She might be just a nineteen-year-old hire car hostess, but she's bleeding right on the ball with our grim situation... all three of us are in almighty deep, deep shit.'

Grabbing the radio microphone, I responded to the good lady Robyn,

'Robyn, we have received all of that negative stuff thank you very much. Might I remind you that I have on board the Vendal III Mr Roger Gayton the Administrator for the North West of Western Australia and the most senior Civil Servant in this area. I also have Senior Sergeant Thomas Corker, the most senior Policeman in the Kimberley. I will remind you Robyn, that I am your boss and would appreciate a little more respect, decorum, and secrecy regarding this delicate matter'

Quick as a flash Robyn got back.

'I don't care a fuck who they are. After dunking the Crown Prince of Thailand and his officers in the Ord River those blokes won't have a job by this time next week, and you might as well close up shop too, cause this put's you and me out of a job as well. As for secrecy, well I will remind you mister smarty pants radio man boss, this here radio transmitter is an open channel long range HF radio call, and every bastard in the top end of Australia could have heard this conversation.'

There was a long emotional moment of silence. Nobody spoke for some time as the magnitude of that statement sank in to our feeble brains. Now it was my time to cringe, Robyn was of course right, there was now every chance that I could kiss goodbye to any further government work orders. We all sat thinking and looking glum... this was indeed a very bad day for us all.

As I reached forward to switch the HF radio off, it sparkled to life again and a voice said...

'I reckon that Robyn bird is right, you are all in the smelly brown stuff...' then another.

'Why don't you all just walk the plank and get it over with ha ha ha...'

As I again reached to turn the radio off a heavy, Russian accent said.

'How mucha you want for dat boat mate, musta be going cheap by now eh.'

The click off brought a welcome silence.

***

They say time heals all problems, and a diversion from the problem creates the needed time. This is how all politicians manage to survive their political disasters, and that is just how Roger, Tom, and I managed to survive this right Royal Thai misfortune.

Some years later after relating this story to a group of strangers at a business dinner, a guest who had been listening intently gave me yet a further reason to regret the Royal picnic experience, he said.

***

'Niven, you don't by chance still have that twenty Baht coin. You may not be aware that the coin given to you by the Crown Prince of Thailand was most likely very special indeed. I am a collector of rare world coins and have some considerable knowledge on the subject. The twenty Baht coin would have been uncirculated having the head of the Prince and the date stamp of 1972, when the Prince first conferred as the Crown Prince. As in most sovereign countries around the world, only the heads of the reigning Monarch is on the nation's currency.

To have a coin with the Crown Prince's head on it while the King is still sitting is very rare indeed. I would say it would be worth quite a bit by now especially as King Bhumibol Adulyadej of Thailand is still very much alive. I would be most interested to see this coin.'

As my new business dinner friend was talking, I was trying hard to remember just what had happened to this very special Thai coin... and then I remembered everything clearly... After I looked at the coin, I had just put it into my white footy shorts pocket to join all my other loose change.

We had had an unusually harrowing day that day, so what would any man do in that situation... Yes, you guessed right; he would simply go down to the local pub and have a few relaxing stress free beers with the boys, and talk about the day's boring events.

This pleasant memory has now moved gracefully into history.

I was most surprised, and honoured that circumstances allowed me to meet the Crown Prince of Thailand, and I am sure that the Prince did enjoy his rather eventful Ord River picnic

At the time of this event, His Royal Highness the Crown Prince was only 23 years old.

The Crown Prince of Thailand Maha Vajiralongkorn was born 28th July 1952.

HRH was conferred the Crown Prince and heir to the throne of Thailand 28th December 1972. His Highness holds the following distinctions.

Bachelor of Arts (Military)"University of NSW Australia"

Royal Thai Army Command College

Bachelor of Law "University of Bangkok"

Air Chief Marshal Royal Thai Air force Pilot Rotary and Fixed wing.

In addition, many other international Military and training tours in Australia, UK, USA, Germany, Belgium, and France.

---- The End ----

Part Two: Are black trackers black?

Chapter One:

No hire car, no Japanese

The eastern sky was black with heavy cumulus tropical rain clouds. It had been raining heavy on and off all morning and the MMA (MacRobertson Miller Airlines) Fokker F27 Friendship propjet was due in from Perth in about 15 minutes.

This was not going to be a good meeting as the clients hire car had not returned from the previous hire and no other hire vehicle was available.

Hire vehicles not returned on time was a regular thing for a number of reasons. A friend may have offered to drop off the hirer at the airport and agreed to return the car for them later. It could be the hirer decided to leave the car at the motel and get the shuttle bus to the airport, or as was mostly the case. The hirer just decided to keep the vehicle for an extra few days without ever advising me. Whichever way, it was all in a day's work, now it looks like I will have to meet this new hire client without a hire car available.

The year was 1972, and for the town of Kununurra and the Kimberly region, it was proving to be a very busy year. Busy with many prospectors and mining exploration companies searching for oil, gas, silver and lead, uranium, gold, and now diamonds.

As would be expected, my hire fleet consisted mostly of heavy 4X4 vehicles especially fitted out for mining and exploration. The hire fleet also included four small sedans primarily for tourists and visiting company representatives. However right now, it would appear that one of my new Datsun 1600 sedans had gone missing.

There were few sealed roads in the area, and the local gravel roads were sometimes difficult to identify as to which was actually the primary road. By city dwellers standards, these unfenced and un-named roads were extremely primitive. These facts required a newly arrived hire-driver to use additional caution in both driving and navigating around this remote area. Getting lost in one of my hire vehicles was an every-day event for the over adventurous visiting tourist, and might I add some overconfident Geologists.

***

The Perth aircraft was about to land, and I still had no news from the depot if the hire car had returned. Like many times before, my one and only hire car hostess nicknamed Stubby (as her name was Helen Bottle) or I, went out to the airport to sign-up, or pick-up the client.

In the event of a vehicle not being returned problem, the standard plan was to hope the car, or any car would be back at the depot when I got the client back to sign up. Today, well it was my turn to go to the airport and face the angry client.

Today was a steamy hot 40°c on the airport tarmac and around 100% humidity, being quite normal weather for this time of the year. It was late February with lots of monsoonal water still about, and not a good time to be visiting the Kimberley. Just then, I felt the tell-tale cool wind of a fast approaching weather front, a glance to the north confirmed that another tight tropical rainsquall was almost upon us.

The MMA Fokker F27 pilot was way ahead of this type of weather front. This was just another small tropical weather-flying problem expected at this time of the year, and as per normal; the pilot had decided to take our visitors on a short ten-minute free sightseeing flight, keeping well away from the airport and the path of the fast approaching tropical squall.

A wall of thunderous rain arrived like a silver curtain to cool the hot tarmac, which was now steaming like a bar-b-cue hotplate being water cleaned.

It will take a great deal more rain than this short downpour to cool this scorching hot earth. All the locals just stood in the hard pounding rain chatting away. There was not much point sheltering under the tin awning, as the noise would be deafening. Anyway, we would all be dry again in about ten minutes, most likely, well before the plane had landed.

These monsoonal weather cells were small and tightly localised. A number of times I had noticed that it could thunder down raining, causing a mini-flood in the town and be completely dry without a drop of rain at the airport, only six kilometres away.

It was all over as quick as it started, we were now in a thick steam bath watching as the Fokker F27 lined up for its landing. I had a quick glance around the airport hoping that the car may be there, my new Datsun 1600 hire car was not in the airport car park. The Perth propjet pulled up on to the hardstand and began disgorging its hot bewildered passengers. I had another thought, and then quickly ran into the depressingly hot, non-air-conditioned arrivals and departure building that the local Shire called an airport terminal lounge.

This was my last chance, with a bit of luck the keys and a note might be in the key drop-off box. All hopes were soon dashed; apart from the remains of a dead cockroach and a smug looking fat spider, the airport key box was empty. I was now starting to get a little concerned; the hire contract stated that this was the hirer's departure flight. If this hire client has already booked out of their Hotel and then misses this Darwin flight, I might have no other option than to report this missing hire car to the Police as lost, or possibly stolen. This had happened before.

Standing in this hotbox of a terminal building was not helping me think straight at all. I had to get outside quickly before I passed out with heat stress in this hot and humid heat.

I soon found a cooler spot so I could watch the passengers tumble out of their air-conditioned aircraft, as always amused to see their shocked faces as they experience for the first time this oppressive Kimberley heat.

It is an interesting time to watch the new Kununurra arrivals. Mainly how they cope with the sudden shock of a large temperature and humidity change. I was thinking how strange that people would quite easily jump on an aircraft to travel to a known hot part of Australia and then suffer in the heat.

Repeatedly I have witnessed the complacency of people who are completely unprepared for this harsh tropical climate. The local heat hits them like a surging wall as the unsuspecting passenger step through the aircraft's open door. They make a natural steadying grab for the blistering hot aluminium stairway rail and quickly retract there scorched hand in pain. Confused and blinded by the bright tropical light and no doubt wondering why they had decided to wear a city business suit on this particular trip. Some passengers would still have on heavy winter outfits and raincoats, providing quite a strange sight.

The experienced airline hostess standing at the aircraft door is ready in position; she has seen it all many times before. She makes a well-timed and confident grab for the devastated passengers arm, giving him or her time to compose themselves before attempting to descend the hot stairs (this time without touching the stair handrail) stumbling down on to the hot shimmering tarmac below.

My next pastime amusement is trying to guess who in this staggering, sweating line of descending passengers will be my new hire client. Little do they know that their quick dash across the hot tarmac to the small terminal building is a total and wasted effort, as they will find no relief from the searing heat in there.

The waiting locals, (including me) are standing outside at the boundary fence, under the large tin awning, catching any morsel of breeze that may be present. Only a few desperate people are inside the terminal building to use the toilets, all will end up outside. This should have offered some sort of clue as to the best place to handle this type of climate. The experienced North-West traveller flying on to Darwin has cunningly learnt to stay on the air-conditioned aircraft, as the pilot's and crew have.

***

To fill in time I like to study the type of passenger arriving at this time of the year. Sorting the passengers into different groups is amusing and most times obvious. I can now see three young sweaty faced, new geologists; all dressed in the same silly Geo uniform, no doubt fresh out of university with new degrees.

My guess is that three different mining exploration companies are the employers of this smart trio; it is easy to figure this out as they ignore one another. This is a time in the Kimberley of big Mining Company secrets for those who have land claim-pegged, and of course... where. The first Geo rule taught is never associate with the opposition exploration employees at any time. Loose lips cost claims.

The way they dress gives them away. Brand new kaki shirt and pants, new tan desert boots with a slouch hat worn with dark polar wraparound sunglasses for style, finished off with a wide brown leather belt. Firmly attached to the belt, and positioned correctly in leather fob pouches are the mandatory compass, pocket watch, army water bottle and of course the indispensable Swiss army knife.

They are all set for an extensive out-back exploration programme... and possible fame. They are all in for one hell of a big shock as most of these young Geo's will be back in the city within three months. Some might be on the next plane out, especially after a brief meeting with their new fellow working mates.

It is a tough life out in the remote exploration camps. Within the next few hours, those nice new khaki pants and shirts will look like all the other crew, saturated in sweat and covered in red Kimberley dust and blowflies.

All my daydreaming thoughts were suddenly shattered by a loud shouting voice on the airport PA system, clearly directed at me.

'DALLAS 'I've been trying to ring you all bloody morning don't you ever answer your frigging phone,' everyone within a hundred metres turned to see what was going on, the voice on the airport PA continued…

'Buggered if I know how you can run a business. Those two Japanese blokes that hired your car from the Hotel haven't checked in for their departure to Darwin, it looks like they've missed this damn flight because of you.'

***

Dan was the senior dispatch officer for MMA (MacRobertson Miller Airlines.) He was using his new walkie-talkie wireless microphone while standing right in front of me, the loud scene created to embarrass and heckle me. He did not like me much, or my little hire vehicle business, well not since he found a large pile of my hire-car handout brochures on his dispatch desk, and more on the MMA front check-in counter.

He was after all a confirmed diehard Avis and Budget rent-a-car man. In the past, Dan had pinched many of my vehicle hires, and now in recent months I had become even more successful at pinching his. In fairness, no love was lost between us. I suppose hate would be a better description as he had little time or tolerance for me as a local town smart-arse bloke… yes it was sometimes tough to be in business in this small town, but fun.

Thinking I had best try to ignore this outburst as people were looking at me, no doubt absolutely sure that I was the cause of some pending disaster. Then I remembered about my newly arriving hire client, and then politely asked Dan.

'Dan 'is there by chance a Mr Tony Bates on your arrivals manifest?'

Dan's already hot and bright-red puffed face was expanding further in the sweaty steaming tropical heat and now turning a dark purple, not a good sign. After all, this was top-secret airline information that I was asking for. I quickly decide to interject before Dan blew an eyeball out, or had a heart attack.

'Hang on their Danny boy old friend,' Dan absolutely hated the name "Danny Boy" whistling the song when around him did not help ether.

'Now just listen here a bit my good friend. If you do not know where your passengers are, and the Hotel Kununurra where they were staying reckons they have not checked out yet, then that is a matter between the Hotel and you… not me.'

I paused to think…

78

'Simple logic tells me that as I have never seen them and my hire car is not at this airport. Then we must come to the obvious conclusion that these two Japanese tourist blokes are still in or around Kununurra. They must still be out, and about somewhere in my beautiful new Datsun hire car... possibly just ran out of fuel, or lost, or they might be'...

Dan stopped me in my tracks, he was not in the least bit interested in my theories, with bulging eyes Dan stuck his face forward into my face blasting out...

'For starters I am not your bloody good friend, and never will be. Anyway in one of your shitty little hire cars Dallas, they are probably frigging well broken-down in the bush somewhere... maybe dead.'

Well he said the "dead" word first. Dan's dislike for me was more than obvious. However, those comments were uncalled-for as the vehicle in question was new, in fact being only some five weeks old. The vehicle was a nice new Datsun 1600 air-conditioned white four-door sedan.

On the other hand, Dan did have a point; these people could easily be lost... I was not prepared to agree with him about them being dead. I could see the city newspaper headlines "Two Japanese tourists lost in the Australian outback," no doubt provided by Dan, and then. "Kimberley Car Hire Company fuck's up again, two Japanese men found dead in the out-back visiting a local scenic beauty spot near Kununurra."

As a parting blast, Dan announced that my hire client Mr Bates had missed his flight out of Broome, adding that he would be offering him a nice big Avis hire car on the next arriving flight, then as a parting insult. No doubt your missing little car was the same vehicle offered to Mr Bates.'

Dan was suggesting that my new car was not a reliable hire vehicle, an excellent hire client pinching strategy; it appears Dan was not the complete dill as I had thought. I must keep an eye on young Dan because he is learning my tricks very fast, and getting far better these days at pinching my hire car clients.

Well no hire client had arrived, yet another daily hire car problem solved. Also another apology averted, well at least for the time being. It was now time for me to put in some serious thoughts into what may have happened to my hire vehicle... and more important, what may have happened to the two Japanese tourists who had hired it.

Chapter Two:

Just a bad pub Map

As an enterprising young businessperson, I had what I thought was a great idea to expand my newly founded hire vehicle empire. The plan was simple enough, being to offer the local Hotel, Motel, and Caravan Park and others a ten percent cash along the finger commission on any vehicle hire they promoted for me.

Being a small-town of only some 3500 local inhabitants this incentive should work well as everybody knows everybody's business. It is a known fact throughout the world that "cash along the finger" works wonders.

The Hotel had recently employed a new front desk receptionist who had apparently totally misunderstood my ten percent commission deal thinking it was some sort of personal offer. The new receptionist had figured that this commission opportunity was a good way to make a few extra bucks on the side, a sort of part-time income, all while working for someone.

I had to admit that this ten percent cash along the finger offer was getting some good results and coming up with some excellent ideas. I soon had a substantial increase in the number of positive vehicle hires, and was later to find out that unfortunately one idea came with a little extra-added Kimberley style of business brilliance.

***

One would assume that the locals in any small-town would all know the best picnic areas and scenic spots right. Well this may be so; however, unknown to me the Kununurra Hotel's new blond receptionist had thought up a brand new way to create additional hires for my vehicles. This idea was achieved by simply providing the hirer with a selection of maps and directions to find the various local scenic spots.

The new receptionist Pia (who liked a few drinks with the boys,) had figured out who were the best people to get all this local area information from…

To her this was simply obvious; the old road maintenance blokes who hung around the workers bar would know all the best local areas. She introduced herself by buying a round of beer, and started a long chat with some of the local bar flies and drunks who permanently live in the Hotel front bar.

Over some time, Pia managed to get them to provide all sorts of local information in the way of maps and directions to some of the best local scenic picnic areas. Then after some considerable time drinking together, these drunks then managed to produce a series of incredibly hard to read spider-inkwell style crappy maps.

The idea was to assist some unfortunate tourist who may wish to hire a vehicle (one of my vehicles) drive to a few of the Kununurra bush scenic spots, helping them by providing a choice of easy to follow maps and directions.

***

I had called in at the Hotel, hopeful of some news or any information on the missing Japanese tourists. I guess I was lucky as Pia; the new Hotel receptionist was on duty at the front counter. I introduced myself as the owner of Multi Agencies hire cars, pointing to a small stack of my hire car handouts on the counter in front of her.

I was later to find out that Pia was a full representative of the classic dumb blond profile. She may not be very smart, but she sure as hell qualified in the good looks department, and we were short of single females in this remote town. I could understand why Cam (the Hotel owner) had her positioned in the front reception, kind of on show. Her large blue eyes, beautiful face, and dual assets had easily distracted me.

Staring at her in a sort of mesmerised way, I had this male thought cross my mind. One would think that a small bit of local girly talk would have been well-intended advice to a newly arrived city girl. Especially as in the hot tropics, copious amounts of city slicker style make-up and the forces of gravity had an undesirable effect on ones attempts at looking your best, especially in 40°c+ of tropical heat. I decided simply to put that lack of advice down to outright local female jealousy.

I was looking into her cute but streaking face, when my view descended to her ample well-formed breasts where Pia had clearly taken into consideration the local climate by reducing the amount of her clothing to a minimum... no doubt to keep cool. Her eyes followed my gaze, and then I noticed that she had noticed that I noticed... I then awkwardly blurted out.

'Have you seen any Jap's around lately?'

'No' was the slow reply, her eyes looking me up and down with a (I know what you are looking at) smile, and then she perked up. 'Oh you mean those two little Japanese men; you know they can't even speak any Australian, cep't what we taught them,'

'Which was'... I asked suspiciously.

'They were very nice little guys, we had a lot of fun together in the workers bar,' crooned Pia. 'They wanted to learn some Australian words and they quickly got the hang of, "g'day mate," "we pay mate" and "our shout mate." Pia then looked up at the office ceiling, searching for some inspiration, casually adding...

'You know I haven't seen them since they asked about doing some sightseeing. I rented them one of your little hire cars, Oh yeah, and when will you pay me my commission?'

I advised Pia that it was the normal thing to get the bloody hire car back and the hire signed off before we can work out any commission. Then advising slowly with a grin, otherwise how would I know what to pay you. I then continued explaining in simple words, that was the very reason why I was here today, to find out just where these two men might have gone with my hire-car. I could tell this

83

conversation did not register in this woman's limited brain as she continued with...

'Oh and another strange thing about these guys, they haven't checked out of the Hotel yet. I think they were supposed to fly out to Darwin today'

***

The shock of this unbelievable statement made me lose my line of gaze; this dumb blonde-haired Bimbo would have known that these Japanese guests were supposed to go to Darwin today.

Apparently, these two non-English speaking Japanese tourists had missed their Darwin flight and were probably still out in the bush... who knows where. Possibly lost somewhere in one of my hire vehicles and all this dumb bird wants to know is when will I will pay her commission on the hire?

It was at this time I almost missed the stack of untidy papers on the edge of the reception desk, held down with solid glass ashtray full of burnt-out cigarette butts. A closer inspection of this pile of loose sheets of paper revealed them as copies of some poorly made crappy hand drawn maps.

'What are these?' I asked, lifting the heavy ashtray off the bundle of photocopied papers. With a beautiful beaming smile, Pia was happy to explain.

'Oh those, those were my idea' crooned Pia, 'lots of the guests were asking what there was to see around here so I thought some maps and directions might help. I got some of my friends who know the best places around here to help me draw them. Yeah, and these maps can be a lot of help to tourists, especially when hiring out your cars.'

***

Pia stood behind the reception desk smiling and batting her long eyelashes at me like a Barbie doll. Then it hit me like a bolt of lightning, it was all starting to come together... It was now becoming crystal clear, I quickly enquired.

'Were any of these crappy scenic area maps given to your Japanese tourists?'

Pia's wide smile went in a flash as she looked at me dumbly, batting her eyelashes in confused childish thought. She was about to cry, obviously upset at my unflattering description of her map drawing abilities. I urgently needed her co-operation and decided to change my brutal tact...

'Beautiful Pia, could you please tell me, which of these local scenic maps did you give to those nice Japanese tourists?'

Pia licked her finger and thumbed through the stack, then pulled out a poor quality photocopy of a map titled Black Rock Falls. I studied the map, from all angles for a full two minutes in utter disbelief.

I have been to Black Rock Falls so many times; for crying aloud, it is only forty kilometres up the road, and it is very well signposted. This nice waterfall, has a little rock-pool, and frequented quite often by the locals. Most days someone is usually at the pool. If this map did not have the title "Black Rock Falls," I would never have known where or what this map gave directions to.

The poorly drawn map was in a childish scrawl with arrows pointing in various directions. A left and a right arrow had been drawn every so often, no doubt to give some sort of idea of which way to turn. This was grim news indeed. Our unfortunate visiting Japanese tourists were by all accounts, and by this poorly drawn map, most certainly lost. All of this disaster was happening right now... just down the road in the Australian bush, not far from this town of Kununurra.

Chapter Three:

The Rescue Mission

Back at the Multi Agencies hire depot, I explained the grim situation to the staff. The entire Company of three then swung into rescue mode. The first thing to do was to checkout Black Rock Falls. Stubby (the hire car hostess) and Gordon (the mechanic) jumped into my Toyota 4X4 vehicle and went out to Black Rock Falls.

I had hoped they would only find two very unhappy Japanese tourists in a broken-down hire car. Ben (the aboriginal car cleaner) remained to operate the office; and I, well, I went back down the pub... to gather some urgently needed information from the MRD (Main Roads Department) local road service crew.

I had previously telephoned the MRD office, was and advised by old bluey, who always answered the phone as to where the road crew were. Seemingly, the road maintenance crew were at that very moment out on a most important road repair job. They would not be back into the Kununurra depot yard until late tomorrow morning. With this extremely accurate and valuable information, I could now easily identify the exact location and whereabouts of the MRD road crew.

These MRD blokes were very familiar with all the roads around the Kimberley including the Black Rock Falls area. After all, they maintained and graded the gravel roads to all of these scenic spots.

As I entered the Hotel front bar, old Bert the MRD supervisor was sitting on his usual bar stool. He was clutching firmly onto a large cold beer with both hands. He had obviously just arrived at the pub, as he still had a drink-shake timing problem. He must lift his beer off the bar to his lips without spilling any of the valuable amber liquid before his next bout of shakes kicked in.

This was, by all accounts only his third beer this day. He will need to down another two beers before he will have total control of his shakes, and appear to the outside world as normal. Out of courtesy, I waited until he completed this important task. I then pulled out a copy of the same map given to the two missing Japanese, handing the map over to Bert.

'What do you think of this Bert?'

Bert held the paper close to his face, studying the map in detail. Bert badly needed glasses, however for Australian male macho reasons he refused to wear them. He reckoned that he did not want to look like a four-eyed weakling poofter; as such, he was quite happy putting up with his bad eyesight, and the inconvenience. Screwing up his eyes, and straining to see the crude map, he turned to me, and said slowly.

'I think this is the same bloody map we helped Pia draw up a couple of days back mate.'

Turning on his reserved bar stool, he addressed the bloke sitting next to him who was wide- eyed just about to skull down his second large handle of frothing chilled beer.

'Fred, ain't this the map what we helped big tit Pia with?'

Fred reluctantly swung his untouched glass aside, and with a disinterested glance at the sheet of paper and positivity announced.

'Yeah mate, that looks like one of em mate. I think so, but couldn't be real sure though.'

This hazy, half-pissed version of events was not helping my task. My frustration was becoming more than evident as I was running a bit short on patience and time with these two. Raising my voice in anger, I blurted out.

'For Christ sake you blokes, give this some of your bloody time. Two Japanese tourists are now lost using this crappy map,' waving the sheet of paper menacingly in the air, 'could you blokes find your way to Black Rock Falls using this shitty, childish fucking map?' In unison, they both replied.

'We sure as hell could mate, cos we helped make it.'

***

This map thing was not going well at all, thinking I am wasting my bloody time here. The only consolation was the small relief of hotel bar air-conditioning, and the couple of cold beers I had downed to recharge my system for tackling the forty-three degree hot world outside.

The local Hotel was by good business location and planning only one street away from my hire-depot and office. I walked back to the office, to see that Stubby and Gordon had already returned from their reconnaissance trip to Black Rock Falls, and was surprised at this speedy return.

'You guys weren't long?'

'Well it's not very far is it' replied Gordon in his usual slow dry tone.

'Well tell me then, is there any news on the missing Japanese tourists?'

'Nope, only a few locals there having a party, been there two days and reckoned they would have remembered two Jap blokes. Not many Japanese around here you know. Mind you, the pissed state they were all in, I doubt they would have noticed if a bloody flying saucer had landed next to them.'

***

Staring at the office floor as if it could provide me some sort of inspiration. I was thinking to myself terrible thoughts; this could turn out to be very bad. We could be in real deep shit if my hire car was the cause of any injury out of all this. We just have to find these two missing tourists... and soon.

Then it came to me. Maybe it is time to call in the cops; we should get some of our taxpayer funded government work force on the job. After all, that is what cop's job is, find missing and lost people.

Ring-ring, ring-ring, the phone kept on ringing then a click told me that something was about to happen. Leaning forward and listening intently screwing the phone into my ear I could hear the faint wheeze of a heavy smokers breathing, somebody was about to talk....

'Coppers'a shop who'sa that?' came a thick Italian accent.

'Who the fucking hell are you' I said knowing this was not the usual crisp phone response from our enthusiastic local constabulary.

'Theees ess'a Ernesto Cigarillo cough, cough' came the wheezing reply in a heavy Italian accent.

'Are you a new Kununurra cop or something?' I enquired, knowing the Police recruit in despair from just about everywhere and anywhere these days.

'No no sir I am e prisoner ina jailhouse. Ah been ina locked-up fo two days, a tink for a drinking fight down e pub eh.'

'Where the hell is the Sergeant, and that new dumb young copper?' I asked politely in a concerned voice.

The rough scratching of a fingernail on thick chin stubble told me this Italian was thinking of a suitable answer.

'They both gona fishing I think. They tell'a Ernesto to looka after e cop shop ana da phone, an no collecta any cash fines, hee hee hee.' Laughing at his own little joke like a Kookaburra.

I was now rapidly getting the gist of this situation. Yes, I can see it now, a trusted model prisoner looking after the town cop station. After all, this was Kununurra.

'When will they be back?' I asked in a more normal voice.

'I don'ta know mate' came the reply, 'maybe whena they catch'a some fish, or run outa booze hee hee.'

This guy was not only a failure as a barroom brawler but a failure as a comedian too. In my best haughty tone, I replied.

'Well thank you very much Mr Prisoner, do let the Sergeant know that I called' and hung up the phone with a loud crash. Well it looks like we are not going to get any needed bloody help from the Kununurra cops today.

Chapter Four:

Black Trackers are black

I could see we urgently needed to form some sort of plan, and quickly. It was now obvious the Japanese tourists never got to Black Rock Falls, but where the hell were they?

Just then, Ben the aboriginal car cleaner breezed into the nice cool air-conditioned office, leaving the door wide open as usual....

'SHUT THE BLOODY DOOR...' all three of us chorused, Ben reluctantly obeyed the harsh command, glaring indignantly, then waving his long dirty pointed finger across our faces in a watch-it mate sort of way. Then in a serious voice, he warned.

'Now you listen me whitey people, you all bin in mah country long-time now. You not notice we abo people not have any doors, or windows.' Ben leant a little closer to Stubby to make his point. 'Dis "man-made" cold air not so good for any fella, black or white... not natural bush thing; dis is all wrong bloody air mate.'

Stubby reeled back a bit. This was too close for her as Ben's wrong air was very apparent.

Ben may have spent a lot of time working with water washing vehicles, but he cunningly managed to avoid ever getting any on himself. Now it was Gordon the mechanics time to have a go, turning to Ben with a big grin, he pointed out a cultural observation.

'Ben mate, you Aboriginals don't have windows or doors because your lot have never built or lived in any bloody houses. The houses you blokes ever get to live in are what we white blokes give you, then you wreck and burn them.

Then when given a bloody good house, the first thing you lot do is smash out the glass and burn all the doors in the front yard to make a cooking fire and to keep warm. Then you go complain to the government that you're cold at night and State Housing come along and fit new doors and glass again... why do we even bother with you lot.'

Ben was stroking his chin in thought. He was winding up to a suitable reply to this white man's keen observation of the Aboriginal way of life, when Gordon interrupted his thoughts. Moving the conversation on, by asking nonchalantly.

'Don't by chance know any good black trackers do you Ben?'

Ben put on his standard Aboriginal elder's face, head held high piously looking down his flat battered nose with hunched shoulders in a regal aloof pose.

'You mean like dem blackfella tracker bloke who helps da police find a man... I can do dat... My uncle he been do dat for long-time now.'

I was starting to think this was interesting. It is not such a bad idea at all, as these black trackers were good. The cops used them all the time, although I have to admit mostly to find the best fishing spots around the Ord River.

'Where is your uncle now' I asked out of casual curiosity.

'Oh him bin gone long-time now, he bin stone dead for sure. Croc got him good when he fishin ina river last year.'

Gordon, Helen, and I looked at one another in utter disbelief; Ben was up to his old tricks again... making fun of white people... I exploded.

'Well your dead uncle Brumby is not going to be much fucking help with our problem then is he, I snapped... I mean for Christ sake Ben can't you be serious about this. We've got two lost tourists to find, and they've been missing for over three bloody days now.'

Ben resumed his wise elder look, and continued talking as if I had never spoken. My ranting was a wasted effort... or was it?

'Mah uncle Brumby he bin teach me everything ah knows. Anyways, for starts da coppers always give clue to go on first time out.'

Stubby thrust the crappy spider map in front of Ben's face.

'Try this Ben, for a good start clue' pouted Stubby.

Ben held the piece of paper at arm's length intensely studying it while again stroking his chin with the long dirty fingers of his other hand. We all looked on in wonder and silence, in anticipation.

After a short while, Stubby briskly removed the map from Ben's outstretched hand and turned the paper around, right side up, placing it back in Ben's grubby hand. Without a moment of surprise or hesitation, Ben then announced...

'She's be right now mate, it no problem now mate, I got em now, let's go.'

This confirmed statement had us all believe that he could track down, and lead us to the missing Japanese.

'How faraway do you think they are Ben, do you think they might be all right, unhurt and safe?' I enthusiastically enquired.

Ben looked indignant and sniffed quickly up his nose, then giving me another pious look of a superior being...

'Now you look em here boss, am bin blackfella tracker now see, not a "majestic" man, how de hell I gonna know all dat dem things eh?'

Just then, Gordon came alive with a flood of new mockery.

'Ben you mean a Gadichi (magic man.) Anyway you're a bloody black car washer, not a black tracker,' droned Gordon in a sarcastic voice.

Ben was not at all amused at this dry understatement of his newfound tracking skills. Ben stared Gordon in the eye, unlike Stubby Gordon held his ground firmly, and stared sternly back. Then Ben, nose to nose with Gordon let fly with his Aboriginal wrath...

'You listen me good whitefella. You gotta be a "blackfella" to be a black tracker, and you ain't black.' Ben snorted and continued.

'You bin out all bloody mornin lookin fir dem blokes and you gone found nuffin, smat asshole, shit-head whitefella.'

This direct comment on Aboriginal superiority in these tracking matters went completely unnoticed by Gordon who had heard Ben down the pub rant and rave many times before, mainly on black Aboriginal rights.

Nevertheless, Ben had not forgotten past problems created by Gordon. It was his workmate Gordon, who had convinced him that his Aboriginal flag was flying upside-down. Pointing out to Ben that he was sure it was the red part of the flag to the top, being "red communists over black" not the "Aboriginal black's over red communists."

Ben thought he could see the logic in this flag design. He then went about his native rights activist business down at the pub, by enthusiastically preaching his newly found flag logic to his few followers, and anybody who would listen to him.

It was not until a many weeks later, that some taxpayer funded; Pakistani Aboriginal legal aid lawyer, managed to convince him he had the flag thing all wrong.

Ben on the other hand did have a strong point with this particular black tracking matter; we had little choice but to give him a go. Time was against us, and he was now our only chance. Things were looking a bit better now; at least we had some sort of a plan. We were now about to do something to try find the missing Japanese tourists.

***

Ben fuelled up a Toyota HJ45 4X4, and Stubby organised the food provisions, crisps, pretzels, and other substantial bush tucker snacks. I grabbed a cartoon of cold beer out of the fridge loading them into the Esky of ice, and Gordon heaved his steel toolbox onto the tray-back. We were all ready for the big search and rescue, and then Stubby had a flash of great female logic.

'Why not ask Chan the China-man to go along with us; he may be helpful looking a bit Asian. He may even know a few words of Japanese, well you never know, he could be some help.'

'That's great, where did you get that idea from.'

'Well Chan the China-man is standing just outside on the driveway filling up his truck, then it just sort of well... you know came to me.'

'Good clear-thinking Stubby.'

I strolled outside to have a chat with Chan the China-man, just as he looked up to greet me.

'Hi Chan, we are just about to go looking for two lost Japanese tourists, Stubby thought that you may know a few words of Japanese and might want to come along with us and help?'

At the same time realising, and thinking, why would Stubby think Chan the China-man might know any bloody Japanese?

'Hi Niv, no problem mate' replied Chan in his broad Australian accent. 'I speak the Japanese lingo fluently.'

'Well,' I said in surprise,' what a stroke of luck; a China-man that can speak Japanese.'

'Not so unusual mate,' replied Chan. 'learnt the lingo from me Mum and Dad when I was a nipper.'

Curiosity got the better of me, leading me down a complicated path I was later to regret.

'And where did your Mum and Dad learn Japanese I enquired?'

Continuing to refuel his truck Chan replied in a matter of fact way.

'Easy one mate, me mum and dad, they're both Japanese mate.'

'Well that would mean that you're Japanese and not Chinese.'

Chan stopped fuelling his truck and stared at me with a look of outright horror on his oriental face.

'Not bloody likely mate, I'm a bloody Australian born right here in Australia. I'm more bloody Australian that you are mate, cos you're a bloody pom.'

This last statement sailed straight over my head. It did not even register in my brain cells for I was in deep, confused hereditary thought. He was right about being more of an Australian than I am, since I was born in Scotland.

'Then why does everyone call you Chan the China-man when you are... well a... Japanese... err man?'

'Beats the fuck out of me' replied Chan with an amusing air; 'my great grand parents' arrived in Broome from Japan to work as pearl divers over 90 bleeding years ago mate. That's four frigging generations ago of ignorant bloody Australians calling us Chinese when we was always from bleeding Japan.'

Chan and I stared at each other in silence. No more words flowed. After all, what more could be said in reply to such a statement and after such a long time? We agreed that we were both real dinky-di Aussies, and walked off toward the waiting Toyota with big grins on out faces.

***

I was later to find out that most of these early Japanese pearl divers took to calling themselves Chinese. This was mainly because at those times, all Japanese nationals were held in internment camps for the duration of the Second World War. The Broome residents knew the pearl divers were Japanese and went along with the deception. Covering for them at every chance as many of these Japanese people were lifelong friends and a very much a part of this small close family community. Chan was obviously not aware of this part of his family history.

It occurred to me that Chan's family would have been in the small pearling town of Broome on the 3rd of March 1942. This was the memorable day when Broome was raided by six Japanese Zero fighters, destroying fourteen flying boats in the harbour and killing 35-40 people. Those must have been hard times for all.

Ben climbed up onto the back of the Toyota, holding a short length of tree branch. He then and yelled down into the open cab for all to hear...

'Hope you bloody white fellas don't mind too much' he said, 'I can't stand all dat white-man body stink close in da front, even with all dem windows wide open.'

Yet another problem self-solved, and what luck. I politely replied to Ben's body odour observations.

'I must tell you Ben I'm a little offended about your obvious concerns at the state of our personal hygiene, but that's okay Ben, that suites us all just fine... mate.'

Chapter Five:

On the right track to nowhere

Stubby decided to stay and man the office phones. We were now ready to set out on our mission. Gordon and Chan sat in the front seat with me driving, with Ben on the back of the Toyota hanging on to the loading bar. A thump, thump of his tree branch on the roof nearly blasted us all out of the cab, followed by a loud yell from Ben,

'Boss, you follow all what a say; now you head-em out all way along dat old Wyndham road okay.'

Gordon was first to speak, and with some explosive frustration.

'Look we're just going back out to Black Rock Falls again; I was there only three hours ago. This is going to be just another bloody waste of time. We would be better looking in other places close-by, like Fords Crossing.'

Then Chan enquired in a casual voice.

'Is Black Rock where the Jap's were supposed to be heading out to?'

'Yeah' Gordon replied with a sneer.

'Well then it's a good place to start. These Japanese blokes must have at least headed in the right direction... eh mate.'

'But we've just been out there' groaned Gordon.

After about 10 minutes there was another big bang on the roof, I could see the large dent from inside the cab. Realising, this was no doubt the very reason why all Aboriginal vehicles were always covered in huge dents. Apparently, they were just giving road directions to the frigging driver.

'Turn dis way' yelled Ben banging this time on the left side of the Toyota cab I complied with the instruction and turned left on to a narrow bumpy gravel road. More silence then Gordon erupted in frustration.

'He's going out to Black Rock Falls, Ben's just following that bloody Hotel map... Black fucking tracker my arse.'

I thought to myself about that map for a moment and then... a sparkle of light came into my dim road-jarring mind.

'I tell you what Gordon. I hope Ben is following that map because following that map was how our Japanese tourists got lost. If Ben tracks the exact same way as drawn on that dumb blond Pia's silly map, then with a bit of luck we should find our lost Japanese tourists… what about that for an idea?'

Gordon just had to have the last word on this tracking matter.

'You guys don't really believe all that crap from Ben, about him being a "black tracker" do you? For crying out loud Boss he's only a fucking car cleaner, and not a very good one at that.'

I thought I would tryout some of my basic Kimberley logic on Gordon.

'Gordon, do you agree we are heading out in the general direction of Black Rock Falls?'

'Well yes' said Gordon.

'Then tell me this; did you or Stubby ever tell Ben where these Japanese guys were heading to at the time they got lost?'

'I don't think so' Gordon replied, 'but then again Boss, Ben has got the bloody map with the name and all the crappy details on it.'

'Ha yes,' I replied with childlike glee, 'but Gordon remember, Ben can't read or write, so he doesn't know where the hell the Jap tourists were supposed to go. I hope Ben is taking us along the same track to where, and what that stupid map is showing.'

'Good point' mumbled Chan with gritted teeth, while being tossed around in the Toyota cab like a pea in a tin whistle by the rough gravel road.

Again, thump, thump on the cab roof, and then bang on the left side. Ben had trained me well in this short time to understand the sacred aboriginal directions code. I swung left off the gravel road on to a much smaller gravel road. Another loud bang on the left and I took a left fork in the road.

Chan sitting in the centre seat position and was hanging on to the large handle firmly bolted to the metal dashboard, knuckles white with a powerful grip. Just as well, and very thoughtful of Toyota providing such a device. Without this handle to hang on to, Chan in the centre seat would have smashed his teeth into the metal dashboard and bashed his head violently on the stout steel roof. Gordon and I were okay, as we had assumed the standard Toyota bush driving position of clamping an arm firmly over the open windowsill, up to the armpit, and clinging on for all merry hell.

Chan yelled out through clenched and chattering teeth.

'If we carry on much further down this road mate, we'll be in the bloody Ord River among the fucking salt-water crocs.'

'Maybe that's what happened to our Jap's' as the unnatural high-pitched voice of Gordon rose above the road noise. 'They probably drove off this same bloody road and went down the river-bank into the water; it would be easy to do in the dark.'

This was not sounding good at all. Clutching the steering wheel harder a thought suddenly occurred. If that was in fact what had happened, I may end up being blamed for everything. I was going to increase the hire company insurance cover, something that was on my mind to do, when I had thought up a better and more brilliant devious plan. A plan that would save me money and put the vehicle's responsibility directly on to the hirer (or so I had thought) by including an additional clause in the hire contract stating that;

"Sedan type two wheel drive vehicles must be driven only on gazetted government roads. Any damage to the vehicle caused by failing to comply will be at the cost of the hirer."

Only thing was, this new clause had not been included into the hire contracts yet, and anyway, in this particular case there may not be a hirer left to pay for any damages.

My dark grim thoughts were suddenly interrupted by a large thud directly above my head, followed by a bash on my side door.

'Dis way, dis way' yelled Ben at the top of his voice.

I wrenched the wheel hard right on to a better-looking gravel road. To one side was a large metal sign, bent over and burnt by many bush fires, but still easy to read.

"STOP No through road Main Roads property."

I could sense the level of excitement in Ben's voice. I thought we must have been getting close... to something.

'How far now Ben' I yelled above the roar of the road noise.

'Not long, soon see boss".... I think' Ben yelled above the din.

I yelled out aloud above the road noise to Chan and Gordon,

'This is a better road', to which Chan shouted a loud urgent reply.

'You had better slow down a bit mate; we're back on the old Wyndham road. We pulled hundreds of tons of gravel out of this area to make the new Wyndham road. The bloody gravel-pit must be just down the road a bit from here.'

Just then my eye caught an unusual sight that created some confusion in my mind, a sort of cut or break across the road with a lower skyline, maybe the crest of a hill. I had never seen that before.... Then Gordon, Chan, and Ben yelled out together...

'STOP...'

I slammed on the brakes in a long locked four-wheel sliding skid, then thought of poor Ben on the back. Glancing in the rear view mirror for any sign of him before the large clouds of gravel dust engulfed the vehicle. No need to worry Ben was already off the back in one bounding leap. By the time the Toyota came to a stop, Ben was facing me through the side window.

'You gone dun close thing der boss, we nearly go join dem'

'Join who' I said?' coughing and spluttering in the massive cloud of red dust.

The gravel dust settled quickly unveiling the dramatic scene ahead. We were only some two metres away from the edge of a large, deep gravel pit. Luck was with us, having only just pulled-up in time.

We were on the high side of the gravel road, looking down onto the top of my white Datsun 1600 car, the Datsun partly submerged up to the roofline in murky brown water.

Two slightly built Japanese men were perched on the roof of the car. They were badly sunburnt, stripped to the waist, and covered in mosquito bites. The look on their faces was worth a thousand photos, "utter terror." They could hear the Toyota coming and had thought that we were about to land right on top of them. If only they knew, just how close we were to doing just that.

***

This was a large gravel pit, obviously mined away from the lower side of the hill in the road. Huge amounts of pea gravel material had been removed over some time, digging into the high side of the gravel road providing a spectacular drop of about four metres. From this high side we were looking down on a large pool of dirty brown water provided by the recent monsoon rains.

The Japanese tourists were, by their lively action obviously not injured. In their excitement to see us, they were waving franticly and were now jumping up and down on the roof of my almost new Datsun car.

Everyone in my group were all gently waving back and smiling except me. I was waving harder with my fist clenched and yelling at the stupid bastards.

'Stop jumping on my bloody car roof you idiots. Chan for Christ sake tell those fuckers not to do any more damage, and to get off the roof of my car.'

Chan opened up with his fluent Japanese. After which the Japanese in their excitement jumped even harder on the roof, causing the roof to cave in while pointing to something at the edge of the murky pond.

'What the hell's going on now Chan?' I asked in my fuming anger.

'Well mate, they are a bit worried about the three big salt crocodiles that are hanging around over there at the edge of the gravel pool?'

I followed Chan's pointing finger, there on the edge of the murky pond was the clear and unmistakable outline of three very large mud covered salt-water crocodiles. The Jap's had been perched on the roof of the car for three days and had now accepted this situation; they were going to be the next meal for the crocodiles. Chan continued his Japanese interpretation.

'They had all but given up mate. I think they've gone a bit loony too. They aren't making much sense; they keep saying that I talk in a funny Australian accent. I think this might be a straitjacket job mate.'

'Tell them that they are in the crocs waterhole and the crocs just want their bloody waterhole back again.' Then as an added afterthought, 'And tell them if they cause any more damage to the roof of my car I'll leave the bastards in there for the crocs to eat.'

That got some results as the Jap's quietened down a fair bit. Ben then went down to the waterhole with his gun and had a loud chat with the crocs. With a few rounds over their heads, they reluctantly moved out the way for a while to watch us from a safe distance.

We soon pulled the now-dented Datsun out of the gravel pond; lucky that the pond floor being a firm gravel base, so this was quite an easy job.

***

On the way back to town, towing the Datsun behind, Chan got the full story from the still very terrified Japanese tourists.

The Japanese guys had followed Pia's crappy map as we did to find them. They soon got confused and ended up lost driving at night.

In the dark, they could see in the distance what they thought were the lights of the town and decided to drive in that direction. It is obvious now they were confused and frightened, attracted by the lights of Kimberley Research Station, driving away from Kununurra heading towards the small government research centre.

All of a sudden, the car launched itself off the edge of nothing into the gravel pit. These frightened blokes had no idea that it was just a shallow pond (only a metre and a half deep) and had spent the first night on the car roof. The next day they decided to wade to the shore to find help when two large salt-water crocs chased them back onto the roof of the car again. Then another croc arrived to add to their terror.

During the day, they crawled back inside the car through an open window to stay out of the sun, but only had about five inches of airspace in which to breathe.

I was trying to imagine the discomfort these two men must have endured crouched inside the small Datsun car by day, with their faces held above the waterline for hours on end. The following night they remained inside the car while constantly reminded by the crocodile movement in the water, all while savagely bitten by millions of hungry mosquitos.

On the second day when nobody came to save them, they thought they would die in this Australian crocodile infested mud hole. They had to face yet another night trying to get some sleep on the roof of the car, again eaten alive by more mosquitoes. They endured all of this while being constantly aware and terrified of something far worse, the almost certainty of being eaten alive by several large salt-water crocodiles.

***

As we had guessed, these two Japanese blokes had enjoyed an evening on the booze with the friendly MRD boys who had shown them photos of some nice local picnic spots. They had this bright idea just around pub closing time to draw up a few maps with directions on how to get to a local tourist place. The two very drunk Japanese liked the look of, Black Rock Falls.

After their boozy night in the lounge bar, Pia redrew and photocopied all the maps. She got a few lefts and rights mixed-up and the names of some of the maps to different scenic areas. The rest is now history.

The two Japanese tourists departed Kununurra on the next MMA flight out. The very same flight I might add that my missed flight hire car client had arrived on. Dan as promised had pinched my client, hiring him an Avis car... We were all too busy making sure that the two Japanese blokes got on the plane and out of Kununurra to worry about this small matter.

My new Datsun hire car eventually went to Darwin for extensive repairs, as nobody could repair such damage in Kununurra. Unfortunately, on return, the Datsun hire car never looked quite the same as before. The sad part was I paid for all the vehicle damage costs as my insurance company refused the claim. The reason given was the vehicle suffered damage while being driven on a non-gazetted road, the old Wyndham gravel road no longer being a government maintained road.

The next morning Ben arrived later than usual and gravely handed me the short tree-branch he used yesterday to bash on the roof of my hire Toyota. I thought he was apologising for the damaged roof when Gordon spoke, holding back a crooked smile.

'Ben has something to tell you boss. He's giving-up his job as a car cleaner and has put his resignation in writing.'

I looked at the rough piece of tree branch and noticed three notches cut evenly along one end. Studying the branch from all angles, I was lost for an answer.

'What the hell is this about Ben? I asked waving the branch around.

Ben took-up his pious official elder look again and announced in a steady voice.

'Whiteman not knows mah peoples writing. Ah, readum for you mate,' taking the branch back he stared at the three notches, 'dat der is Abo message stick. It telling you I quit as now got better bloody job; tracker work with da Police.'

***

I could not for the life me of figure out if Ben was having a joke with me or not. However, I could not detect any sign of humour. This could be serious stuff.

'I suppose you will need a good job reference for the new job. Well you did do a fine job as a tracker yesterday, and your car cleaning work was ok, so I will write one for you.

Taking the branch back from Ben again; and with the help of Gordon's Bowie knife, I had noticed on his tool trolley. I then proceeded to cut two further deep notches in the other end, and then handed it back.

'That should satisfy your new employer, I have told them you are a good bloke, and not a bad tracker, especially for your first go. I mentioned in a short post scriptum side comment, that we are sorry to see you go and a job will always be waiting for you here should things not workout in your new job.'

Ben shook hands with both of us, stating he never knew that I could write a message stick, and he would be happy to teach me to read one when he had some spare time. He then turned and was gone.

Gordon said that was a nice thing I did for Ben; stating he will buy him a beer next time down the pub.

As for the two Japanese tourists, well I never heard from them ever again. I do not think we will ever see these two blokes back in Australia for a holiday any time soon. But then again they sure had some exciting Australian experiences to tell all their friends back home.

---- The End ----

Part Three: Did the best man win?

Chapter One:

Not lost mate I just can't move

Secrets and more secrets my anger was obviously starting to show, no matter what I do, it all appears to end up as my fault these days. I will have to pull myself together; all these negative thoughts could drive a man into some sort of depression. By all accounts, it looks like we have misplaced, or possibly lost a geologist... again.

It was late November 1978 in the small but modern new town of Kununurra, located in the far north of Western Australia. I had just taken an urgent phone call from Normandy Mining in Perth. The company was a little concerned, as they had not heard from their field geologist in over a week. Since he was driving one of my Toyota 4X4 hire vehicles, would I know, or have any idea where their Geo might be. They also wanted to know if I had heard from him since he hired the vehicle nearly a month ago... My reply was less than polite as this type of call was becoming all too frequent.

'No sir, I do not know where your geologist is except it was hundreds of kilometres out into some remote bush area. I signed out that hire myself, and as per normal, I did ask in what area the vehicle was going to work, and told that information was a company secret; your company orders. I wouldn't know where the hell to start looking, but you must know since you were the people who sent him up here on this top secret field trip?'

There was a long pause on the phone as the manager went about slowly digesting what I had just said. Before he had time to reply, I suggested he should get back to me when they decide if they can tell me something useful. I was still a bit upset over this silly phone call, suggesting that I should know or do something. Then advising, when and if they get back to me, I expected to be enlightened as to what their geologist's field plan was. At the least that would be a starting point.

***

These were crazy times in the Kimberley area. The whole of this vast area was crawling with exploration companies looking for oil, gold, diamonds, and uranium. My little hire company was flat out servicing their demands. The fleet consisted of twenty-two off-road 4X4 vehicles fitted out for exploration fieldwork.

Exploration companies were the worst offenders for keeping vehicles longer than the agreed hire term. This caused me endless problems; mainly because most of the vehicles had been booked again well in advance by other clients. I did feel a little guilty at my curt response to the phone call, assuming the best place to start on this missing vehicle investigation, was with the hire contract.

The contract revealed all the usual information such as drivers name, address, company, age, licence number and so on. From the geologist's age of forty-eight, I could feel a little relieved in that he was not a novice. He should have a great deal of prior experience in fieldwork, and how to handle a 4X4 vehicle in the rough out-back.

My Toyota Landcruiser hire vehicles were well equipped for remote geological work. Fitted with heavy-duty bull bars, sidebars and a tow bar, two spare wheels, long-range fuel tanks and water tank, plus a tool-kit, tow snatch strap and kangaroo jack. An optional hire RFDS long-range HF transceiver and larger first aid box were also available but rarely hired.

The only other worthwhile detail mentioned on the hire contract was the date it went out, now over four weeks ago, and the date it was due back. This confirmed that the vehicle was not due back for another two days. At this time, we had no reason to worry. As a hire company, we were a long way from considering, or declaring a lost vehicle... This was not the time to panic.

The driver had said he was collecting rock samples and required a flat tray-back vehicle. I also remember telling the Geo, the payload was a maximum of one ton on rough terrain and not to exceed this weight or the springs will snap.

Our last parting conversation was the Geo asking out of curiosity, the reason why the Toyota cab roof is painted bright orange. With a large white dot in the centre, and a large black number on it. Well I was thinking all this to myself, just as the phone rang. Within the next day or so, he will soon find out why these things are there.

It was the project director Sam from Normandy Mining, asking again if I had heard anything at all from his geologist. These people all acted like spy controllers being very reluctant to give out any information. Even to someone who might be the only person who can save his geologists embarrassment... or possibly his life.

'Sam, all I can tell you is your Geo has plenty of provisions and good equipment. He struck me as knowing what he was about in the bush. Without a location we don't know where to start looking for him.'

There was a small pause; Sam was deciding something of great importance. That being should he trust me with his company secrets.

'If I give you our geologist Bart's most likely ground position you must promise me you will treat the information I give you as highly confidential.'

It was obvious that Sam did not comprehend the gravity of this situation. Sam's Company had lost reporting contact with their Geo over two weeks ago, and were only now concerned where their Geo Bart might be. The possibility that this bloke might be injured or dead never entered the conversation.

This was yet another good example of the high-level of exploration fever that was gripping these companies at this time. They had not only lost touch with their geologist but with reality and their staff's safety. To what depths will these people sink to guard against information leaks about their possible mining gains, seeped in suspicion, and greed?

***

'Can I tell you this Sam, if your Geo is injured and needs medical help? Within a week, the entire bloody world will know where your silly secret place is. Sam, we have good experience with these situations, this is the way things are done up here. You can declare this situation as an emergency, and we will be part of a search and rescue team organised by others. Alternatively, you can give me a company order to search for your geologist.

I will fly my Cessna to the locations you provide to me, and I will tell nobody... unless I come across an injured Geo. If we find the vehicle broken-down, caused by my equipment failing, while being used within its designed capacity, then I will cover all the costs. On the other hand, if this breakdown was caused by your problems or the misuse of my vehicle, then you will cover all the costs. Do we have a deal?'

There was another long silence and a crackling as Sam covered the phone to talk with someone, someone who no doubt controlled the tight lid on the cash box.

'You have a deal, I'll telex you an order number, and the map locations for Bart's sample programme. Can you start the search for Bart now?'

'I'm on my way Sam but don't expect any results for some hours as I will be in the air for a while; and relax, these situations usually turn out okay. Most times it's just a fuel problem, or a split water radiator or something simple.'

As I hung up the phone I was thinking, I hope I was right. We had just recently lost old Joe the cook from the Lake Argyle Tavern in very mysterious circumstances, never to- be seen ever again.

***

Old Joe was a bad boozer but a good cook. He told me one day while having a drink at breakfast. (I was drinking coffee he was drinking gin.) That all his best creations in the kitchen were always produced while he was half pissed. One of the main problems he had in his life was to get the booze-cooking balance right.

Tavern guests considered Joe's breakfasts were about the best around while his lunches were most times booked out. The small Tavern-restaurant midday lunch was also popular with the Caravan Park, and day tourists. Then there was the evening meal, it was, well... crap. Joe had only just figured out a way around this sad dilemma. That was by preparing all the evening's dinner food well before his three o'clock cut-off sober-time, after which time he was usually well and truly drunk beyond all acceptable cooking results. Then one day he jumped into his old car and just went missing... forever.

Many of the locals joked about his disappearance saying they reckoned it was an assassination by the jealous opposition, as old Joe had pinched much of the local weekend restaurant trade. Nevertheless, I was there when this strange disappearance took place, and I had my own theories on what happened that odd day.

***

At that time, I had a really great government contract up at Lake Argyle, a contract to provide my boat the Vendal III, and a Captain... me. The contract required a three-day a month charter to the PWD (Public Works Department) for water sampling and monitoring work on the newly created Lake Argyle. My last day of the boat charter usually finished at around seven, and in the dark. As such, I would normally stay the night at the Tavern, and get an early start back to Kununurra first thing in the morning.

This way I could then enjoy one of Joe's great early breakfasts. I was in the bar that last night, drinking with Joe and some of the locals. Old Joe was quite pissed and quite excited about going on holiday the next day. He was looking forward to going back to Queensland to see his family, planning to start at midday tomorrow, driving his beloved ancient Toyota Crown sedan. When I left the Tavern bar at about ten that night, Joe was still knocking them back with a bunch of tourists and locals.

The next morning I just knew there was something wrong, as the breakfast was very mediocre, in fact it was crap. On complaining, then bluntly told that Joe had suddenly decided last night to start out on his planned holiday. I thought to myself, Joe was as pissed as a parrot when I left him at ten last night. Surely, Joe had not decide to drive to Queensland after he left the pub. Well that is just what Joe did. In in his pissed state, he had decided to go to Queensland right there and then.

***

I was driving slowly back to Kununurra on the lake road, towing my 24-foot, three-ton boat, still grumbling to myself about the crappy breakfast, when I came across a lone copper about twenty kilometres from the Argyle Tavern. He was leaning on the roof of Joe's beat-up old Toyota Crown sedan. From my view, it looked like Joe had skidded, and come off the sealed road onto the gravel roadside, now pointing down the roadside-drain, facing into the bush. As I pulled up the young copper said in a much-trained policeman-like voice.

'Now move along sir you are blocking the road traffic.'

I took a good look around and noticed that we were the only two people on this road for three kilometres in each direction, and I knew for a fact I had not passed anybody since leaving the Argyle Tavern ten minutes ago. We were very much alone. Slowly getting out of my Toyota, I walked up to the surprised young police officer who I had never seen in these parts before.

'Where's your police car officer, are you out here all on your own. You might require a lift back into town or at the very least a cold drink,' handing the young copper a can of cold coke, and then nodding my head at the car. 'This Toyota Crown belongs to old Joe the Argyle Tavern cook.'

The young Policeman held a grim face staring at me in textbook fashion.

'We are aware who this car belongs to sir, I have been stationed here to guard this accident site while a senior constable goes into town and returns with some expert help.'

Then noticing my dubious look, 'We were on our way up to the Lake on some early morning police business.'

Thinking yeah, I will bet, Barramundi fishing most likely. I started looking in and around the car then under the vehicle, and then at all the footprints around in the gravel, and then at the police officers size eleven standard issue police shoes.

'Well officer, I do hope the expert help is an Aboriginal tracker, as that's the only expert you need here right now. I was drinking with Joe until ten last night and I can tell you he was well and truly drunk then. My guess is Joe fell asleep at the wheel and drove off the side of the road, ending up stuck across the road drain.'

The officer pulled out his notebook and started to ask me some police type questions.

'What is your name and address sir, and where are you going at this early hour of six thirty in the morning?'

I continued as if the young copper had not spoken...

'Write this lot down officer, I think Joe was okay when his car skidded and stopped as he has tried to reverse out... quite a few times. He was a victim of bad luck, too much booze, and a dark moonless night. Joe's Toyota Crown landed on a sharp granite rock, which as far as I can see has done a nice neat job of cutting the car's tail-shaft in two. This car was going nowhere, and Joe knew that. That's when Joe decided to walk back home to the Argyle Tavern in the pitch-dark, as I said, there was no moon last night'

The young copper looked at me with suspicion and started scribbling into his notebook again.

'What makes you so sure sir that he has tried to walk back to the Tavern?'

'Easy, Joe knows this area quite well and that this is just a big bend in the road. If he walked back cutting off the corner, he could be back at the Tavern in under an hour. In addition, the engine is stone-cold so this all happened over six hours ago, which would be shortly after Joe left the Tavern bar. He knows nobody would come along this road for the next five or six hours and so decided to walk back to the Tavern.'

Climbing back into my Toyota I leant out through the window,

'By the way, I hope the tracker can sort out Joe's footprints from all of yours; anyway, with a bit of luck Joe will be back at the Tavern bar by now. If not, you're going to need a helicopter to search for him in this rough country.'

***

Joe never did get back to the Tavern. His personal effects were still in the car including his money and bankbook No doubt the very reason why the young copper was guarding the vehicle. There was an extensive ground and helicopter search carried out over many hundreds of square kilometres. Unfortunately, old Joe the cook just disappeared in the thick bush and never found. Not even his remains have been found to this day, some thirty years since that sad and tragic event.

Joe had apparently wandered off into the bush, less than seven kilometres in a straight line from the Tavern where he worked, and lost his way in the dark night. The Aboriginal tracker followed Joe's tracks for many kilometres going in the wrong direction before they faded out, along with Joe's chance of survival.

***

'You must have had another bad night again boss.'

This was Gordon the mechanic, his way of waking me out of my daydream state being deep in thought about old Joe the cook, and his untimely end.

'Yes Gordon, today we have an important mission for you and me. That is, to find one of our clients who is apparently overdue on reporting to his company? This problem is a minus two-seven.'

Gordon looked at me intelligently, pushed his frameless glasses back up to the bridge of his sweaty nose, and said.

'Two days to the end of the hire contract and Toyota unit number seven. This doesn't sound very urgent to me with still two days left to the hire return. Anyway, I had spoken to the Geo who is driving unit seven before he left for the bush. It looked well provisioned and he sounded to me like he knew what he's doing, so what's the big deal?'

'His company are very worried and want him found urgently, and guess what, they are actually prepared to pay for all our time in finding him.'

116

Gordon cocked his head to one side and looked at me in genuine surprise.

'Well what do you know, that's certainly a first. An exploration company that actually does care about one of their people being lost in the bush. I am amazed they are prepared to pay to find their bloke. This bloke must be important.'

Gordon was correct; it is a tough business. An exploration Geo is only as good as his or her next profitable find. That may well be what this was all about, then adding my view.

'Or what he has found is something important... adding, if you can come along with me in the Cessna as observer, I will get Pedro my brother-in-law to sort out a vehicle ready to go bush on a search and rescue mission. That's assuming we find the bloody missing Toyota.'

As I was talking the telex machine started rattling away with a message from Normandy Mining. Containing an official request to find their geologist, an order number, and three sets of map co-ordinates. I noted that two of the areas identified were now quite popular prospecting areas, especially with the escalating interest in gold and diamonds.

This Geo would have come across many other geologists looking and working in those same areas. That left the third location, forty kilometres north-west of Spring Creek at the fork of Nine-mile creek and Cow creek. This position, like the other two was in very remote bush country; however, this particular area; to my knowledge was of little interest, and rarely if ever visited. This was then the obvious area to start my search for the missing Geo.

It was a 40-minute flight out to the search area. We had decided to fly over one of the other positions on the way out as it was almost on my direct flight track. My company aircraft is a Cessna 182RG; however, I considered it was not suitable for this particular task of search and rescue. RG stands for "retractable gear" having small wheels and not recommended for any possible rough gravel road landing. For this flight I was flying a borrowed normal fixed gear Cessna 182 with large wheels suitable for landing on gravel roads if needs be.

On the other hand, the main reason for using this particular aircraft was that it was fitted with a powerful external PA (public address) system. Used for frightening the living daylights out of cattle in an attempt to muster them. There was a choice of twenty different hideous noises to drive the stubborn cattle along, and at the flick of a switch, the pilot could blast the drovers and jackaroos with loud instructions. This was a very handy gadget for attracting people's attention and talking to people on the ground.

***

We were flying along low and slow at around 400 feet, with ten degrees of flap down, flying the first leg of a grid search pattern. All of a sudden there was a bright flash that lit-up the already bright cockpit, Gordon yelled out in terror.

'For fucks sake what was that.' Screaming at the top of his voice above the engine noise, 'Oh my god, we're going to crash.'

Gordon's arms were moving around in panic and his hand accidentally knocked my prescription sunglasses off my face on to the cockpit floor. This situation required firm assurance.

'Now just hold on their Gordon, do not panic old chap we are okay, it looks like the bloody Geo has found us, and he is just flashing us with a mirror.'

The inside of the Cessna continued to be flooded with the bright light. As I attempted to fly clear of the light, the light continued to follow us blinding me. This was dangerous; we were only at 300 feet and 10 knots above stall speed. I revved the Cessna engine in an attempt to let the bloke on the ground know that we had seen him but he continued to mirror dazzle me into blindness. I could not even work out his ground position.

With the application of full power I made a gentle climbing turn until the bright light faded then held that track. The instrument panel was a sea of sparkling whirls as my eyes readjusted back to the darker light. That was close; too close to tell Gordon about right now, because right now he needs to get his brown stuff together. I thought I had better try to defuse this situation.

'Gordon, I am happy to advise that we are both going to live to drink another few beers. Could you do me a small favour and rummage around on the floor and try find my sunglasses that you knocked off my head nearly bloody killing us both.'

'Sorry about that boss, I've never been flashed by a mirror before. Hell, I never realised that a simple mirror could be so bright. As a kid, I used to flash lots of people on the freeway with a mirror and never gave it a thought.'

'Well who knows what happened to the poor buggers you mirror flashed back then. You might have succeeded in killing some unfortunate innocent bastard, and never have known about it?' Then remembering that Gordon was a practising Catholic, 'Think about this matter next time you're in the confession box chatting to your friendly Priest. I'll bet you will get quite a few Hail- Marys?'

With my sunglasses in place and my eyesight gradually returning to normal, I decided to try my rescue attempt once more.

'Gordon, you look out and try to figure the location where our flashing Geo is and I will keep my eyes down and on flying this plane. When you have a ground location point your finger directly at it, and hold the position. I will fly in that direction, and then we will blast him with the PA system. That should shut him up.'

'Over their boss,' I followed Gordon's finger and turned the aircraft gently until he was pointing over the nose of the aircraft. 'He's dead ahead now, and not too far away.'

I could see by the brightness of the cockpit the Geo was still using his mirror on us but kept my eyes low and on the instrument panel. I picked up the PA microphone, turned the volume up to full chat, and pushed the button.

'Toyota hire vehicle number seven you're overdue in reporting to your bloody company and stop flashing that fucking mirror at me you shithead, you almost caused me to crash.'

That did it the flashing stopped abruptly. I was then able to look out of the Cessna windows again; however, Gordon was now complaining, as he could not see a bloody thing. I then proceeded to fly in low slow circles above the Toyota with its bright orange roof and a big number seven easily seen from a distance. I pushed the button again,

'Wave both your arms above your head if you are okay and not injured,' the Geo waved his arms he was okay. 'Hold your arms out steady if you have vehicle problems.' The Geo held his arms out, so he had broken down, 'Hold one arm up if you have water and both if you also have food,' The Geo held both arms up.

'Okay I'm going to drop you a walkie-talkie by hanky parachute, watch-out for it and don't lose the little bastard it's expensive. If you don't find it, I'll charge the bloody cost of it to your company.'

This system was a well-tried and tested method of getting a radio or small medical kit on to the ground from a slow, low flying aircraft; even so, it was a very difficult task to judge the target point. I had practised many times and still could only get the landing point within 100 metres of the target, and that was with a weighted streamer, a parachute was much more difficult.

The trick was to use a small parachute to keep the decent rate at the maximum that the goods could stand without smashing it into a thousand pieces. That is why this particular radio is set into a foam beer stubby holder and then wrapped in a number of layers of bubble wrap. The required aircraft approach speed was 50 knots at 200 feet above the ground. The package release-time was just as the nose of the aircraft goes over the intended target.

Well that is what I did but the Geo still took half an hour and my help from the air to find the bright yellow parachute. I could now appreciate the problems that World War two bomb aimers had… it is not easy. Bart eventually found the parachute, and held up the radio and immediately started talking.

'What seems to be the trouble Bart, I notice that you have quite a load on the back that Toyota and you're heading up a very steep slope?'

There was a crackle and a few squeaks and then.

'I can't hear you very well pilot, can you hear me?' then back on the PA again, I gave him another blast of the mustering horn.

'Yes I can hear you okay Bart but then again as you can hear, I do have my volume turned up.'

The next communication was much better, in fact perfect. Bart explained that he had been broken down for eight days and was about to walk out that night. The problem was a twisted off tail-shaft while trying to climb a small hill, and now the vehicle was bogged and immovable.

He was a bit pissed off and not very happy about the situation, left stranded in the bush for so long. In addition reckoned that my vehicle was a heap of crap as the rear tail-shaft had twisted, broken in two. I advised Bart that I was getting dizzy flying around in circles. The quickest way to resolve his immediate situation was for me to fly in a mechanic by helicopter to fix the Toyota.

'Bart, listen out for the chopper and don't dazzle the bloody pilot with your mirror. One or two flashes is all he needs, anyway the pilot will be listening out on this frequency, give it a few hours for me to sort this all out.'

***

It was eleven o'clock in the morning as Gordon and I got back to the workshop office. My first job was to organise a helicopter charter from Sling Air to take Pedro out to the stranded Geo with another tail shaft. My second job was to advise Normandy Mining that their geologist Bart was found and safe. For some reason they requested that Bart call them the second he got back into Kununurra.

Pedro my new service manager had only been with us for three weeks. Arriving from the City of Perth, having never had any experience in working in remote places before. This was to be his first flight in a helicopter. Pedro is also my brother-in-law and has a healthy family trust in me not to get him hurt, or put him in a position that might get him killed too soon.

I waved bye to Pedro and the helicopter at around one o'clock. The Bell 47G will take about an hour and a half to get to the broken down Toyota. I figured about one hour for Pedro to replace the twisted off tail-shaft and around six and half-hours to drive back to Kununurra. This should get the vehicle with all people and equipment back by around ten o'clock tonight.

Alas, as Robert Burns once said "The best laid plans of mice and men often go astray." No truer words thought, written, or spoken in a Scottish accent so difficult to understand, yet so befitting of this day.

***

We were worried; very worried, it was well past ten o'clock, and nobody had turned up. My wife Lesley wanted to know what had happened to her brother, what had I done to him?

Yes, it was my fault again, I was starting to develop a complex, and a guilt that I may have in some way been responsible for... something. A phone call to Sling Air Helicopters confirmed the chopper pilot had dropped off Pedro with a new tail- shaft at the Toyota around two thirty. Just as I had calculated, so what had gone wrong?

Just before midnight, we received a phone call at home from Pedro, who had just a few minutes earlier driven back into town, and was now in the service workshop.

'What the fuck happened, your sister was just about to shoot me. I thought you must have snapped the flange bolts on changing the tail-shaft or something.

Pedro's excited voice tumbled out in a torrent down the phone,

'Oh no the bolts were okay but the bloody tail-shaft was the wrong one. The parts ticket said it was the right one but the bloody thing was too short. Wait till you see the tail-shaft it's twisted like a stick of liquorice.'

'If the bolts haven't snapped what would have caused the shaft to twist off?'

Pedro gave one of his little chuckles, and then told his story.

'The Toyota must have had more than two ton of rock samples on the back. The Geo was trying to drive up the side of a steep rocky slope. It looked like a mountain to me. He reckoned everything was going well until he selected the 4X4 low transfer range, and I guess that's when the tail-shaft

122

twisted off. Not surprising with all the engine torque and all that weight on the back.

The stupid fucker forgot to engage the front wheel 4X4 locking hubs. All I did was to remove the damaged tail-shaft then engage the front-wheel locking-hubs and simply drive the bloody thing out with only the front-wheel drive. We drove all the way back into town like that. Another thing, he insisted that we bring back the bloody two ton of rock samples.'

'Jesus, this lot is going to cost the exploration company a bomb but why did it take so long to get back. I reckoned it would only be a five-and a half-hour drive back into town?'

'You're right again but the Geo said he would do a little bit of prospecting while I was changing the tail-shaft. I told him it would take less than an hour. He was away over five hours.

It was bleeding hot in the sun and nothing to drink but one bent can of hot coke, I can tell you I was more than a little pissed off with that Bart bloke. When he got back to the Toyota, I was sheltering under the thing. It was too bloody hot in the cab. Then he tells me he'd been lost for the last four bleeding hours.'

***

Pedro never did forget his very first outback vehicle repair breakdown, while working in the Kimberley. From then on, Pedro always carried plenty of water, and a Codan 6924 HF portable radio transmitter... and his own signalling mirror.

It is hard to believe, but proven true many times over. In the bush, stupidity can kill you instantly; however, ignorance takes just a little bit longer.

At the very least, this lost geologist should have taken with him an air-band walkie-talkie. He could then have called any number of passing aircraft for help. I have never been a boy scout, but I do practice the code. I think everyone who travels, or is about to enter into a challenging situation should. "Be Prepared."

In addition, I did know that this Geo Bart was not in the right place to find the now famous AK1 diamond pipe.

Why, well my claim pegging company West Coast Surveys was at that very time in the "hot spot." Laying out a number of tenement claims on behalf of another mining company client. But then again, at that time, I did not know what the significance was of all this secrecy. However, I did know the active and most interesting area being worked was just south of Lake Argyle. This was eventually to become the discovery area of world's largest diamond mine... AK1.

Chapter Two:

The Ron pegging the right way

The pace of mining exploration was rapidly moving into top gear. Many exploration companies and prospectors were pegging and registering mining exploration tenements almost every day. The local claims registration office, being a part of the Kununurra Courthouse building; was managed by the Clerk-of-Courts John. John was also carrying out the dual role as the Mining Registrar and having a tough time meeting the demand for his services. It was clear to all he was a busy boy.

One of my hire clients was a small claim pegging company operated by two young blokes. They would sometimes hire my 4X4 Toyotas, use my servicing facilities, and had rented some space in my yard for their equipment. Both partners were very good at their job, however as time went by they had big problems keeping up with the enormous amounts of legal and government paperwork.

This paperwork was a necessary obligation for correctly submitting applications for mining tenements and prospecting claims. One of the pegging partners had decided to leave the partnership, to work exclusively for their largest client. The remaining partner Ron and I decided to go into business and so WCS "West Coast Surveys" was born.

Ron, now my partner ran all the demanding fieldwork. I on the other hand looked after all of the submission paperwork, which I will admit was a total bureaucratic nightmare. The claim registration forms being required in five sets, or more for each claim, then every bit of paper was required individually initialled and dated, and the claim-form signed. All the claim sheets had to be time-stamped by the mining registrar and then accurately assembled with detailed location maps for the Mining Registrar claim submissions.

Two full sets of claim copies were required for the Mining Registrar. With a further, two sets for the prospector client, and then a copy for my own reference file. Many of these claims were at multiple ground sites in and around other interesting ground pegged and owned by other companies, as such these "other" exploration companies were always challenging the accuracy of our claim pegging work.

Claim jumping was rife, over pegging; another prospector's claim was an everyday event presenting yet further problems. Accuracy was important. We did however have an edge, as Ron was exceptionally good at getting the all-important datum peg in the right place first time.

Getting the datum peg in the right place was of little value when the annual bushfires burnt the mandatory regulation wooden stakes to ground level. Then there were the hungry ants who decided that this dry wooden object was an excellent foundation to build their new anthills. To be a properly pegged claim one must comply with the letter of the law being the Mining Prospectors tenement claim-pegging act of 1904.

This mining claim act clearly states the exact size and the type of material that the claim pegging stakes made from. Apparently, nobody in the mines department thought about the normal yearly bushfires.

Many a valuable prospecting claim has been lost in a Court challenge because of not adhering to the 1904 tenement act, by simply using metal star pickets in place of wooden stakes. One important claim was lost just because the tops of the wooden stakes were not painted white on the top eight inches.

As a precaution, Ron had taken to always placing a steel star-picket alongside his wooden datum pegs topped with a bit of bright foil and some survey streamers for an easy location to future wooden peg replacement.

***

This was 1979 and the very first land satellite was now available for spot positioning called "Geosat" (now replaced by GPS.) This technology was not available to everyone. Apart from being expensive, it was very slow taking up-to four days to get a latitude and long ground position-fix within an accuracy of six metres. Satellite high definition photography was not available to the private sector, being still a top-secret USA government tool mainly used for spying on the Russians.

Ron had two experienced pegging teams, each with their own 4X4 and equipment trailer. Ron would dash around the vast Kimberley region from one pegging job to the next.

His job was to plot and set-up the all-important datum reference corner king peg, and layout the trenches for each claim. Then a waterproof pouch fixed to the wooden datum corner stake containing the claim details. The pegging crews would then go about setting out the full claim area using an accurate survey compass sighting and knocking in the smaller wooden intermediate stakes every 100 metres along the surveyed boundary lines.

Not many men could handle this; it was hard hot work. The area ground temperatures were often in excess of 46° C. As such, the crews were at most times close to their physical limits. They were required to carry bundles of wooden stakes, a heavy hammer, and two litres of water.

Ron is one of the smartest men I have ever known, a real bushman. This man had developed along the way, some very interesting and accurate ways of positioning the all-important corner stake at the correct datum location.

A map reference point is a fixed geological position like a mountain peak, sharp bend in a river creek bed, or some other immovable easily map recognised fixed landmark. The datum stake position or starting point is located from the clients designated map position showing the clients intended mining tenement claim. It all looks simple from studying a flat paper map. However, we all know the ground is not flat.

Nonetheless, the challenge is to place the all-important datum reference, ground stake accurately. Preferably, within a few feet of the registered tenement map datum, using a standard government survey map. Ron thought-up the (spot-on) signalling mirror idea, with a hole in the centre, and a simple string cord looped through the hole.

This mirror was also a handy lifesaving gadget; it is so simple, worn around the neck when not in use. Every member of the pegging crew carried one and I later supplied the Ron signalling mirror to all my air charter pilots. I still carry one in my flight bag to this very day.

The big problem in using a mirror to signal a moving object flying at 3000 feet altitude and eight kilometres away is how do you know you have the mirror light spot on the target? The standard or old way was to put the light spot on the ground in front of you then move it in a vertical sweep up in a line towards the target. You would have to do this many times, rapidly to make sure that by chance one of the sweeps hit the target, or the flash seen by the pilot.

With Ron's mirror, you simply placed a pencil, or stick through the neck string holding the pencil out in front of the stretched loop. You then look through the hole in the centre of the mirror, while at the same time placing the top of the pencil in line with the hole. Sight and align the hole, the pencil top, and the target in one line, then reflect the sunlight onto the top of the pencil. This will place the sunlight spot right on to the target every time and you can also track or follow the moving target. It works perfectly every time. Its simple rugged and safe, and has no batteries or moving parts.

***

The pegging business is all about being first to claim the ground, being accurate, and registering the claim correctly with the mines department. This would include all the required government paperwork accurately lodged, and of course, the tenement fees paid in full. These fees always presented the biggest problem. The fee payment had to be a bank-cleared cheque before the claim considered fully processed.

Some of these fees were, well to put it quite bluntly, to me... enormous. It was normal to have the fees in excess of

$30,000 for a large and multiple set of claims. The post office mail was not very time-reliable in the Kimberley. True a jet aircraft service brought mail every day, however part or all of that day's mail could remain in Port Hedland or Broome a thousand kilometres away. The mail off-loaded without notice. Mail was then loaded on to approved Royal Mail passing trucks or a small charter aircraft to reach Derby, Fitzroy Crossing, Halls Creek, and Kununurra, who knows when. It could take between three and ten days to receive mail from Perth even though the Royal Mail considered a priority.

To help speed things up a bit, mining company clients would bank-telex claim fee funds directly into my bank account. I would then draw a local bank cheque to pay the clients mining tenement fees. On many occasions, the slow transfer of telex funds back into my bank account would create a massive shock to my bank balance. It could take two weeks or longer to settle and clear the funds leaving me with a massive money problem. Dumb as it may sound, I was actually paying large overdraft fees to help my clients secure their mining tenements.

It was at about this same period that I noticed that my hair was rapidly turning grey. You see, once the mining tenement fees were cleared and paid, the urgency to answer my pleading phone and telex calls for payment seemed for some reason unimportant to the client. After being burnt, broke, and forgotten a few times. On more than one occasion, the pegging job was complete and the entire set of documents ready to lodge and register, but if the lodgement funds were not forthcoming, we waited... and we waited.

Ron was a very busy man who tried very hard to get all the pegging jobs completed on time. Just getting around the remote Kimberley outback was a massive challenge. On many occasions Ron was needed back in Kununurra to set-up the next few pegging jobs, then to order and road-freight many tons of the approved type of wooden claim stakes from Perth, and or to resolve some claim irregularity with a client.

Ron would manage somehow to get a lift to the nearest landing strip, most times just a straight bit of gravel road, advising me via his HF Royal Flying Doctor radio with the location and pick-up time. I would then fly out and bring him back to Kununurra. One day I received a radio call on the RFDS (Royal Flying Doctor Service) HF radio to fly in and pick him up at Kingston's Rest Bow River station airstrip.

I told Ron I was not very happy with that particular airstrip, as the aircraft had to land and take-off on a one-way narrow airstrip, and under a low-slung power line. Ron quickly advised me there was an all-new Bow River station airstrip just three kilometres from the homestead and he would be there at eleven o'clock tomorrow. Could I pick him up from there and bring him back to Kununurra.

I checked the new strip location with the Kununurra flight service, they had heard about the new Bow River strip but had no details as the new strip was not yet ALA (authorised landing area) approved. On the other hand, they advised Bow River station had applied for the approval. On hearing of that impending approval and another pilot telling me, he had a friend of a friend's friend land there without a problem, so I decided to fly out to the new strip and pick-up Ron.

I arrived over Bow River station homestead, and could easily make out the old airstrip with the XXX markers but could not see the new strip. This cattle station area is on the Bow River run-off flats. The whole land area was the same light-brown sand colour for twenty kilometres in every direction.

On the ground, various features do normally stand out from the air, but this land was all the same brown and featureless. After ten minutes flying around Ron mirror flashed me but I still could not locate his exact spot or for that matter the new airstrip. I decided to do a little grid search pattern in the most likely area I suddenly came across Ron waving his arms like windmills, standing beside a patch of rusty corrugated tin. I lined up for a landing then franticly waved off by Ron.

On my second approach, Ron was indicating to his right. When I was just twenty foot off the ground, I could now see why. I was previously about to land on the wrong side of the runway markers. It was only when I had landed and shut down the engine that I noticed the line of half-buried tyres, indicating the correct side of the runway. I then noticed the two dirty-white painted truck tyres indicating the airstrip threshold. The strip markers and even the once white windsock were now Kimberley brown. This airstrip was invisible from the air due mainly to the surrounding terrain being the same colour as the gravel airstrip.

Ron was really pissed as he had been waiting in the hot sun without shade for over two hours. Then to see me flying around in circles almost overhead just made him all the madder.

The next day a twin engine Baron landed on the same airstrip except on the wrong side of the strip dividing indicators. The aircraft was a total write off, luckily with nobody hurt, the charter aircraft was picking up people from Bow River Station.

The unfortunate Baron pilot being advised that Dallas had landed there yesterday, telling Kununurra flight service "if that shithead can land there, then anybody can." Then again, that pilot did not have a good bloke like Ron on the ground to guide him, which was I guess rather unfortunate for him, and very fortunate for me.

***

Mining companies were now entering panic stage to have their land pegged, and their claims lodged. This experience was very much like watching a feeding frenzy of hungry dingos on a dead calf. The tenement claim frenzy went on day and night well into the wet season, making work in the remote outback both difficult and dangerous. It was quite a common experience for a slow, low, water ford crossing to change within an hour into raging, wide flowing river. Many times changing from a pleasant dry creek-bed to full raging flood.

Numerous inexperienced prospectors and tourists have lost their lives from camping on those nice flat sandy creek beds. A day without rain means nothing as many have been washed away in the dark of night by water that had fallen in a tropical thunderstorm over sixty miles away. While others have tried to cross the same creek that only an hour ago was dry, and perished in the powerful floodwater.

Ron and his crew helped, and possibly saved many from an outback disaster as he managed to convince people to stay on high ground and well back from the creek-bed or water... However not everyone listened. I know that he and his crew risked their lives on a number of occasions to retrieve people and equipment caught and washed away in the fast tropical flooding creeks.

The pegging frenzy brought with it other challenges and risks to get the best land claimed first. Time was running out as untrue information carefully leaked on what was about to happen.

***

The monsoon season made accessibility by vehicle difficult, and so helicopters were used more and more to reach the prospective claim sites. Some of these sites were a great challenge for the chopper pilots to get in and out of, requiring a high-level of flying skill. Even so, some pilots paid the price for being just a little too complacent. Maybe just a little too distracted for a second. As that is all it takes to turn a tiring days flying into a memorable disaster... assuming the pilot survived.

Ron was not a pilot but had seen good and bad flying and had been involved with aircraft for many years. Being in a helicopter crash was not a new experience for Ron.

He had figured out long ago that with all the high-risk chopper flying he was involved in; it had to happen at some time or another. His best insurance was in picking a good pilot that he trusted and knowing just what to do in the event of a problem... This careful approach is what saved his life on this occasion.

***

It had been a long tiring day starting at first light. The mission was to get seven datum positions located pegged and mapped in one day. All the helicopter fuel dumps had been carefully arranged weeks ago to refuel the Bell 47G-2B for this job. Ron would set-up the claim datum while the pilot went off to refuel at one of the fuel dumps.

132

The plan was to land at last light and then camp for the night getting an early first light start next morning to do the same tiring thing all over again.

This chopper was an early designed Bell 47G-2B, a machine with a good flight safety record. A similar helicopter is used in the TV series "MASH" or the Australian "Skippy" series. All helicopters have a well-tested and documented set of flying limitations, and all flying machines have detailed performance envelops. However, as we all know, limitations and performance envelops are just numbers; and numbers can be changed... Just like the old aviation saying goes, "bold pilots may never become old pilots." Then again, there is always mother luck to rely on.

It was a hot and muggy 32 degrees in the desert at 6am in the morning, with a depressing 100 percent humid monsoon air. They were a bit overweight for the temperature and elevation, at a ground elevation of 1689 feet above sea level. There was no mistaking the WAC aviation chart numbers; this particular position in this desert was high. Then again, sea level temperatures would be 34 degrees suggesting an acceptable, small, but normal inversion.

Considering the hot humid weather, sloping ground and nil wind the pilot decided on a transition take-off. This style of helicopter take-off only taught by the military, and always considered high-risk requiring considerable skill.

The advantages are the helicopter is moving away from the take-off point the instant it leaves the ground thus making it much harder for an enemy to target. Except this was not the reason for this particular pilot. The other reason for using this style of take-off gets the helicopter into a quicker conversion of forward lift with a lower or narrow power margin.

The recently rebuilt Bell 47 failed to clear the trees at the edge of the landing site. Now with three feet of the main rotor blade torn off, the Bell 47 crashed heavily to the ground. Immediately the helicopter then flipped on to its side with the engine screaming at full throttle. Apparently, the noise was deafening, with bits of the helicopter flying in every direction.

The main rotor blades had instantaneously sheared off to stubs with the stabiliser bar beating a large hole into the soft ground just a few feet from the recently refuelled, and now ruptured, high-octane fuel tanks.

Both Ron and the pilot knew the crash survival drill. Hang on tight and stay strapped-in, shut the engine down, turn off the fuel, and switch off the electrical master. Then the second the engine and airframe stops all movement; get out of the thing and run for your fucking life, hopefully before the inevitable fire and possible explosion.

Ron and the pilot escaped from that Bell 47 crash without so much as a scratch; however, the helicopter was beyond help soon engulfed in flames, burning into a twisted molten mess. To this day, I still have the photos taken by Ron as he witnessed and photographed this close shave with death.

I arrived at the crash site just three hours later with the replacement Bell 47, piloted by the owner of the helicopter company.

Ron still had a day's work to do, so with his pilot he jumped into our Bell 47 and continued with his claim-pegging job. There was nothing left to see or do except take a few photos of the smouldering wreck for the insurance company

***

About two weeks later Ron had reached his physical limit. He had suffered a complete physical breakdown, and rushed into the Kununurra Hospital suffering from extreme heat exhaustion. I arrived at the hospital to see that Ron was still unconscious, out cold and hooked-up to an intravenous drip. Ron slept deeply for three days straight, I know since I was their most of the time. When this tough man came around and returned to the living, all he wanted to do was get back out bush with his boys and finish off a few more pegging jobs.

Reluctantly, I had some bad news for Ron, news that would spell the end of his pegging days, and his beloved company West Coast Surveys. Nevertheless, we still had a little more time, and a few more pegging jobs to complete before his company and Ron's mad survey pegging career all came to an historical end.

Chapter Three:

Diamond fever epidemic

Sir Charles Court, the Premier of Western Australia, under continuing pressure from the mining and prospecting sector, bowed to the heavy political lobby by bringing in sweeping new mining legislation. New legislation regarding the way in which a mining tenement is now to be field claimed, and registered in Western Australia.

It would no longer be necessary, or required to first, physically peg a mining tenement claim. One could simply make a mining claim by marking out the wanted area on a government mining survey map.

Should the requested claim-area found to be vacant on the master mines register, and not currently plotted, it was now considered available; as such a mining or prospectors claim could be granted without stepping a foot on the land.

Only then is the tenement marked with a datum stake and trenches. This procedure was a complete reversal of the current system whereby the proposed tenement claim was required to have all the corners correctly pegged with a datum stake and corner trenches completed, before the claim application. Under this new law, no labour is required to peg a claim prior to registration.

Ron bounced back to good health after four days in hospital. This was enough for him, which was evident by the fact the next time I saw him he was knocking back a large beer in the local Hotel cave-bar.

I had noticed Ron's Toyota neatly parked in the shade at the pub and thought I should call in for a drink. Ron had to be in there, knowing that nobody but nobody ever allowed to drive Ron's personal Toyota HJ 47 tray-back Land Cruiser.

***

The cave-bar was busy for this time of the day. Ron was in deep conversation with a few mining company blokes, as I approached the bar I called out.

'Hi there partner, how are you feeling now, you look like you have lost a few kilos?' Ron turned on his famous radiant smile and held out his hand.

'Good try partner,' shaking my hand vigorously, 'but you'll need to send me a lot more pegging work than that to kill me off matey, I lost six bloody kilos somewhere in that hospital. I've got a lot of eating and drinking to do to catch-up to fix my weight and fluid deficiency.'

Then turning to the four khaki dressed mining company men at the bar,

'Niven, I think you know all these blokes?'

'I sure do, and they are all from different mining exploration companies, it's a wonder they haven't started a nasty bar-fight by now over something.'

The big man in the corner with the large unkempt red beard was Mal Macleod the CEO from Afro-West mining he laughed aloud.

'We've only been here for fifteen minutes Dallas, give us a chance. Stick around you might see blood on the ground before this days end.'

Ron winked at me over his full glass of beer. We had a firm understanding that we would never discuss our business or our clients business with anyone, especially in the pub.

Our client's secret business matters and instructions were normally discussed in my double-glazed and padded soundproof office, well away from the pub and exploration spies. That is just how serious this exploration paranoia had become.

It was our fixed company rule, if any of our staff caught or reported discussing our clients business in the pub, or anywhere. This would bring about an immediate termination of their employment. The offender then put on the next aircraft out of town.

These were heavy secret times. Keeping ones mouth shut and being discrete was the only way to guarantee that we could be trusted. Trusted enough to carry out contract work for the various mining and exploration companies that required and used our services.

Last month Ron had sacked (or is that railroaded) out of town one of his loose mouthed pegging crew. He had made an example of this bloke, hence all the other crew knew exactly what to expect if they talked about their well-paid job while in town. This was a necessary action to reassure our clients that we could be trusted, but then again, could we trust our clients?

There were more unfounded crazy rumours distributed around the town by the exploration company management themselves, than any of their workers down the pub. The idea behind all of this silly diversion tactics was to steer the opposition away from their own areas of most interest. The net was quickly tightening… it was now only a matter of time.

***

Ron and I had witnessed some very elaborate dirty tricks. Cunning plans, devised to achieve the complete distraction of opposition from their company sensitive exploration areas. Some games were funny, some tricks were very expensive, and some were just outright dangerous. This was a very serious game to be a player in, with only one eventual winner.

The bar atmosphere was more than a little spaced-out as were the six men standing along it. All four of these mining men needed information urgently, as time was running out, and the best place to get it was still the Kununurra pub.

The four men looked and acted quite pleasantly towards one another. Yet Ron and I knew all too well that underneath all that casual charm and smiling, they all seethed with rage and hate of one another.

They each had at some time or another, over the last six months. Having been the instigator or victim of one or more of the others expensive time consuming and wasteful diversions.

They were all hoping that after a few more drinks someone would let slip with a small microscopic piece of information that may prove useful enough to give them an edge in this serious race.

***

These four men were responsible for the spending of a considerable amount of money in the area, making them all-powerful identities in this small-town. Now it was close to payday, with the huge rewards known by all. As such, the tensions were now extremely high.

This was a multimillion-dollar high stakes game and there were some big players at the table. Included were the giant DeBeers diamond cartel, CRA/ Rio Tinto, and a number of other smaller, however nonetheless powerful players.

The time was September 1979 and the sweet smell of success was powerful and close. They almost had the spoils within their grasp, but which of these four companies will be the one to find and own the world's largest producing diamond mine?

***

Those that know, say that all diamonds were formed in the deep earth more than three billion years ago. Deep down in a dip in the Continental mantle, at a depth of about 100 kilometres. At that great depth, any carbon being nicely pressure-cooked at temperatures of between 900°C and 1200°C for a billion or so years would form into diamonds. A small variation in the pressure or cooking temperature will spoil the cooking pot. Too low or high, then all you would end-up with is graphite, suitable for making pencils.

Over millions of years, diamonds are then brought to the surface in a volcanic rock flow, now known as "Kimberlite." This is the name given to diamond bearing rock first found in the Kimberley area of South Africa.

Apparently, this is not quite the case with the Argyle diamond mine AK1, which is actually a "Lamproite" rock, not "Kimberlite" rock. Then again who cares about the name of the rock, in those days we already knew that quality diamonds existed. We were all trampling over vast areas of the Kimberly in an attempt to discover the diamond pipe, or source of all these little sparklers?

As my partner Ron would say, "That's what this game is all about mate, and may the best man win." I on the other hand, had another view. I had become a little fascinated by the various methods used in trying to locate the diamond pipe.

***

The large wealthy exploration companies started with using modern Geophysics to target the Kimberlite rocks. However, not all Kimberlite rock contains micro diamonds.

The poorer companies just went out into the field and used the standard Geological textbook prospecting practice. This method required a good logical Geo nose to find the Kimberlite samples. The only problem was that you can find Kimberlite, or should I say Lamproite in huge areas of hundreds of square kilometres in just about every direction and nearly all of it did-not contain the required and sought-after micro diamonds.

Then again, none of this information was new. A number of good Kimberlite samples and Lamproite micro-diamond bearing rocks; were ultimately identified and confirmed many years ago. Nevertheless, the samples were from such diverse, far, and distant locations that to identify a source was all but impossible. Some other strategy and new thinking was required.

All of the prospecting exploration companies soon found out that the old ways of prospecting were proving just as successful as the all-new and expensive electro-magnetic resonance and gamma logging systems, currently used.

These mining companies spent many millions of dollars on the extensive sample-drilling programmes, which rapidly drained the company exploration funds for little gain in knowledge.

The thing to remember was in the beginning the small and poorer companies were doing quite well, using the older techniques such as UV (ultraviolet) hand-held lamps, a simple acid test, a jeweller's eyeglass, and a lot of legwork.

I discovered that initially these small companies had the jump on the big rich companies, so at that time it was still a level playing field.

I will try to attempt summarise my un-qualified but observer's view of this great race, company-by-company. A race to how the world's largest diamond bearing pipe eventually became a reality.

In the process, it may provide some interesting background on a few of the great characters who were involved.at that time. I might add most of who had used our business services at some time or another.

***

Lindsay Doig (33) was the project manager for Stockdale Prospecting (owned by DeBeers)

Lindsay was a tall good-looking, softly spoken very likeable Scotsman with a good sense of humour. He also had a sharp eye with a distracting interest for what other exploration people were doing in the Kimberley, which was a great pity.

Ron concluded that was because he never used our excellent pegging services. However, Lindsay being a real nice bloke just made it all the easier for the well-practised and unscrupulous opposition to take maximum advantage of his nosey interest in their business, and they did.

Lindsey was out of his depth and class in this devious tough business environment.

***

"The diamonds hunt by Stockdale Prospecting."

They drilled many holes and had taken many samples from all over the Kimberley. This company had been in the area carrying out exploration sampling for some fourteen years... ultimately discovering nothing-interesting, mostly barren Kimberlite and a few small-scattered diamonds.

They had also found small alluvial diamonds in the Ord River and in many of the creeks flowing into the Ord. I have no idea what type of geophysical modelling they used, but I do know they missed just about all the indicators and markers needed to target the diamond bearing pipe.

140

On the other hand, I do know they had accumulated a massive amount of data. This data collected, spanning over many years while prospecting in the Kimberley. All of which would have been of great significance to form a more complete picture of what was taking place in other mining exploration company models. Stockdale it would appear was a long way from identifying the target, even though they had previously explored all of the now known "hot spot" at an earlier date. To add further misery for this company. Amazingly, they still held through Uranex NL some control to the mining tenement lease containing the "hot spot." Was all this extremely valuable data eventually acquired by any of the others… who knows?

***

Malcolm Macleod (39) was the MD & CEO of Afro West Mining.

Mal is a big-hat and boots type of field Geologist with a happy-go-lucky laid-back sort of character. He liked to play my guitar, sing, and drink lots of my booze in my office. Every business meeting turned into a party but he never gave-up on asking me what the opposition were up to; and well, I never told him.

***

"The diamonds hunt by Afro-West."

With Mal, about half of his work diligently carried out in the field using a combination of standard-practice Geo stuff, laced with some Mal-style good common sense. The other half of his work expertly completed in the pub checking out rumours and sifting through the town gossip. Mal was no dimwit as he watched very closely to what was going on and applied his cunning mind, mixed with good field geology to arrive at the "hot spot."

Mal the ever-practical Geo quickly figured out the pattern and type of Lamproite changed in samples, that being only a few small alluvial diamonds actually found in the Ord River above Ord River Station, with many more found below. As such, this must be close to the source. Nevertheless, there was still a considerable amount of land area to cover and sample.

141

Then a few loose lips down the pub confirmed that he was in the right "hot spot" area, and then the pegging started.

He had us peg a number of areas including a nifty move in claiming the lower Smoke Creek area, which later proved to be a good move as it was rich in alluvial diamonds. The other areas claimed were in very significant positions in the "hot spot" and carried out as midnight claim pegging jobs.

Although correctly pegged, these so-called midnight claims swiftly were challenged by AJV (Ashton Joint Venture later to become CRA.) These claims were just a bit too close to their area of interest for comfort. Then again, nobody would dare show, draw attention, or admit to this touchy situation.

***

Tony Gates (42) (Gatesy) was representing Gem Exploration,

Gatesy, was a well-respected Geologist and a smart businessperson with a keen eye on a mining company deal. Nearly all of our dealings were through his Perth city office, Gatesy would quietly go about his fieldwork without attracting much attention.

I would say that Gatesy was the best at working out the possible location of the diamond pipe. His exploration company may have been small, but Gatesy used what I would say was more useful technology and better geological modelling to arrive at his conclusion, which as it happens, was spot-on. Gatesy was so close to a discovery that he was on fire, and he knew it.

***

"The diamonds hunt by Gem Exploration."

Gatesy is a persevering methodical style of Geologist. Gatesy took a standard targeting approach and applied a new angle. He devised a new geological model using wear, distance and time. I do not know exactly how the system works, however as far as I can understand, Lamproite and Kimberlite rock containing micro diamonds has a wear factor.

Gatesy worked-out a radius curvature wear of Lamproite rock travelling away from the source over some time, and converted that tumbling wear factor to distance travelled. We are talking time spans of hundreds of thousands of years, in short, the sharper the Lamproite rock edge sample, the closer the sample would have been to the source. Alluvial mini diamonds have the same wear factor so when they are at their sharpest, is when considered the closest to the pipe, or source.

All Gatesy had to do now was plot all the positions of the sharpest samples and cross-reference them into a grid, and then into a cross point star to get to the "hot spot." This was very smart Geological detective work. We then carried out Gatesy instructions to peg mining claims in his identified "source area," which just happened to be in that very same area that Ron and I called the "hot spot."

Later on, Ron had asked Gatesy how he had known he was so close; to which he replied that his barefooted assistant started complaining of cut feet. Gatesy knowing that fresh Lamproite and new diamonds are sharp, he then knew he was very close. I think Ron made him buy him another beer for telling that porky one.

***

Pat Donnelly (59) & Frank Hughes (57), Pat was the admin manager for Ashton Joint Ventures owned by CRA (Conzinc Rio-Tinto Australia.)

Old Pat (his local known name) was always available for a chat, a smoke, and a drink. However, behind his disarming endless smile was a hard-nosed, and much focused businessman.

It has been said by many, that Pat could charm the venom out of a dead snake. They also say that he was very good at poker, but I was never about to try my luck to find out.

On the other hand, the other three exploration companies did in a way play poker with Pat, and as history was later to prove... they lost the game.

Pat under Frank Hughes instruction, had the week before the discovery, gone out and hired all of my remaining fleet of vehicles for an indefinite time. Pat provided me with a CRA standing company order to hire all of my other vehicles, including all those returned at the end of their hire. Pat now had sixteen of my twenty-two vehicles locked-up tight in his secure company office yard. I knew then that something big was about to happen.

***

"The diamonds hunt by Ashton/CRA."

These people were a well-funded lot, and had a number of large field crews operating under their senior Geologist Frank Hughes. They made extensive use of helicopters and must have had a very good geological model as they had systematically zeroed in on the target.

Even so, the land area was still quite large, and needed more positive samples to narrow-down the target area to find the elusive diamond pipe.

One of the Geo methods was to sample for elevation. The idea being, since diamond bearing Kimberlite rock then driven up from the depths of a volcano in huge lava flows over thousands of years. It then forms a "Tuff ring" with material that runs down the side of the volcano into the valleys and rivers.

As luck would have it, and later confirmed by Frank Hughes who was the Ashton/CRA field operations manager.

On that particular sunny-day, Frank was out sampling and was busting for a piss. He instructed the Jet-Ranger pilot to land urgently. While relieving themselves against an anthill a Geo noticed, a glint of something stuck in the side of the anthill.

On a closer inspection, it turned out to be a one-and a half carat octahedron diamond with very sharp points confirming the site-find as a possible pipe tuff-ring diamond. Frank had landed on the rim or edge of the diamond pipe. All they had to do now was to figure out in which direction the pipe tuff was facing, then peg and claim the area. Which as it happens was almost in the middle of the calculated "hot spot."

There was one major problem… Stockdale Prospecting through Uranerz NL already held the mining lease to this "hot spot" area. That is correct; Stockdale already had access and a means to control the land and exploration rights to the world's largest diamond mine. However, Ashton soon found out the tenement lease was due to expire in just seven days. Other mining exploration companies were also sniffing around this same area, and they were all very close, very close indeed.

CRA had a big problem... how could Frank Hughes, Maureen Muggeridge and Pat Donnelly keep a firm lid on this mammoth find until the land became available in seven days? Easy one, just play a game of bluff poker, Pat was good at poker. He suggested creating a massive diversion away from the area. This would achieved by hiring every available vehicle and helicopter capable of going bush, or used to prospect, or peg a claim... and that is just what they did.

***

The smiles at the bar were starting to wane and the sarcastic comments began to flow with the booze. Lies and diversions were not going to work now, not today. Now it was a matter of the best bluff, but just who of these four had the best poker hand to play. Who could play the game best... who will be the winner?

This was not at all Lindsey's style, but just how did they stack up against one another at this critical point in the game.

The tension in the air was now so thick. It was like a cloud of heavy air weighing down on us all. Each move, and each word, was carefully analysed with suspicion, eyeballs swivelled at the slightest movement in expectation of a useful clue, verbal miff, or comment.

***

As Ron lent forward to pick-up his drink from the bar, he said quite casually into my ear.

'She's on for bloody-well young and old now mate. Hang on to your bloody arse, because we're off for the ride of your fucking life.'

Ron being a man of exacting and descriptive words would shortly have his theory confirmed.

The four mining moguls beamed false smiles and kept their equal distance from one another along the short bar. Ron and I exchanged knowing glances as we felt the tension build further and noticed the body language of shuffling feet and roving eyeballs.

Ron kept up a light banter of conversation, on subjects such as the Government bastards that had recently changed the mining act so now he was out of a job. Launching into would any of you rich mining blokes like to buy 120,000 survey pegs and some 4Kg hammers, all going very cheap.

***

Old Pat lit yet another cigarette from his old one, and with a tight smile that looked like he was passing wind, ordered another round of drinks for everyone.

Pat then gently puffed a large cloud of smoke into the non-smoking Lindsay's face obscuring his head for a moment, opening the conversation with a fierce verbal right hook.

'Well what do you know blokes, this month's almost gone. It will soon be October and the beginning of the wet. Are you guys going to close-up shop and get away early this year?'

This was a not-so-well disguised inquiry as to what were they all going to do in the very near future? Everyone got the message and the snooping intention all mumbling something in reply. Except Lindsey, he had a worried look on his face then piped-up in all seriousness with a silly grin.

'Thank God you have reminded me what month it is Pat. Shit, 1 still have over three million dollars left in my exploration budget account, I must spend this money before the end of the year. First thing tomorrow, I will hire two more Jet Ranger helicopters from Darwin to finish off our annual exploration project… most likely out where your ground-pegging crews are busy scratching around in the hot sun.'

Everyone forced a loud and false laugh at Lindsey's attempt of tongue-in-cheek dry humour. His boasting about the control of large amounts of company exploration funds being at his disposal was a true and genuine boast. Lindsey was innocently naive, as all at the bar thought him amusing.

There was good reason, as he was the only one standing at that bar who did not know that Frank Hughes and Pat Donnelly of Ashton/CRA. Had some days ago hired every available helicopter and 4X4 hire vehicle in the North-west from Darwin to Port Hedland

The fact of the matter was; Lindsay's boast was true. At that time Stockdale Prospecting were most probably the best-funded mining company in the Kimberley, if not all of

Australia. Although, tomorrow he would not be spending any of his large funding-budget on more helicopters or exploration 4X4 vehicles, there was none left to hire, Ashton/CRA had hired the lot.

After fourteen years, Stockdale had set-up a very nice town yard and office. They had their own fleet of Toyota 4X4 exploration vehicles (which was why they never hired any of my vehicles). They also owned a full workshop and sample lab, staff accommodation and even a helicopter-landing pad right in their town backyard.

Yes, they had almost everything, except for one thing, and that was local knowledge. Knowledge that they already had in their possession access through Uranerz NL to the mining tenement lease, which included the "hot spot" later to be known as AK1... the worlds largest producing diamond mine.

***

Of the six men, drinking at that bar that day five knew what was coming down. Lindsay was in complete ignorance as to what was going on around him.

The smart-arsed reference that Lindsay had made to Pat about hiring additional helicopters to jump the Ashton/CRA ground-pegging crews caused a genuine hearty laugh at the bar. This was because we all knew that it was a Pat contrived deception. A smart plan to keep Stockdale and others away from where all the real action was, the "hot spot."

The sad state of affairs was that nobody in this group could talk about this weird and bizarre position. The reason being as we were all in our different ways legally held to commercial secrecy. The saddest thing of all was; being a true but strange fact, that Ron and I knew far more than they did, while bracing the bar that day. We knew pretty well what everybody was up-to.

Ron was enjoying the teasing but could see things were going to get out of hand very soon and added his bit to Pat's enquiring comment.

'Well I can tell you this Pat. Niven, and me are folding up the fucking pegging business, and I will be going on holidays permanently. We've still got a few jobs to finish off and Niven has got a pile of bloody paperwork to write-up and lodge, then I guess after that it's all over Red Rover, well for me it is.'

Mal came back to life with what he thought was a very cunning slippery question asking…

'How many more pegging jobs have you got to complete then Ron?' Ron was just as quick.

'Nice try Mal, but you'll get fuck-all out of me mate, we run a survey pegging service not a bloody gossip newspaper mate. But if you want some real juicy information, I can tell you one thing for sure, it's your bloody turn to buy a round of drinks… mate.'

Mal joined us all in a thinly disguised laugh and promptly bought a new round of drinks. Ron had managed to reduce the bar tension a little… or was it just the booze?

***

These people should all know by now that Ron and I can keep our mouths shut about their business. On the other hand, this was very much a cat-and-mouse game for the others. Each hoping that one of them might slip-up.

They most certainly did not want Ron or me to say anything about their exclusive business dealings. It was a dicey situation for Mal, Pat, Lindsay, and Gatesy as they wanted to urgently know what each of the others were about to do.

Out of the four of them, the only people that Ron and I did not have all of the detailed information on was Ashton/CRA as they kept their company secrets very close in-house. We did on occasion hire them the odd Toyota 4X4 (except for last week when they hired the lot). We also serviced their vehicles, and repaired their field camp HF radio systems, but we had never carried out a claim-pegging job for them.

They had their own pegging crews. They always brought the crews in especially to do their claims, and then flew them out again, immediately after they had finished the job to avoid gossip.

***

Gatesy, the ever-watchful geo was strangely quiet. I think he was a little worried about the fact the claim paperwork I

148

was working on was his, and would I be sloppy enough to let anything slip out in this bar room chat. "Loose lips sink ships."

He need not have worried as this type of barroom interrogation was now becoming quite normal; as such, Ron and I were masters at changing and steering the nosey conversation subject elsewhere.

Gatesy leant forward and ordered a round of drinks then said to Pat,

'If you want to know what I will be doing soon I don't mind telling you at all. I'm going to finish up this last drink and then I'm going to piss off home to the Motel and get a good night's sleep... good night all.'

On that brief note Gatesy skulled down his beer and left without another word, the others soon followed except for Mal. There was still plenty of drinking time left in this day.

I left Ron with Mal both grinning away, wiping the beer froth from their untidy beards, these guys got along quite well, but then again Ron got on well with everyone.

***

Our overall information on what was happening with all the exploration company business in the Kimberley was by far the most comprehensive and complete. Far more than most mining exploration companies working in the Kimberley could have ever guessed.

I do admit that we never knew the exact detail, though we still acquired all the necessary information to form a good picture of the unfolding events. Although we had no more than around 35% of the possible mining claim field work in the area. The fact was that we covered a very large area of the Kimberley every day, and had direct access to the many other exploration companies and field crews working in the bush and desert, including, Ashton/CRA and Stockdale.

On many occasions, Ron provided survey stakes, cold beers, and the use of his RFDS Codan HF radio to other pegging and exploration companies in the field. As Ron would say. "This was the bushman's law of help." I must admit I had some trouble understanding this code of the bush. Especially as I had to replace all the bundles of wooden survey stakes, food, and fuel, he handed out to people wandering about in the desert.

Then again, it was Ron's company too, and I was soon to learn that there was another useful and covert reason for all this generous action. Ron being smart, soon found out everything that was going on with all the other exploration companies who were busy in the out-back pegging mining claims. Ron is a very smart man indeed.

If you can just imagine for a moment the scope of services that my five small businesses provided to the mining and exploration companies.

***

Under the company name of "Multi Agencies," we provided a Toyota 4X4 vehicle hire service, set-up for mining and exploration. We supplied, repaired, and hired, long-range HF Codan radio systems, and provided a full mechanical service and repair workshop, specialising in mining and exploration vehicles. We also provided a full confidential survey pegging service and then we had our own light aircraft. Nobody could match that service at the time, and the information gathered was nothing short of astonishing.

Although we never carried out any pegging services for Ashton/CRA, we did however know every place where they were pegging claims and sampling. They used chartered Jet Ranger helicopters for many of their covert field-sampling missions, and our office as a matter of normal operations monitored all the aviation HF and VHF radio traffic frequencies.

The CRA helicopters would give regular SAR (search and rescue) position fixes, a CAA (Civil Aviation Authority) mandatory requirement for all commercial flying operations. We easily worked out that the CRA geological work around the Gibb River road, and other areas were shams to keep Stockdale and others off the scent. We could see that CRA were very busy in the "hot spot" as our own pegging survey crews were bumping into them on a regular basis in that area... yes that same special area.

We had recognised that a situation was rapidly intensifying, a situation that we were having some difficulty in fully understanding.

Over the next few days, things started to rapidly fall into place. Things were hotting up fast; WCS were suddenly asked to peg a number of areas for Gem Exploration, Northern Mining, and Afro West, right in the middle of the "hot spot." We also knew, as no doubt did the others, that this same area was still under lease to a well-known local exploration company Uranerz.

Then the penny dropped when I noticed that the required lodgement date for all the claims. They were listed be lodged at first opening of the Kununurra mining registrar office, 9am on the 2nd of October 1979. A quick check exposed that Stockdale and Uranerz held the mining tenement lease over that same area of land. This was the actual area containing the "hot spot," a long held lease that would expire at one minute past midnight... on that same date.

The question that came to mind was... had Stockdale renewed the Uranerz lease in the last few days, or had they just let this land go as uninteresting. On the other hand, had they just simply forgot to renew the tenement lease? Was this the real thing; history was about to be made?

Ron and I looked at each other in silent amazement... was the elusive diamond pipe actually on this area of land. Ron and I suddenly realised it must be. It was now a foregone conclusion. Should we keep quiet about this, or maybe make better use of this information, or should we simply sleep on this valuable information?

I decided to adopt a wait and see attitude as our company was in the business of providing a range of services to all these mining companies. As per our company rules, we must remain neutral and impartial, regardless of the outcome of any future events. Nevertheless, was I correct in my assumptions? If I am indeed correct then somebody was going to be very, very rich tomorrow morning at a little after nine o'clock. As that was when the Kununurra Mining Register Courthouse opened for business.

***

On the way home, I called by the Post office and checked my mailbox. There was only one item of mail, a bright yellow envelope marked with a diagonal red urgent. I opened it-up on the spot, and was relieved to see it contained a large Bank cheque from Gem Exploration.

They were now back in the race again for tomorrow's big opening event. The cheque was for the full amount needed for their mining tenement lodgement fees.

This was a close thing, since without this bank cheque I would have had no reason at all to front-up at the mining register courthouse tomorrow morning... As for now, I must go back to my office and complete around two hours of mining tenement paperwork to be ready for this historic event tomorrow.

Chapter Four:

Facts about the name Kimberley

You know, after more than twenty years living in the Kimberley, I must have heard every story and variation about how the Kimberley got its proud name. The most common story is that of Dutch Captain Willem Janszoon of the Duyfken, who in 1606 while trying to navigate the Malacca Straits to China.

It has been said that Captain Janszoon accidently sailed a little too far south, ending up sailing east along the north coast of Australia. A few days later he was then reported to have sighted a land mass that reminded him of Dutch South Africa, naming the northern Australian mountain range the Kimberley.

Wrong, wrong... so wrong, the Dutch were not in even in South Africa at that time. The Dutch settlement of South Africa began in March 1647. This being much later in the great Dutch sailing explorer's history... what then is the truth.

***

Who was it that said, "The truth is stranger than fiction, only because fiction is obliged to stick to possibilities; and the truth is not." Ah yes, the master himself Mark Twain.

***

It is a fact that in 1873 Lord John Wodehouse, being the 1st Earl of Kimberley, known as "Lord Kimberley" was appointed by Her Majesties Government to the office of the British Secretary of State for the Colonies.

Shortly after this appointment, the Earl then left for a posting to South Africa just before the discovery in the region of a rather large 22-carat diamond on the banks of the Orange River. This find caused a small diamond prospecting rush.

The diamond bearing area was right next to the Northern Cape and known to the local prospectors as the "New rush."

The Dutch settlers wanted the name changed to "Vooruitzigt." However, Lord Kimberley complained to everyone that he could not pronounce or spell the Dutch name, also that the proposed "New rush" name was vulgar.

This minor bureaucratic matter then passed on to his Colonial Secretary J. B. Currey, who being a very smart young diplomat indeed suggested the perfect solution. He recommended the new Provence must have the name Kimberley since he knew the Secretary of State Lord Kimberley could both spell and pronounce that name quite well.

A short time after, the new area became a small thriving mining town, known as the Kimberley. Named after the first Earl of Kimberley.

This small South African town of Kimberley was later to become the centre to the world's largest known diamond mines; also the future DeBeers brother's diamond mining and trading organisation. In those early days, geological surveyors had recognised a special type of rock-type and formation in the diamond bearing area, and named the magna rock type "Kimberlite"

Now Kimberlite is just a rock type named after this new place in South Africa, on the banks of the Orange River called Kimberley. However, the name Kimberley originally comes from a small coal-mining town in the County of Norfolk, being the fifth largest County in England... yes indeed true.

The name Kimberley first originated from a granted Royal Peerage; the "Earl of Kimberley," created by Queen Victoria in 1866.

As we all know, on the other side of the world, we have the rather large Continent of Australia.

***

In the year 1879 that is right, only some six years after the Earl of Kimberley gave his name to a small province in South Africa. The Earl again recognised by Her Majesty, by then he had been swiftly promoted to the "British Secretary of State for the Colonies."

Remember, at that time Australia was just another of Her Majesties many Colonies, so the Earl was a very powerful man indeed. He was in fact the very man who paid the wages to all the British Government employees in the Colonies, including Australia.

***

At about that same time the Governor of Western Australia Sir Harry Ord, decided one day to find out what was going on in the remote parts of his state. This led to him to sending a young man, keen to make-a-name for himself type-of-bloke called Alexander Forrest, all the way up into the remote far north of the state. Quite simply to see if there was anything worthwhile grabbing up there.

A year later Forrest came trudging back to Perth and reported to his boss Harry. Forrest reported that right up in the top end of this massive State of Western Australia there was this bloody great place.

He had in fact discovered a vast fertile land with a thundering almighty freshwater river running through the middle of it, with good soil suitable for growing feed, and raising cattle. He then suggested to his boss Harry (that is Sir Harry Ord) that they should offer the land to new settlers.

Forrest had a keen eye for making a quick dollar, or was that a pound then? Anyway, he suggested a settler deal should ultimately proceed under some sort of government grant, with a fixed term lease. This smart idea removed any outright land purchase, and the government could hold full control and title to the newly discovered land. This cunning grant/lease proposal went ahead, as later on, the State could make big bucks by releasing the land repeatedly.to new pioneers. Alternatively, the government could sell the land in the future when the land was fully developed with other people's hard-

155

earned effort and money. Thus making huge profits... a nice little state government earner eh.

***

Nobody at that time considered, or thought the local owners; the indigenous people should be included in this great plan. However, they had a major problem to resolve first, they would need to give this new fertile land-area a good name.

Young Alexander Forrest was no dill when it came to big sums and slick business. Forrest had not received any pay in over a year, and he knew the name of the bloke who would be signing his pay-cheque. He suggested to Harry that they should call the place the "Kimberley" after his boss's boss the Earl of Kimberley, because after all he was the "British Secretary of State for the Colonies."

Forrest pointed out that this would go down well when Harry had to ask his boss for some further funding to get the new land grant deal started.

Young Forrest could see that Harry was a bit miffed at that idea, and figured out the reason why. He quickly suggested that the bloody great river he had found up there should have his name as the Ord River, and so it was.

Sir Harry Ord, shortly after this event had quickly retired to a warm place in the sun; now replaced by a new Governor, Sir William Robertson. Forrest had another small problem rapidly brewing; the new Governor Sir William wanted his name on things, including this new land area up in the north.

Forrest pointed out that the new names had already been previously requested by mail, so five months later in August 1880, a letter arrived by ship from the Earl of Kimberley. He had finally granted approval of the new names, and everybody was pleased and happy ever after... except for Sir William.

Up until that time, the Earl of Kimberley had never set a foot on Western Australian soil, and had no idea what the new Kimberley area looked like.

Another matter that needs clarifying is Alexander Forrest suggested the name for the Kimberley simply because that was the name of his boss, the Earl of Kimberley... It was not because the area had similar features to the South African Kimberley. The Earl of Kimberley had never seen the West

156

Australian Kimberley, so he had no idea what it looked like. On the other hand, Andrew Forrest had never been to South Africa so he had no idea what the African Kimberley looked like.

The truth is set in documented history. The Kimberley in Western Australia was "not" as first thought named after the Kimberley in South Africa. On the other hand, one must agree what a magnificent coincidence, and what a weird set of odd circumstances; both places ultimately named after the same man.

***

Anyway, shortly after, Forrest quickly resigned his job, dumping the poorly paid, government, remote area, surveying business. Then with his brother went into the real-estate business. Alexander Forrest soon proved to be a smart and diligent businessperson. He quickly became the government land-grant agent for... yes; you guessed it the Kimberley...

The Forrest brothers were criticised for the way they obtained control of their investments in North-West station properties. Accusing them of exploiting their government paid survey work for profit.

To remember the great sacrifice Alexander Forrest made in discovering the Kimberley in Western Australia, the government saw fit to erect a bronze statue of him in St Georges Terrace Perth. The traditional Aboriginal owners never got a mention. Mainly because they knew, the place was always theirs... It had been for over four million years.

No matter the reason, possibly just a minor coincidence in the huge government land profiteering scheme, that some say, continues on to this day.

***

So just where do we go from here... What do we have?

We have the Kimberley area, being on the Orange River in South Africa.

Then almost half a planet away, we also have the Kimberley area, on the Ord River in Western Australia.

Apart from a short street in Phuket, a small family park in England, and his own hometown name. There appears to be no other significant places, areas, or towns named after the Earl of Kimberley.

Now we must ponder, just what would be the odds, or the chances, of a person from the northern hemisphere. Who gave his name to, two vastly separated land areas in the southern hemisphere on two different continents. Later being the sites of the (not known at that time) two largest known diamond producing areas ever to be discovered in the world.

Also weird, and noted. Both named "prior" to the knowledge of that fact, and wait there is more to this strange story… and it is not a set of free steak knives.

***

Back in the 1886 Halls Creek gold rush days, micro diamonds regularly turned up in the Kimberley. The old prospectors working the Ord River area would report small diamonds, seen while panning along the riverbanks from where the Bow River and the Ord River junctions meet, all the way down to the Cambridge Gulf. However, in those days, they were all looking for gold and nobody attached much importance to these micro diamond finds.

Many of the old gold prospectors were immigrants from all parts of the world, and a number were from Dutch South Africa. They had noticed how similar the mountain formations and landscapes in the newly named West Australian Kimberley were so much like the Kimberley region of home in South Africa. In fact, most of the older Dutch prospectors thought that this was the very reason why the area eventually called the Kimberley… How wrong they were.

It was not until the early seventies when the focus turned to oil exploration, that sample drilling produced clear evidence of what they had identified as Kimberlite in many of the core samples. (Kimberlite in volcanic rock is a good indicator of the possible presence of diamonds.)

It was also a time of new technology using the new military, declassified "Passive Magnetic Resonance" systems.

If you knew the right people, and had the money, you could also get a nice high-resolution photo of your prospecting area from a satellite whizzing around in outer space. These were magical new geological times.

Helicopters now used regularly to take spot samples from interesting areas made sampling quicker and easier. A number of the older, world-experienced Geologists prospecting in the Kimberley area for oil also recognised the unique likenesses of the Western Australian Kimberley region to the South African Kimberley. However, they had simply thought the same as the early Dutch gold prospectors had; the name Kimberley just named after the South African Kimberley because the local scenery looked very similar.

These oil company Geologists were turning up increasing amounts of Kimberlite rock and olivine Lamproite containing micro diamonds in their drilling samples. Then the penny dropped... this must be an archon formation area, having the same type of old crypto-volcanic rock formations as seen in the South African Kimberley. There had to be a diamondiferous pipe close by, and considering the number of the samples and the wide coverage, it had to be a big one.

***

As a wise old sunburnt Geo once said after his seventh large re-hydration beer down at the pub.

"Listen hear mate. If it looks exactly like the same place you found something interesting before, then by the standard law of basic geology, as taught in the second lesson of Geo School to be a Geologist. There is every chance in the world it will have the same interesting bloody stuff there... do you understand what I am saying mate?"

***

I must admit that all sounded like basic common sense to me, and I only had two beers at that stage. I must also admit I was very tempted to ask him what the first lesson was, and then decided that too much knowledge in one day might damage my fragile head. These were strange times, I must be careful.

By 1976, the word was out, and the race was on for the source of all these diamonds. There are diamonds in them there hills, and funnily enough, them there hills are now known by exactly the same name as the place in South Africa as discovered in 1873... a place where they have also discovered diamonds.

Alexander Forrest discovered and named the Kimberley in 1879, only six years after not knowing anything about the other place called Kimberley in South Africa. Then in 1979 yes, that is right exactly one hundred years later, this new West Australian place called the Kimberley became the site of the world's largest producing diamond mine... AK1.

Then we have just one last strange question that I have often thought I should ask. Just why did Ashton/CRA name their magnificent diamond mine AK1 (Argyle Kimberlite 1.) The bloody tuff pipe diamond bearing rock is diamondiferous "Lamproite" magna rock, and not "Kimberlite" rock. Did Ashton/CRA not know this obvious and basic geological difference when they named the significant world famous diamond mine? Now how dumb was that.

The name should have been AL1 (Argyle Lamproite 1.)

***

I was thinking about these strange and interesting world diamond producing areas, coincidences, dates, and names as I drove home that night. The plan was to get an early night, as it will be a very busy day tomorrow... and no doubt an historic day. A day that I will be a part of forever.

Chapter Five:

You do agree, I was here first

My eyes opened in the dark shuttered bedroom, the only sound inside the room was the low hum of the air-conditioner and the gentle breathing of Lesley lying next to me. It would be another hour before the first light of dawn will signal the field crickets outside to stop calling out for a mate, and the frogs to stop croaking with the delight of the easy advertised meal.

In the tropics, having a backyard swimming pool had its many relaxing advantages... and disadvantages. The little slimy bastards were having a cricket party, and fornicating in the pool again. I glanced at my luminous watch on the bedside table it was exactly 5am. Who needs an alarm clock, this was my normal time to meet the new day, and who knows just what special memories and events this day will bring.

I crept out of bed so as not to disturb Lesley and the children. Normally I would put the coffee on and have a shower, then checkout the leftovers in the fridge for breakfast. Today I would just have a quick shower and have my coffee at the office.

Gatesy had been promising for days the mines department fees cheque for the recently pegged claims was on the way. 'It should have already arrived by now,' he kept saying, that it was posted from his Perth office "urgent express mail special delivery" over six days ago.

I will ring Gatesy when I get to the office and let him know the good news, the cheque had finally arrived, and that I could now lodge his set of claims exactly as he had instructed me to at 9am this morning. I guess Gatesy will be relieved to know that all his hard work has turned out okay.

Gatesy was very frustrated at this slow royal mail delivery, but to me, and all the other permanent residents of Kununurra this was all quite normal. Frankly, it was all a silly game of who will do the job for the least money, since the government always gave the mail contract to the cheapest tenderer.

This was a time when the national newspapers arrived three days old, with express mail taking six to eight days to arrive; it is easy to see which has the most priority. Many trucks and air-charter companies could have delivered the mail much quicker, alas they were not duly registered, and contracted "Royal mail" carriers.

Newspapers were not mail finding their way to Kununurra by any, and all means within two to three days. However, not all was lost as this slow mail system could be used to great advantage. Especially when it came to the application and lodging of mining claims, and other legal documents.

Each day, all of the Kununurra Mining Registrar's claim application paperwork was mailbag posted down to Perth to update the master records in the Perth City office.

By the letter of the law, a mining claim was not a legal binding transaction until the original claim duly entered into the public master register, and plotted onto the master mining tenement map. This public master map always held at the Perth City Mines Department.

In those times, it was not all-that unusual for large parcels of mining claims to disappear in the post for a short while. This gave even more reason for the clients to insist on individually time and date-stamped copy documents.

Nevertheless, a prospector or exploration company could easily telex down the information to their Perth office or dictate the information over the phone. Then have someone in

Perth lodge the mining tenement claim direct with the Perth City Mines Department.

In 1979, there were a considerable number of slight-of-hand, smart-arsed dealings carried out by the major diamond players. This done with the easily created confusion of two sets of mining claims being lodged and accepted for the same area, from two different registrar offices 2800 kilometres, and up-to three weeks apart. Paying two sets of claim registration fees was not a problem, as the duplicate funds were eventually returned within a few weeks.

The new Mining act of 1978 was being executed slowly with a crossover of the old and the new parts of the legislation. This being somewhat ambiguous, and still having problems. It was an easy matter to bog down your opposition to a claim. It mattered little who had a pending application for the same exploration claim. The claim-jumper simply objected to the claim in the Wardens Court.

If that was not resolved to your satisfaction, then an appeal to the claim always immediately lodged. The whole claim dispute would now be heard against you again in the Supreme Court. This type of claim-jumping defence added enormous pressure to defeat the opposition's objection, by simply stating that the claim-application already correctly lodged with the Mines department office in Perth. The company lawyers then producing proof, that the application was already processed and appropriately entered onto the Perth public register.

They would then deny to having had any prior knowledge that this same area had a previous application lodged in the Kununurra mining registrar's office over three weeks previously.

Once on the public register it was very difficult to amend or change. The local Kununurra date and time stamped claim should have had priority over the later Perth claim. However, this appeared to have little benefit and no advantage at all if the claim jumper happened to be an international multimillion-dollar mining company.

**

The damn copy machine was running hot as hell again. I had used-up three rolls of thermal copy paper and I was now running low on supplies. All of the original claim submission paperwork had to be in "permanent ink," this carried out using my new computer dot matrix printer set to "letter-quality." It certainly didn't look as good as my golf ball typewriter, but it was much cheaper per A4 sheet as the golf carbon ribbons were very expensive, and there were a good many pages yet to copy.

Much noise was coming from the outer office. The staff had been in for some time, and they knew well not to disturb me when I was in the middle of producing all the copies for a mining tenement lodgement. I glanced at the clock, shit it was nearly 8:30am and I wanted to get to the mining registrar office no later than ten-to-nine. I still had the map locations to plot and draw-up, just then Sue stuck her head in the door,

'You look like you need a cup of coffee and some help. If you want, I can carry-on with the copying while you get on with something else.'

'Both are great ideas Sue, I am reaching the stage of utter frustration with all this paperwork. I was here until gone midnight last night and thought I had the applications all but finished, well I was wrong, I've got to be out of here in twenty minutes.'

Everything went much faster with a little help. The stacks of paper were finally completed and collated into bundles with a separate mines department lodgement set and the all-important cheque placed in a large brown envelope. One large gulp of my coffee and I was out the door heading briskly for my Toyota land cruiser.

The Kununurra Courthouse, which also held the Mining Department Registrar's office, was by luck only about a five-minute drive from my office. I paused for a second at the tee junction before turning right. Then looked across noticing that one of my hire Toyota Land cruiser vehicles was just pulling-up to a halt under a shady tree opposite the Courthouse.

Within a matter of three seconds, I drove my Toyota up and parked almost touching the other vehicle, identical bull-bar to bull-bar. Pat was head down lighting another cigarette, but he would most certainly have heard me pull-up.

This was a very cool display, just what in the hell was Pat up to? Pat then looked-up and nodded his head in acknowledgement before filling the inside of the Toyota cab with thick white smoke. I thought to myself that will only hide you for a second chum, just what do you intend to do after that.

***

It was now five minutes to nine and John, the Clerk of Courts, who was also the Mining Registrar, walked up the short path to the Court's main double glass entry doors. The staff inside let him in but the sign on the door still said closed. John appeared not to notice the two waiting Toyotas across the road under the only shady tree, or if he did, he never once gave a hint to show that he did.

Pat was lighting yet another cigarette, this time from his old butt as he sat looking at me through the windscreen with his usual grinning smile. His eyeballs rapidly swivelled to his left and I quickly followed his line of sight. John was standing behind the Courthouse entry glass door with his hand on the sign, which still said closed however this time he had a big grin on his face from ear to ear.

The little bastard was having his moment of joyous fun, what is he waiting for, why not just turn over the bloody sign to open? John's big grin was starting to bother me.

Then it all started to filter through my brain, this was a showdown. It was like an old cowboy movie, "pistols at high noon." Just who was going to draw first and shoot the other dead in his tracks?

There was a loud creak of a dry Toyota door opening; Pat had caught me by surprise as he got out of his Toyota, my hire Toyota. In response I quickly started to do the same, however, Pat was quicker walking over to me and standing at the half-opened door of my Toyota looking at me. I noticed that he did not have any documents in his hands; he was not armed.

The thought did occur to me, this is my chance. I could quickly push my door open hard, knocking old Pat over and then make a dash to the mining registrar's office.

I hesitated; Pat was staring coldly at me, and then in another cool gesture threw away a perfectly good cigarette, for a fleeting second distracting my evil thoughts. Then he casually lit another cigarette from a pack he magically produced from somewhere. I must confess that I was a bit side tracked by this cunning manoeuvre; as Pat lit-up again, I clearly heard him mumble between sucking puffs of his new fag.

'Niven we both know what's in that large brown envelope,' gesturing towards my vacant passenger seat, 'and you would know that I have a similar envelope in my Toyota,' he then continued in a soft caring fatherly voice.

'We need to think carefully about this important situation and what the final results will be, are you with me so far?'

I was not expecting this. Well for a start, I had thought that I would have been the first to lodge my client's tenement claim, but hang on what happened to all the others.

Where was Mal from Afro-West, he should be here, I knew Mal always lodged his own mining claims.

Then there was Stockdale, maybe they had just simply renewed the old Uranerz NL mining lease, with a quick telex renewal request from their Perth office, had I misjudged all of the information and the players? Who would know, we were all alone… just Pat and I.

Ron and I knew just what was about to take place this special morning. Were all the others still a few streets behind, not knowing, or aware of what was about to happen. Remember, at that time, we were just a lowly pegging company.

This really was a typical Mexican standoff. Here we were. It was just Ashton/CRA and me representing Gem Exploration. What shall I do now?

Just as these confusing things were slowly going through my dim brain, Pat sharply interrupted me from my deep thoughts with a polite smokers cough.

'Niven you need to consider a few facts. One of us is going to walk through that door before the other.'

Old Pat was playing his well-practiced poker hand, then staring me straight in the eye still wearing a wide grin,

'Niven I would suggest to you, and expect you to agree that I pulled-up here in front of the registrar's office first?'

I looked over Pat's shoulder, John the Mining Registrar had just turned over the door sign. The mining registration office was now open for business.

John would have been the next best-informed person to know what was actually going on with the frantic diamond fever.

He would have very easily worked out that an important claim was about to be lodged, and would have guessed that this morning was going to make history in some way... but whose way?

I was rapidly running out of time... and ideas. I went through a few possible action plans. Pat was fifty-nine years old, a heavy smoker and not very fit; I on the other hand was a very fit thirty-six year old.

The thought did cross my mind. I could jump out of my Toyota, and beat old Pat in a sprint to the Mining Registrars door; I would then be the first person to lodge the claim to the mighty Kimberley diamond pipe.

However, these thoughts were all starting to sound a bit silly in my head; this was just not me... I could accept the simple suggestion that Pat was correct, he did in fact pull-up in front of the Mining Registrar's office first. I then reviewed my sensitive position thereby accepting and allowing Pat the right to walk into the claims office first to lodge his Kimberley diamond mine claim.

Well... that is just what I did. Words would not come, and I just nodded my head to Pat in acceptance to his proposal... he had played his poker hand well.

I watched with regret as Pat casually walked across the road and into the Courthouse, throwing his cigarette on the ground just before he entered through the glass doors.

The record shows that my clients claim was lodged some eighteen minutes after the Ashton/CRA claim since that's how long it took John the Mining Registrar to date and time-stamp all Pat's paperwork.

I had no doubt in my mind that Ashton/CRA at the very same time had lodged a similar claim in the Mining Registrar's office in Perth. This would have been their form of insurance. At the Courthouse door Pat stopped and shook my hand saying, "you've done the right thing Niven." Then he walked out to his/my Toyota, driving off with yet another newly lit cigarette, bellowing smoke out the window... mission complete, claim 79/106 lodged.

***

AK1 was a huge discovery, and about to change the Kimberley, Kununurra and Australia forever... but not me, or my family.

That was the last time Pat and I ever spoke. Pat became a very busy and important man, involved in the setting-up of ADM (Argyle Diamond Mine) Joint Venture and Ashton Exploration replacing AJV (Ashton Joint Venture.) The plan was initially to mine alluvial diamonds from Smoke Creek area

Pat Donnelly sadly died of a massive heart attack five years later. He had been part of Australian history and had seen an Australian dream come true... such is life.

***

The next day Ashton/CRA returned all my hire vehicles. Although within a week, they were all out on hire again to the many prospectors that flooded into the Kimberley after hearing the news of this massive new diamond pipe.

They came in the hope of securing some small land claims in and around this new discovery; apparently diamondiferous pipes are rarely, if ever, single events. However, Ashton/CRA were kept busy with other serious and demanding matters, trying to resolve the unbelievable situation, in that their company mining exploration licence had lapsed at the time of registering the AK1 mining claim lodgement. Yes that is correct... they had no valid exploration licence.

If I had lodged the Gem Exploration claim first. I have no doubts Ashton/CRA would have then lodged a solid objection, using their large legal team. However, in the knowledge of later discovering that Ashton/CRA had not renewed their exploration licence. The company being not licenced to register a claim. This would have gone a long way in supporting my client's claim to the world's largest diamond mine. At the very least, forcing Ashton/CRA into some sort of negotiation.

***

Four months later Ron and I had finished all our commitments to the survey pegging business and wound up the business of West Coast Surveys. We had all been looking forward to a quieter time, but this was not to be. A few weeks later, with all the surrounding mining claims filed and lodged... then the mighty legal battles began.

As the saying goes, "Today is tomorrows yesterday," and as Ron would say, "The shit has hit the preverbal fan mate, and there will be no way any of us can avoid being covered in the brown stuff."

What Ron was referring to was the instant and bitter legal fall-outs that started after the claim lodgement explosion. Gem Exploration challenged Ashton/CRA because of their claim not properly pegged in accordance with the Mining act. (We were lucky on that score, as Ashton/CRA never did use our claim pegging service.)

Ashton/CRA challenged both Gem Exploration and Afro-West for claim jumping. Then and Stockdale challenged everybody for over-pegging their mining prospecting claims on their registered mining lease... and that was just for openers.

Everybody was suing everybody over claim infringements, and worst of all was that Ron and I were the meat between the sandwiches. Our daily lives became hell, continually called into court as material witnesses for both the claimant and the defendant.

Refusing to attend court hearings or to be a witness brought threatening letters of a subpoena from some very powerful people. Our extensive time and costs resulting from attending the various mining company court battles never fully compensated for. Any money we may have made from the pegging business was soon gone.

It was a very grim and costly experience for the both of us. When Ron eventually moved down to Perth City, the mining company's well-paid lawyers moved the Court battles and hearings down there and continued to make Ron's life a misery.

Ron and I were walking on eggshells, as we had to remain unbiased to any of the companies involved in the various cross litigation cases. The barristers and lawyers were trying their damn best to get an angle on us, both in an effort to help, and support their individual court cases.

Life as we once knew it was now a miserable daily matter of sifting through all the old mining claim lodgement files and notes. I had, had enough of the phone calls from mining company lawyers demanding copies of my old mining claims information... a curse for keeping good and accurate business records. Something had to change... and soon.

***

The door to my office opened and in walked Ron with a cartoon of beer on his shoulder. Followed by Mal from Afro-West with a large bottle of Bundy Rum and a half cartoon of coke. Things were looking up, as both were grinning from ear to ear. Ron and Mal had just returned from yet another bitter Court hearing; judging by the grins it had all gone well for them today. Ron decided on an announcement...

'Okay partner you can stop all that fucking work stuff, let's have a singsong and a party. I'm driving down to Perth in the next couple of week's mate, so this can be one of my half-dozen or so farewell parties.'

Ron and Mal looked like grinning twins while gently placing the booze on my office bar.

'Well I must say you guys are a sight for sore eyes I could do with some happy playtime, give us a tune Mal,' handing Mal my guitar while I made some drinks at my now well stocked little office bar.

Forty-five minutes of singing and drinking had put us all into a much better mood, however I was still waiting for one of them to tell me what the hell had happened at the Court hearing. While refilling the drinks I ventured to ask.

'You guys have been quiet about what happened at the Court hearing today. Do I have to beg you guys for some info, what the hell was the result?'

Mal grabbed his rum, and Ron grabbed his can of beer then Mal spoke for the first time instead of singing and playing his favourite Beatles songs.

'You would never believe it Niv; the Court Warden was going through the long list of my claims. Throwing them out one after another then when he got to the lower Smoke Creek claim he stamped the bloody thing as my legitimate claim. Ashton/CRA forgot to include the lower Smoke Creek area in their log of claims.

I can't understand why they missed that, but they are really pissed off about it. To make it all worthwhile I got the Smoke Creek assay results back last week. The area is confirmed as a good alluvial mining prospect,' then raising his glass, 'I would like to present a toast to the new Afro-West Alluvial Diamond Mine.'

We all toasted the yet to be formally registered; and might I add funded new mining venture, and then carried on singing and drinking. Grim matters are never as bad as they look when you are having a bit of fun with friends. But then again, diamond matters were never simple. Ashton/CRA was not about to give-up so easily.

About six weeks later, with Ron still hanging around town, Ron came into the office for a final coffee and a casual chat about business matters before he left for Perth. Discussing Mal, he mentioned that Mal and Afro-West were in a bad way. They were having a big problem in trying to float the new Afro-West Smoke Creek alluvial diamond venture.

The ASX (Australian Stock Exchange) in a curt letter to the CEO (Mal) had knocked back his company float application as not viable. They had doubts about its viability, as a mining tenement lease. It was in their expert, and advised opinion, being much too small an area to support an alluvial diamond mine.

It was not difficult to guess just who their advisor was in applying political pressure to get the new float thrown out... the fight was on again.

Ron pulled out the WA lands survey map of the lower Smoke Creek area, which he knew well and studied it for a minute while stroking his unkempt beard. I watched with interest, and then broke the long silence.

'You know, I think we could find a bit more land for Mal. Mal still has the option to make a marine mining claim over the entire area that forms the Smoke Creek discharge into the Argyle dam. His existing claims only go down to the water edge at the Argyle dam.' Ron looked up and said, 'I think it's worth a bloody go mate.'

I studied the survey map closely looking for any clues or additional land.

'If you think it has a chance Ron, however the only bloke who will really know is Mal. I will give him a call and see if he wants to come over and chat about this possibility,' then a thought came to mind. '

This may end up as your very last pegging job Ron, how about that.' Ron snapped back at my ignorance.

'Just how the fuck do you think I could peg a bloody claim under water you dumb assed shit. Marine claims are just lines on a bleeding mining survey map mate.'

I cringed at my exposed stupidity and picked up the phone. Mal had already thought about a marine mining lease idea and considered that this would still not gain him enough land to satisfy the ASX. Mal reckoned Afro-West had little choice but to sell the lease to ADM/Ashton, after all this was their carefully planned objective… He was admittedly out of his depth in slimy business matters. Ashton knew the game well, delivering a well-played blow.

Ron yelled out in the background for Mal to come over to the think-tank to try and sort out all his troubles.' Then he roughly grabbed the phone from my fingers.

'Come over here you dumb shit. You never know what a couple of simple-minded bush bastards like Niven and me might think of. Anyway we need some musical inspiration,' then he slammed the phone down and sat in my nice leather office chair, at my desk... Ron was not a happy man.

'If that big fat Geo arsehole doesn't come over here and talk to us, he and his bloody new company can go and get fucked... we're only trying to help the bastard.'

Ron was cranky; he could not see why Mal was not responding to our offer of help. I was starting to agree with Ron, after all what did Mal have to lose, and then I thought Mal had played a risky game of poker, and his company debts would be high. Selling out to ADM would no doubt resolve all of his company debt issues.

I was now sitting where Ron was previously sitting opposite at my desk as Ron had now taken up residence sitting in my nice desk chair. The maps of lower Smoke Creek spread out in front of me, with all the Afro-West claims clearly marked in the upper left-hand corner, positioned almost off the survey map.

Then I glanced over Ron's head to the back-wall of my office, a wall covered with a number of WAC (World Aeronautical Charts) covering the whole of the Kimberley and Northern Territory.

I had months ago pencilled in a number of the active mining company camps and lodged leases to show my tech's and mechanics how to get to the various camps to service our hire vehicles. A cunning plan was forming in my brain and Ron sensed it.

'What the hell are you thinking of now Dallas, you've got that crazy bloody look on your face.'

'Well Ron, I'm looking at the WAC maps on the wall behind you. These maps cover a much larger area than the mining survey maps in front of you. WAC maps being a scale of 1:100 0000 and the survey maps being a larger detail scale of just 1:25 000.

If you look at the position of the Afro-West, lower Smoke Creek claim positions. There appears to be a considerable amount of land to the west of their existing claims. Yet on the survey map, this does not show as obvious.

The reason becomes clear when you realize that this area is really part of three separate, adjoining mining survey maps. Ron, have you got any of these western area survey maps in your field kit?'

'I'm pretty sure I have them in my Toyota. Look, I can see what you are getting at mate, but you can bet that any land to the west of Afro-West's claim has already been pegged a long-time ago. Or it's just bloody solid granite rock as the Carboyd Range runs down that side of Lake Argyle, ending up at Mount Chambers.'

I could tell that Ron was not convinced about my idea of finding more land. I guess it did sound a bit silly, "missing mining land to be found, previously lost in the borders of other adjoining survey maps," ha ha ha.

'Okay, let's get the other survey maps out, cut them to all meet-up and see what the land looks like. Then decide if my idea is a load of bullshit or not?'

***

For the next hour, that is just what we did. We stood back and looked down at our finished effort; a mining survey map now stuck together with transparent tape. Ron got out the list of current mining claim positions for that area, and started plotting them in as the closest claims to Afro-West. The silly grin was slowly moving off Ron's face as we heard a rumble of voices in the outer office. Mal had arrived demanding entry to my office, bringing gifts of peace and future headaches, launching himself through the office door...

'Surprise... I thought you guys would be getting a little dry at this time of the day,' then looking at Ron and I, and then at the survey maps spread-out on the floor. 'What the hell are you two silly bastards up-to?'

Ron and I were both down on our knees pondering over the map on the floor stuck together with tape. Then in unison, we both cried out together.

'Surprise...' and then Ron filled him in with the new land details. 'Mate we have just found you around seven square kilometres of bloody land, and maybe we will find more, and would you believe it matey it's all adjoining to your existing lower Smoke Creek lease. With this land and the marine claim you should have more than enough land to satisfy those ASX fuckers and the smart-arsed mines department down in Perth.'

Mal was stunned into an immovable position so I got up and removed the bottle of rum he was holding and made us all a drink to celebrate this auspicious occasion.

Two months later Afro-West floated their new alluvial mining company with an IPO (Initial Public Offer) raising five million dollars. The new company was set-up in a very short time. Starting with an alluvial diamond-sampling programme on site at their new lower Smoke Creek mining lease. All Mal Macleod's hard work was finally paying off.

***

So how was the world's largest diamond mine discovered? There have been so many strange stories, with outrageous claims made as to how, and who were the first to discover this enormous diamondiferous Lamproite pipe.

I will state hear and now I have limited knowledge about modern diamond prospecting and field work. However, my information and knowledge on these important matters were collected, and assembled into the most likely truth from an involved observer's point of view. That being one who was living and working in Kununurra well before the advent of any serious interest in diamonds, and then being around throughout the complete discovery process. The information I am about tell you was gained largely through my business activities, and talking to the very people who were directly involved. Eventually leading up to the discovery of the AK1 pipe.

***

Please understand, knowing the hot spot area, the place where the pipe was most likely to be, and knowing the exact location of the pipe were two very different and challenging matters.

My clients and other mining exploration companies already knew the area of the "hot spot" containing the pipe however; Ashton/CRA had in fact actually located the exact position of the Lamproite pipe.

To get a true perspective of the immense problem and the brilliant, or was that lucky geological work by Ashton/CRA, I need to explain some huge local dimensions.

The known "hot spot" covered a vast area of approximately one hundred and eighty-five square kilometres. The recently discovered pipe tuff ring was only some 45 hectors in size or around a 1600 by 450-metres, an area of around half a square kilometre.

175

Micro diamonds turned up in many parts of the great Ord River waterways, it was quite common. Small diamonds were regularly seen in gold prospectors sifting pans over the last hundred or so years. However, the first Ashton/CRA young diamonds were ultimately found in Smoke Creek, and that was only by sheer luck.

Lady luck was proving yet again to be an important part of successful geological exploration. The first stroke of luck was in where they were found, only some twenty kilometres from the yet to be discovered pipe. The second stroke of luck was the way in which these diamonds eventually found.

Ashton/CRA had set-up an exploration camp at Kingston's Rest being not that far by helicopter from the hot spot and close to the Great Northern Highway.

They decided to try out their newly assembled small HMS (heavy metal separation) plant. The mineralogists ran about 250 kilos of recent gravel samples through the plant as a test-run to set-up the new system.

The initial new plant run was also a good time to check out the training and efficiency of the mineral observers who were going to work and operate this new HMS plant. A young minerals observer named Lyn Tagiaferri was pleased to advise the plant manager that she had recovered a number of the new system test diamonds.

Her boss was astonished, and later told Lyn that these were not test diamonds, but real diamonds. Good-sized half carat and larger octahedron sharps, indicating a good sample batch close to the archon origin stone. We must give full credit to Lyn for finding, or exposing the very first existent Argyle tuff ring diamonds.

The race was now on to find out just where these younger diamonds were originally sampled. Frank Hughes was the senior geologist in charge of all Ashton/CRA field operations. Frank immediately put together a number of experienced geo field teams. Arranging them into tight grid search patterns, systematically covering all the old sampling areas. Much of this work carried out by the reliable Jet-ranger helicopter.

During a helicopter survey, as it happens, nature called and Frank asked the pilot to land. While relieving himself on the side of an ant termite mound Frank washed off some surface material noticing a distinct glint. A glint that proved to be a reasonable size one and a half carat octahedron diamond.

Frank later told me, that he then realised what he was possibly standing on, ultimately he must be very near to what was the tuff rim of a diamond pipe. This find was a massive leap forward in identifying the pipe location and easily the most important key-discovery to date. Nevertheless, Frank still had a large problem to solve, and that was in which direction from where he had found the tuff diamond was the elusive pipe. Millions of years of surface erosion had left no clues as to which way this pyroclastic tuff ring might ultimately lay.

Frank assembled several geo field teams to survey various areas. One such geo team led by Maureen Muggeridge given the northern sector to checkout. However, Maureen disagreed with Frank and insisted that the pipe was most likely laying to the south. Maureen went against Frank's orders and took her team to the south confirming the now positive result. The discovery of the huge AK 1 diamond pipe, which is now history.

I would have to say that most of the credit for this magnificent discovery of the century would have to go to Frank Hughes and his powerful urine stream, and of course his weak bladder in needing to stop for a pee… Then again, lady luck and a careful helicopter pilot did pick the place. We must also accept the fact that Frank did know he was close to the pipe as Lyn Tagiaferri had found and proved the existence of tuff rim diamonds in the samples.

This then leaves Maureen Muggeridge who with an excellent geological nose worked out which way the tuff ring pipe would ultimately lay, the result… AK1. The world's largest diamond mine ultimately discovered.

**

Business was booming in the Kimberley's, my biggest single problem was keeping qualified staff to run my small business ventures. Desperate times call for desperate measures. I urgently needed more staff, especially another electronics service technician.

Chapter Six:

Pushed from the nest by Mum

I have noticed over time, sometimes you can have good-luck in business and then sometimes unfortunately you get bad-luck. Most times the duration of each way, and which comes first, are by far more important to any successful outcome than the immediate resolve of a pending urgent problem.

This accepted state of affairs was ultimately tested to the limit after I employed two new additional staff. A Multi Agencies accounts clerk Paula, and a Kimberley Electronics technician David.

I was pleasantly surprised, and had thought myself lucky the day Paula walked into my office in early 1979, applying for the locally advertised job as accounts-clerk and hire-car-hostess. This woman was well qualified, and her resume was impressive, well it was to a small-town businessperson such as me.

She could type and knew how to manage a small office filing system, and as luck would have it, she was the right size for the last remaining company Hire-car hostess uniform. Paula was about 36, with a pleasant personality and smile; she was married with two young school-age boys, and had arrived into town only a week earlier.

Her husband had managed to get a job in the town with the MRD (Main Roads Department) driving a tipper truck.

They lived in their own caravan in the town caravan park, only a short walking distance to my business and hire depot. I thought things were going my way for a change, some good luck at last... or so I had thought at the time.

Paula was an excellent organiser and soon had the office running well in no time. As the months went by, she proved to be a very capable secretary and gradually gained full access to all the company business accounts and records. This employee trust later proved to be my simple bush-style undoing.

In October 1979, the Kimberley region was alive with mining exploration crews. The mad panic was on to find, and claim any land that might have diamond-bearing Kimberlite. The large diamond pipe named AK1 recently discovered by Ashton/CRA did not stop others coming for a look. As they say, there is never only the one diamond pipe. Indicators proved there might well be others in the area so the prospecting activity was intense.

My company provided four- wheel drive hire vehicles, mechanical maintenance, and radio communications sales and services to the many exploration companies who were busy trying to find another AK1 pipe. This diamond-bearing pipe would later become the world's largest diamond mine. However, right now I needed another electronics technician urgently. My last technician had resigned suddenly then set up his own radio service business in town in opposition to me. This was a blow to the business especially since Brian was an excellent radio technician, most importantly, technical people were difficult to find and keep in these remote parts.

***

The beginning of October was an interesting time to be in the north-west Kimberley, being just at the end of our dry season. I think this is the best time of the year with beautiful 34 degree-days, mild tropical nights, and clear, crisp deep-blue skies.

I was expecting a flood of applicants for the position, considering the cold weather down in Perth. My advert had now been in the Perth paper for over a month without attracting a single reply.

I was about to try plan "B" by placing an advert in the eastern states newspapers. Then my office girl Paula received a phone call from an elderly woman in Perth, who claimed to be the mother of the most brilliant electronics technician in Australia. (I think all mothers think like that.) My first thought was why was this bloke not calling about the job himself?

To date, this single enquiry was my only response to the tech's job. The phone call from mum sparked my curiosity antenna. Although a bit odd, and not sounding too good a prospect, I thought to myself, why was this technician's mother was trying to get her son a job? I just had to find out and so I rang mum back.

***

'My name is Niven Dallas; I'm trying to contact a Mr David Bank, who responded to my advertisement for the position of electronics technician with my company,' there was a slight delay then a soft old-ladies thin voice spoke.

'Oh dear I am afraid that David is not at home now, I am his mother can I be of help,' came the soft reply, and then 'I was the one who actually made the enquiry, not David.'

'Well Mrs Bank I would really like to speak directly to David if I may, could you please get him to send me a resume and some details of his work experience...' Mum interrupted me before I could finish.

'Oh I can tell you all those things,' interjected Mrs Bank, 'you see David has always lived at home so I know all about the jobs he has had, and the types of work that he does.'

This was a silly conversation, but again curiosity got the better of me.

'What type of work does your son normally do' I asked mum who replied in an eager flood of words.

'David is working at the moment for a large medical company that sells, services, and repairs all types of complicated electronic equipment used in hospitals,' Mum continued to explain things to me in childish detail.

'You know things like x-ray machines, ultra-sound equipment, and heart monitoring systems. He also fixes the nurses paging systems and even the patient's television sets... sort of everything really.'

I thought shit I am wasting my time here, then as one last try.

'Yes but does he know anything about radio transmitters, two-way radios,' then I started to talk baby, 'you know like the taxi's and a Policeman would use.'

I was trying to make the question simple for mum to understand but then I realised that it must have sounded funny, as Paula in the next office overhearing this call, had started to laugh aloud... mum continued.

'Oh yes he builds things like that all the time,'

'Builds them' I enquired softly.

'Well yes the house is full of bits of radios, soldering irons, box's everywhere cables and things. He's filled all the rooms in my house; David brings work home all the time the house is a mess.'

I pulled the phone from my ear and stared at it... Am I going out of my bloody mind? Here I am interviewing a bloke, through his mother, who wants him to leave home and take a job in the remote North West of Australia. I was rapidly getting the impression that this mother was just trying to get rid of her son... I wonder if this bloke knows that. In frustration, and in a raised voice, I asked a leading employment question.

'Excuse me, but just how old is your son Mrs Bank?'

'David was thirty-three last March came the soft reply,' then more sprightly 'there is no need to raise your voice Mr Dallas I was only trying to help my boy,'

Oh dear I had upset this little old lady with my rough outback ways.

'Mrs Bank you must understand, your son will have to talk to me directly if I am to assess him for this position, could you please get him to give me a call.'

I was about to hang up when Mrs Bank spoke again...

'David is a nice boy but he is very shy Mr Dallas.'

Groan I thought, his mum still thinks a 33-year-old man is a boy. Mrs Bank continued in her quiet way.

'David keeps getting lots of offers for new jobs all the time. He never goes out and has few friends; I am very worried about him. You see I want him to leave home and experience something of the world.' There was a sad silence and a soft click and mum was gone.

I was still holding the phone thinking in my usual crafty way... had lots of job offers has he, he must be good, then again he sounds like a real mum's nerd. We do not have a nerd on the staff at present... well not a real one, we did have Stevo, but he was a sort of bikie without a motorbike.

My deep thoughts were suddenly shattered by the mechanics shouting a loud demand from the workshop floor,

'Hang up the bloody phone. It's been dead for five minutes we need to make a frigging call.' Damn, I must try to get another phone line into this building. We had a small 2X6 line exchange switch, which was nearly always at full capacity, getting another phone line in this town was almost impossible.

The next day David Bank rang himself... well not quite, I could hear his mum prompting him in the background. We had a long chat, he told me in his quiet voice that he was a self-taught electronics technician.

His interest in electronics started as a hobby when he was nine years old, and he could not recall any broken piece of electronic equipment that he had failed to get going again. David claimed he had a current working knowledge of most commercial radio communications equipment. I must admit, that under my intense quiz he did impress me with his range of knowledge in this area.

My phone interview moved on to enquiring about his social background, all attempts to move the conversation in the direction of his friends and in particular girlfriends, politely avoided.

I concluded that David Bank was a quiet, shy, and studious type of man, still very much attached to his mother's apron strings. My immediate concern was how such a sheltered man would handle the challenges of living in a remote town in the Kimberley region of Western Australia.

David did however open up on the subject of flying, saying that his mum had told him that I was also interested in flying. We hit it off... we had found something in common, I offered John the job on a strict three-month trial basis, which was accepted, nevertheless I was still more than a little concerned as to just how David would fit-in up here in the remote north.

Unbeknown to David, his mum and I were on a unified mission, she wanted to get her Son out of the family home, and into a world of new experiences. I on the other hand needed him up here in my electronics service workshop. I had offered to fly David up to Kununurra but he politely declined saying he preferred to drive up in his own car. Anyway, he said, he had some stuff he wanted to bring up.

'What sort of stuff,' I asked?

David replied he had many radio parts, components, and equipment he thought I could use up here. That triggered another line of concerned thought, which was that his mum obviously wanted him to clean out all of his old electronic crap from her house.

'We can freight that lot up here David, it's over 3000 kilometres by road and not worth the risk in driving, and anyway you would need a good reliable car to drive on these rough pot-holed gravel outback roads.

'No problem there,' replied David ("No Problem" it was the first time I had heard this stupid city slicker comment) 'I've got a nice 1971 Mazda Capella rotary'.

I was stunned, I could hardly believe my ears, nobody, and I mean nobody in their right bloody mind would think of taking a 7-year-old Mazda rotary engine powered vehicle into a remote area. If the slightest thing were to go wrong with such an odd vehicle, it would immediately become a "roadside write-off."

This was four-wheel drive country, or at least a good Ute or a truck. He should fly up to Kununurra; confirming I would cover the cost. I then continued expressing my concerns about his intentions to drive up north in that particular vehicle, to which David said he would think about it and get back to me.

I was later to have the confirmed proof that David Bank has without doubt, no knowledge about motor cars or any mechanical things. Then again, I should have guessed that, after all what normal man would own a superseded bloody Mazda Capella, for crying aloud.

***

A week later, I rang David's home in Perth to arrange a flight for him up to Kununurra; his mum answered the phone with a worried voice.

'David had left over a week ago in his car... has he not arrived up there yet?' Now I was starting to get a bit worried, mum continued...

'David has not phoned me at all since he left last Sunday.'

'Well he hasn't phoned me either Mrs Bank; but don't worry Mrs Bank, he can't get lost on these out-back roads if he just sticks to the main gravel road and follows all the empty beer cans and bottles,' (trying to lighten up the developing grim situation.)

There was no laughter response, had I gone a bit too far with that old joke, especially on a worried mother?

'Mrs Bank you shouldn't worry,' I was going to tell her it's a four-day drive to Kununurra then realised that her son David had already been driving for seven days.

'I will call a few people I know and try find out where he is. Everybody knows everybody up here; we all look out for each other. When I find David I will tell him to call his Mum urgently.'

Mum did not sound all that convinced at my casual assurances however, there was nothing more she could do but wait.

I put the word out to some business friends down the track at Halls Creek, Fitzroy Crossing, Derby, and Broome. Surely, he has gone past Broome by now. The only description I had of David was a quiet shy man in his early thirties driving a Mazda Capella sedan, heading north to Kununurra, everybody asked the same question, what the bloody hell was a Mazda Capella.

The first call I got was from a friend in Derby, David had only made it as far as Derby, and he was now at the King Sound Hotel, I thought bloody hell, that was after a full seven days travelling from Perth. Many phone attempts and sometime later with the help of the King Sound owner Frank Camer-Pesci, I managed finally to get David on the phone.

185

'What the hell happened? It takes me four days to drive from Perth all the way through to Kununurra, you've been on the road for over seven days, and you're only just over half way to Kununurra?'

There was a long pause of silence while David no doubt considered my rough attack mood, then in a quiet voice spoke.

'Nothing happened at all.' David quietly replied. 'I always like to drive along slow and enjoy the beautiful scenery on the way. I have taken some nice photos, and met some really nice people.'

I thought to myself what a lot of crap, who is this bloke. There are just endless kilometres of dusty corrugated gravel roads, and miles of shit sand with a few stumpy burnt-down, half-dead trees. What the hell have I got myself into this time? I snapped back to reality. This person thinks he is on a Sunday afternoon drive with his mum, enjoying the outback scenery. With a softer voice, I enquired...

'David, is your vehicle going okay?'

'Yeah' replied David, 'it's a bit hard to start and the exhaust pipe is blowing lots of black smoke... and I now have to put in quite a bit of oil, but the car seems to be going all right.'

David sounded very confident for a man with a Mazda Capella.

'David, please confirm you are carrying in your car at least twenty litres of drinking water and two Jerry cans of spare fuel, a week's food supply, and some basic tools?' I was now on my high horse spouting basic remote area survival strategy to an uninterested city slicker nerd. I sensed that my message was not getting through, and so continued...

'You have been lucky so far David, the Mazda Capella twin rotary engine uses more fuel than a road train. The engine type is plagued with excessive compression seal wear and cannot handle; no correction, will-not handle gravel road dust. No doubt the reason why you are tipping large amounts of oil into the engine. On top of all that, there isn't a motor mechanic within two thousand kilometres who could fix your bloody Mazda rotary engine if it failed.'

There was another uncomfortable period of silence, and then David's soft unruffled voice replied,

"Well I have to admit I never thought of all that. I just loaded up my stuff in Perth and hit the road; everything's been fine so far.'

My brain was racing. It was now obvious that David was completely ignorant of the many dangers in driving on remote area outback roads.

'Listen to me David, promise me you will carry the provisions I have just mentioned. In addition, you must make sure that you take the Fitzroy/Halls Creek road and not the Gibb River road when you head out of Derby for Kununurra. Now listen that is the turn to your right-hand side at the road junction sign, for Fitzroy or Gibb, now this is important... Do not go down the Gibb River Road, do you understand all of that?'

'No problems' replied David with a light chuckle, (again that no problem phrase) from now on I would hear it many times repeatedly. Just how wrong can a silly phrase like that be?

***

I heard the bad news during a short phone call from an old stockman. This bloke had rang me reverse charges from a pub in Derby. David Bank had become a problem.

'You got a right fucking nutcase stuck on the Gibb River road mate. He's bloody broken down about twenty miles from the Great Northern Highway end. I told him he'd be better off coming back to Derby with me. I was going the opposite way you know.'

The old ringer with a grunt of disgust, made this obvious point very clear to me.

'Well mate he decided to stay with his bloody flash car, and asked me to call you and let you know what had happened mate.'

'Is David all right' I asked, 'has he run out of fuel?'

'He's okay for now mate, he's got plenty of petrol, but he had run out of brains, water and food, he's got water and food for about two days now, cause I gave it to him. His bloody engine blew up mate, I gotta go mate. I'd like to crap-on all day but this is a dry talk we're having, and this call must be costing you a bloody bomb.' Then he was gone... no doubt straight to the drovers bar for a beer.

***

It was around midday when we got to David. It was hot for this time of the year at 39°C without a cloud in the sky. He was sitting on a low termite mound sunning himself by the side of the road reading a technical manual on integrated circuits.

David was about five foot nine, and a bit on the flabby side. He sported a full black beard and thick black framed Buddy Holly style glasses. David was wearing long black dress pants and a dark long sleeved shirt. He looked like he had just popped down the road for a bottle of milk and a newspaper.

He was completely oblivious to the level of danger he had placed himself in, later admitting that no other vehicles had been by all that day. Only the old ringer stockman on his way to Derby.

The Gibb River Road is 650 kilometres of isolated rough dirt road. It is just an old poorly maintained cattle stock route. The sign says at the entry both ends "Trucks and four wheel drive vehicles only." My view has always been that City slickers like to come here for brainless adventure, and sometimes to die. I do know this for a fact, as on many sad occasions I have been part of the search and rescue missions to find these troublesome adventurers.

David looked up from his book. I thought he surely must have heard, or seen us. With all that red dust in the air, he would have seen us coming for miles on this dusty gravel road. While still sitting on the termite mound, we shook hands, and then David said politely.

'You must be Niven, my new boss,' I was pulling him forward inviting him to remove his arse off the anthill.

'We're pleased to see that you are safe and all right David, you had us a bit worried there for a while, we'll tow your car back to Kununurra as soon as the mechanic removes the front drive-shafts an attaches the towbar.'

188

I could tell by the look on David's face that he needed to know why we were removing the vehicles drive shafts but he was too polite to ask.

'I noticed that your car is an automatic, even with "N" for neutral being selected while being towed, these type of automatic cars will still turn the inside of the gearbox causing it to overheat and will with certainly destroy itself long before we reach Kununurra.'

My eyes drifted down to the empty two-litre water bottle on the front seat of the Mazda, David later advised me that he had no other drinking water.

'Would you like a cold beer David you must be as dry as that anthill you were sitting on?'

'No thankyou I've just had a drink of water,' replied polite David.

Did he realise that all his drinking water was gone, two more days in this heat and he would have been gone too? Another thing he did not know, was that anthills breath through a purpose made vent in the top, I had assumed that the anthill was barren and nobody was at home, hence my suspected dry anthill comment...

Had that anthill been occupied a construction ant-crew would have been sent to unblock the nests air vent. I can only imagine what David would have said in loud words to the world then.

I had to look away in wonderment that such a supposably smart man that could be so naive and stupid in such a remote area.

I turned my attention back to the Mazda Capella. On a closer inspection, to my amazement, strapped on the top of the broken-down Mazda was a very large model aircraft. I judged this model to have about a two-metre wingspan.

On top of this model aircraft was a large model helicopter, all wrapped in huge amounts of bubble wrap plastic, all of which now covered in thick Kimberley red dust.

Swimming through my mind was our last phone conversation, where we talked about flying. Was this what David meant when he said he was very interested, and knew a great deal about flying?

Well as I was soon to find out some weeks later... this was indeed his total flying experience... David had never been on a commercial passenger aircraft, or for that matter ever flown in a light aircraft.

Chapter Seven:

You've done it this time Dallas

David had never been in an aeroplane in his life before, but he most certainly knew all about them. Two weeks after arriving and settling into Kununurra life, David decided to give me a demonstration on his unique aircraft flying abilities. At his suggestion, we decided the best place to fly such a large model aircraft was, well... at the local airport of course.

Kununurra airport had a flight service centre, staffed by the DCA (Department of Civil Aviation). Now we must respect these truly wonderful blokes who run the flight service unit, and they do know me very well as I lodge my aircraft flight plans there on a regular basis.

Out of courtesy, I asked the flight service blokes for permission to use their airport apron area to fly David's large model aircraft. After noting the size of the model aircraft the duty officers became quite excited about seeing the thing fly, they suggested we should use the aircraft hard stand, this area was right in front of their DCA office building, providing the DCA staff an excellent air-conditioned viewing point for watching David's model aircraft.

I was amazed at DCA granting us flying permission so quickly. I was also very surprised by the jovial attitude and the level of humour at our flying request. The normal assertiveness of bureaucratic supremacy had slipped a little showing a hint of normal human interest.

The smart arsed officer on the flight plan counter laughingly insisted that I should lodge a full flight plan for the intending model aircraft flight. To keep the jovial happy mood alive I quickly obliged filing a full flight plan for Kununurra training circuits, PIC (pilot in command) being David Bank.

Pilots in those days called the blameless DCA flight service officers the "Gestapo." Most of these flight service guys thought themselves very much as righteous tin gods of the airways, with all sorts of aviation powers at their disposal that could cause unbelievable chaos and misery for a simple pilot such as I.

With the flight plan completed as requested, the smart arsed flight clerk, without hesitation stamped and signed off the plan as per a normal flight, giving me a stamped copy. This silly action later proved to be invaluable, saving me many thousands of dollars, not to mention keeping my pilots licence.

It also created for me, over some considerable time, a severe level of non-cooperation with the Kununurra flight service office. Well, until all the current serving officers and staff had moved on to other airports.

***

David assembled the large model aircraft under the watchful gaze of the flight service staff. They were all smiling and cracking jokes that this was probably the best aircraft Dallas would ever fly. David had now finished assembling the large aircraft.

The decisive moment had arrived; the aircraft was now ready to fly. David offered me the radio-control console, I backed away hands raised, promptly declining the offer to fly this complex and expensive model aeroplane.

'Dave I can fly a real aircraft but do appreciate that a certain amount of advanced skill is required to fly a model aircraft from a stationary ground position; and anyway the stamped flight plan has you as the pilot in command.'

The large smile on David's face was well worth the compliment as he went about testing the various aircraft flight-control functions. David said later, he was most impressed, at the acknowledgment by DCA (Department of Civil Aviation) as a proper pilot, even though he was only a model pilot.

Dave carried out his list of pre-flight checks. He twiddled the joysticks, pushed buttons and flicked switches. Eventually he was satisfied with the performance of all the controls, Dave then reached into his bag of tricks and produced an electric drill type gadget with a rubber sucker thing on the end.

Everyone watched closely as Dave place the rubber sucker-thing on the end of the large propeller nose cone and with push of a button the prop spun and the engine roared into life. David quickly pocketed the starter gadget and went straight into taxiing the aircraft about the hardstand area.

This was impressive stuff. The DCA staff stopped making derogatory comments; no doubt still about me. To watch in wonder at this perfectly made model aircraft, moving about the tarmac under its own power.

Without further delay, David opened up the throttle and the aircraft accelerated rapidly and lifted off into perfect level flight. You could see Dave was in his element, confidently steering this beautiful aircraft about the skies. We were all staring, jaws dropped in amazement at this spectacle when David swore… for the very first time in his life I think.

'Fuck-in-hell…the controls are bloody jammed!'

Now, because I was outside, and standing alongside Dave. This unbelievable and terrifying comment from Dave and its consequences were now blatantly obvious to me.

Meanwhile, the DCA flight service blokes who had all retired to the air-conditioned comfort of their flight service office. With beaming smiles, were now peering out of their soundproof office windows, all taking in the wonderment of this spectacle. These smiling flight officers were happily watching this model aircraft event. All the spectators being unaware they were just about to witness a major crash incident at their beloved Kununurra airport.

The aircraft did a low swoop over a line of nicely parked proper sized aircraft then shot up into a magnificent near vertical climb. Slowing down, almost to a stop, and then turning very slowly into a hammerhead stall. As my daddy used to say, "What goes up must come down." The DCA boys thought this was a spectacular air show, put-on especially just for them.

'Can't you fucking do something,' I yelled out

David stared at me for a moment; he was wide-eyed, with his mouth open in a look of sheer terror. No longer was he the cool in control nerd technician. I feared the worst was to come, and was not disappointed, I yelled out in frustration and panic.

'Hit the fucking engine kill button or something'... now that worked.

The large model aircraft abruptly fell silent. Without engine power, the aircraft immediately lost thrust, completing its vertical climb, stalled, and turned into a vertical dive. At great speed the large model flew directly into the front of Robert Dick's aircraft, a very nice Piper Lance parked neatly on the edge of the airport hardstand.

The damage to David's beautiful model aircraft was a total write off, as it burst into many parts on impact. From this distance, I could also see considerable damage to the front of the Piper Lance's windscreen... this was bad... very bad.

I glanced at the flight-service office observation window to see a row of terrified looking DCA duty officers who had watched the whole tragedy unfold before their very eyes. No longer laughing and frozen to the spot; nevertheless in no doubt about who they would blame for all of this... me. David recovered his voice spluttering.

'What should we do now?' I replied with a frantic voice.

'Go pick up your aircraft bits and run like fuck, I will go and talk to the Gestapo, but don't hang around here as they might just put me straight into bloody jail.'

As I entered the flight-service office, I could sense the consolidated conceit. As per the normal DCA disaster manual, the Gestapo had tightly closed ranks and banded together, this was just another obvious case of "gross pilot error" and most certainly not their fault in any way. The elected Gestapo spokesperson piped up and announced his condemning piece.

'You've done it this time Dallas, the department will have your fucking pilots license suspended, you won't even get a ticket on a domestic aircraft flight out of this town after this show is lodged in the duty records.'

The DCA were experts in the art of appropriating blame to others, I have always thought it was part of their basic training, but now it was my time to install fear, yes I had indeed thought of a cunning plan.

'Now just hold on their chap's, (waving the flight plan in the air) I have here a duly signed and stamped flight plan signed by this very flight-service clearing the said aircraft to use this very airfield. You lot, as the local flight control officers have authorised an unlicensed pilot David Bank to use a part of this airport for non-approved flight operations.'

Again, I vigorously waved the flight plan in the air as I rapidly departed the flight service office leaving the stunned flight officers standing in frozen terror, some other cunning work would be required to fix the blame on Dallas... this time.

***

Robert's pride and joy aircraft, his beautiful Piper Lance suffered some $18,000 worth of airframe damage, requiring a new windscreen and some small cowling repairs, grounding the aircraft for a time.

Robert was not a happy chappie, his damaged aircraft eventually repaired with the Department of Civil Aviation's own insurance cover, and the matter as per the disaster manual expertly hushed up in true DCA Gestapo style.

Nobody ever spoke of the incident again, but the hard faced looks, and the obvious hindrance in filing my future flight-plans confirmed that this matter had not been forgotten by any of the serving Kununurra DCA flight-service staff for a long, long time.

***

David Bank proved to be an excellent electronics engineer but a very poor judge when buying motor vehicles, handling of his or my money, and any flying skills. In addition to this list, I was later to find out... also vulnerable around powerful women.

Chapter Eight:

Lust & Trust = Greed & Need

I glanced at the office clock it was past seven Paula was always on time. Just as my mind was absorbing this possible glitch to the start of this workday, the phone rang. It was the hospital, the receptionist sounded quite bright and cheery.

'Hi Niven we have Paula here, she wants a word with you,' then before I could imagine the worst, Paula's happy voice came over the phone.

'I'm sorry Niven I'm at the hospital, I have fallen off a horse and chipped my spine. The Doctor said I'll be lying flat and immobile for the next 6 weeks.'

This was not good news, as we were very busy in the office at this time. Apparently and news to me, Paula liked riding horses, and had been invited out to a cattle station on the weekend for a horsey time.

This sort of invitation was quite common in our business. My many invitations were normally to hunt, fish, shoot guns, and get drunk. Station people in the Kimberley are very friendly that way.

Paula felt bad about her accident since she knew we were extremely busy with all the exploration and mining activity going on. She also knew I would always pay my employee's full wage in the event something like this ever happened. Genuine accidents do happen. Paula suggested that if I could bring the new office electric typewriter along to her caravan, she could get some office work done lying down. I told her I was happy to wait until things improved but Paula insisted, and would feel better that she could still help in some way.

A few days or so later I had a call from Bill the station manager enquiring as to how Paula was, and apologising that he may have in some way been the cause of her unfortunate accident, I jokingly I replied.

'How's that Bill, did you give her one of your wild horny brumby's to ride?'

'No, No' replied Bill, 'she was on my kid's horse, a real pussy cat. The only thing was she was a bit drunk when she fell off the fucking thing.'

'Oh dear I replied, she didn't tell me that bit'. Bill went on, 'If I hadn't filled them up with booze, or for that matter placed that urgent order for a chopper fuel delivery; well I guess she wouldn't have been out here in the first place?'

'Hang on there,' I butted in, 'what chopper fuel delivery?'

'The one your office arranged for me, eight drums of chopper fuel, delivered to four chopper-muster refuelling points on my station. Paula and her husband delivered them out on a tipper truck.'

I knew then that something was very wrong, as I do not own a bloody tipper truck. I smelt a rat then asked a leading question.

'Bill have you received an invoice for the delivery yet'?

'Nope, paid cash along the finger; just as Paula wanted, is there anything wrong?'

This was all starting to sound very odd, things were not right. I was getting suspicious... What was going on, and then I thought.

'Has she done this sort of fuel thing before?'

'Well yes, a few times... is there something wrong mate?'

Ah ha, so Paula had received a phone call at my office from Bill for a helicopter-muster fuel drop. The cheeky buggers; they used the MRD tipper truck that her husband takes home on a weekend to deliver the fuel out to Bill's station. Gets paid cash, and has a damn good time to boot. I could sense that Bill was also getting suspicious about all this and decided to head off any possible client damage.

'Paula has just had an x-ray confirming that she has a small bone chip off her spine. Not anything too serious, apparently six weeks rest will fix the problem, oh and was the fuel drop locations okay?'

'Yeah they got the fuel dump's spot on and the muster went well.' Bill's reply was slow and measured, he obviously knew something was wrong, but this was my problem not Bill's and so I finished off the conversation with a big lie.

'Sorry got another call coming in Bill, I'll tell Paula that you called.'

I then gently hung up the phone in deep thought. This was not good news. It was time to call on Paula for a wee chat.

***

The caravan door was open as were all the windows, this was quite normal, as it was another very hot day.

'Hello,' I called out, 'anybody home?'

I peered in through the fly wire door nobody was in sight. Paula must have gone across to the toilet block. I thought best to sit inside out of the sun and wait, as she can't be far away.

Sitting on the small sofa, my gaze drifted down to my office typewriter on the floor. Paula was in the middle of typing a letter while she lay flat of her stomach, laying on an exercise mat in the walkway. A letter was well under way, and I thought what company business was this about?

My brow furrowed as I read the letter in disbelief. To my surprise, the letter neatly addressed to the franchising manager at Hertz rent-a-car head office Perth. Thanking him for granting and approving a Kununurra Hertz rental car franchise for her in Kununurra... the cheeky bloody bitch.

Paula had apparently applied for the Hertz rental car franchise that I had relinquished only last month. She knew it was available since Paula had typed the termination letter to Hertz for me, a letter that included a number of good reasons for ending our relationship.

We were losing a considerable amount of money because of the Hertz company policy of using a standard Australia wide vehicle hire charge. They insisted on pricing every type of vehicle hire contract the same.

Hertz never thought, or considered the difference in a 4X4 vehicle hired for a family-fishing trip around Melbourne, Adelaide, or Perth. Alternatively, to that of a mining company based in a remote location, smashing the same vehicle to bits over granite rocks and burnt-out desert bush. In addition, Hertz never accepted or recovered any of my billed suspension and vehicle body damage costs, including tyres staked by burnt stumps, and even the end-of-hire top-up fuel. These genuine costs were simply directly charged, and deducted from my monthly hire account.

I was in effect paying Hertz Australia to wave its company flag in the remote Kimberley, with a fixed Australia wide flat hire cost. Still, it was a free country, and I guess if not Paula, then someone else would have taken on the surrendered Hertz franchise. All the same, this was not expected or acceptable. Especially by someone who was using my confidential client info, on my paid time, and on my bloody typewriter.

The creak of the fly wire door announced that Paula had returned.

'Hi Niven' came the bubbly greeting with a big radiant smile.

'What's this' I demanded waving the letter in the air. Paula never hesitated or broke stride in her instant assessment of the embarrassing situation. With a confident still beaming smile, Paula casually replied.

'Oh that, I was going to tell you about that.'

'Sure you were,' I fumed. 'Just like you were going to tell me about all the station chopper-muster fuel deliveries, which were supposed to be my direct business orders.'

Paula continued to smile. I continued to rant on.

'You and your old man were carrying out a shonky delivery deal when you fell off that bloody horse, blind drunk; so I'm told. You also led Bill to believe that the fuel was being delivered to his station as one of my services.'

As we stared at each other eye to eye, my shouting descended into a stony silence that felt like hours, and then Paula still smiling quipped.

'I'll type you out my resignation then.'

'Not on my bloody typewriter you're not' I spluttered like a spoilt child, as I scooped the machine up off the floor and blundered past her, stumbling out the door. As I strutted away in disgust, I heard Paula call after me.

'We can still be business friends, can't we?'

This was the pits of employee disloyalty and mistrust, only one thing for a man to do in this horrible situation, and that's go down the pub.

I had thought just like you, that this was the end of this story; well you are wrong. Small towns have many secrets. Keeping them has always been the biggest challenge, as most secrets do not remain a secret for very long. You would think that a smart bloke such as me would know everything that went on in my own business premises and with my own staff...well I wish that were correct.

***

Some three months went by... I was the last to know, or maybe I should say, last to believe the story circulating down at the pub. The story was, that my technician David Bank and my ex accounts/hire Hostess Paula were screwing their hearts out in my company located, and supplied staff caravan.

By the way, this particular company caravan is located close to the rear of my office, in the hire car depot.

Unbelievable, no by the gods of Zeus, this could not be true. I challenged the deliverer of the juicy morsel gossip to provide me with some creditable proof to back-up this claim. If for nothing else but in an attempt to discredit the whole fantasy story.

Rum and coke in hand, I leant forward, listening in disbelief to Miller as he slowly unfolded his tale. This Miller bloke worked the night shift in the adjoining property, which happens to be a 24-hour fuel service station. It cost me five beers to get the whole story out of slow talking, fast drinking Miller.

Miller worked the 10pm to 5am shift. He reckons that most nights he went out the back of the petrol station about 11pm to pee on my wall... again.

Years ago, I had built this four-metre high wall as the dividing wall between the two business premises. Miller continued...

'As you do while in this relieving situation, I was looking up, gazing at all the stars, and was surprised to see you're ex secretary being helped over the wall into your backyard by no other than Dave, your nerd radio tech.'

'Which way was she going?' I casually enquired.'

'Oh at that time of night she was going in.' Miller firmly replied.

'You sound like this was a regular bloody thing?'

'It certainly was mate,' replied Miller with a grin. 'They were at it almost every night over the last couple of months.'

'I can't believe this, something is very wrong here.' I touted in a raised voice. Everybody in the bar within earshot mumbled in a confirming tone.

'But it's all true Niven.'

I glanced around the bar, at the sea of wise and knowledgeable faces. I then attempted to dispel this most unlikely barroom story.

'Look here you blokes, David Bank knows nothing about women; he's a bloody radio nerd.'

The bar chorused. 'He does now.'

I attempted to add support to my claim.

'He's a fucking thirty-three-year old virgin, he only loves radios, and his mum.'

The bar chorused. 'He's not a virgin anymore.'

I was getting nowhere with this grinning lot. My irritation was obviously starting to show, I tried again in stumbling aggravation.

'And another thing, why the hell would Dave bring Paula over the back wall when he had a bloody key to the front bloody gate and everything else at the depot?'

'That's an easy one,' replied Miller in a matter of fact way. 'Many-a time you were still at work while they were in the caravan screwing away, so she had to go over the back wall. You know mate, to avoid being seen by you.'

'This is crazy,' I snapped back at the gloating faces around the bar. 'Are you lot trying to tell me that Dave the nerd and that Paula bird that I sacked, were in the caravan out in my backyard fucking their hearts out, only two metres from my office desk... And I didn't know anything about it?'

'Sure as hell was,' confirmed Miller. 'Just like when I was on the other side of the bloody wall, pissing on it, only half a metre away from where you sit at your desk in your office.'

The bar cracked up in laughter. Then in a final chorus...

'Dallas that information is worth a drink, it's your bloody shout.'

On the way home, I looked in at the office, and sure enough, the company stepladder was propped against the back wall right next to the company caravan. The light was on so I gently knocked on the door, but nobody was home. David had gone.

David Bank was gone forever, for on that very same night, Dave and Paula had eloped, or as they say in the tropics "shot through." Dave had abandoned his job as my radio technician without saying a word to me. It was now obvious; this sudden departure had a precise plan, most probably devised by Paula while still working for me.

How strange this old world is, David had learnt in his very short time in the Kimberley. All about the opposite sex; how to keep a big secret, and how to deceive his boss.

Paula for reasons known only to herself; had decided to dump her husband and their two young boys, for the love of an innocent virgin nerd.

The whole town knew what was going on with Paula and David, with the exception of my wife Lesley and of course me.

***

It was only a few months later, Paula's badly rejected and depressed husband, sadly committed suicide in his caravan over this family matter, by blowing his brains out with his .22 rifle. As I understand, the two boys ended up back with Paula.

Was this true love? Maybe it was, or was it just lust. I do not know. I sure hope it was all worth it.

***

Lost in thought, and staring over an untouched drink, I began to think about all of these matters. David's caring mother need never again worry about her son's lack of worldly experience. So be it, I wish them both well, and a poor, convenient, and selective memory.

***

I believe you get what you give in this world, as they say Karma… what goes around comes around.

Life still carries on, now I need another good electronics technician, and, as it seems… another office employee.

---- The End ----

Part Four. Two for the price of one

Chapter One:

Urgent Advert one reply

It was all happening again, a sort of Déjà vu. I was starting to panic as time was running out fast. The advertisement for a radio service technician had been in the Perth West Australian newspaper for over three weeks without a single response.

***

"Electronics technician; based in new town of Kununurra. Mostly RF radio communications work, servicing from bench and field. Excellent air-conditioned working conditions. Good salary paid to right person.

Accommodation and vehicle supplied. Applicant must be able to fault trace down to component level, and work unsupervised. Sense of humour would be most helpful. First contact, please Phone or fax Niven Dallas 08 9601 5300"

***

I had taken on a large contract to service the total radio communications systems at Argyle Diamond mine, as such had expected a flood of responses for this exclusive position, my assumption was very wrong. As Antonio Banderas quotes, *"Expectation is the mother of all frustration"*

At the time, I was in Perth with my family enjoying a much-needed Christmas holiday break. It was around the 18th of December 1981. My well-thought-out plan was to employ another technician in Perth, and then fly back up to Kununurra after Christmas in my Cessna 182RG aircraft.

The aircraft was currently undergoing a three yearly major inspection at Perth Jandakot airport. I had in the past, successfully used this very same employment method on a number of occasions with quite good results.

Moreover, it had the added advantage of sorting out any problems a technician may have in regards to flying around the remote Kimberley area in a light aircraft.

**

The 1982 new-year was in, and the party season had come and gone, I was now urgently required back in Kununurra within the next few days. With the scheduled major maintenance service completed on the Cessna 182, and ready to fly. The aircraft was now urgently required back in Kununurra for remote area service work.

I extended my adverts for a radio technician to include the Eastern States newspapers; even so, I still had not received one reply. Reluctantly I then phoned my Kununurra office to advise that I will be flying out of Perth tomorrow without a radio tech, departing out of Jandakot at first light for arrival in Kununurra at around 5pm. Robyn Burford the office accounts girl and sometimes hire car Hostess took the call.

'Yeah, everything is fine up here boss, but there is a big pile of bills on your desk that will need sorting out. Oh yeah, and the bank manager keeps phoning, he wants to see you urgently.'

Hmm thinking, looks as if I have run out of money again. I will need to change this subject quick before Robyn thinks she will have no pay next week…then asking.

'Have you had any office enquires about the radio techs job?' Robin replied brightly, 'no, no luck.' Then a short pause...

'Hang on boss, there was this woman who rang up the other day about her husband who might be interested in the tech's job.'

I thought bloody hell here we go again, some woman ringing up about a job for her husband. Last time it was the man's mother. What is wrong with blokes these days, why can't they speak for themselves? Robyn droned on.

206

'The lady has left a phone number for you to contact her. I didn't think you would be bothered, especially after the last woman who recommended her son for the technician's job.'

Followed by copious amounts of laughter down the phone. Robyn thought it funny reminding me of my last tech who had eloped with my sacked accounts clerk, the very cause of my present staff shortage.

'Yes, yes all very amusing Robyn, you had better let me have that number as this is the only response we've had so far. Robyn promptly quoted the number.

'This is a Port Hedland phone number I noted?'

Robyn added with a giggle.

'Could be, she said her name was Holly Johnston and that she managed the Mount Newman Social Club, and that you should only ring her back during drinking hours?'

'Maybe she has got her job enquiry mixed up?' I said.

'No boss, she did say, "Radio technicians position on behalf of her husband," (mimicking an upper crust English accent)

'She has a very posh English accent. She sounded like an actress out of one of those old British movies.' Robyn carried on with her mimicking... then cutting her effort short.

'See you late tomorrow Robyn' I said ending the silly conversation and hung up.

Then I thought about this for a moment, the last woman who responded to one of my technician adverts was the blokes mum. He eventually ran off with my ex, or better described as sacked office girl, they sort-of eloped and never seen again. This time it was the bloke's wife making the inquiry, my curiosity got the better of me... yet again.

I rang the number Robyn gave me; the phone answered on the first ring. A gruff voice blasted out.

'Newman Social Club 'ear mate.'

'Could I talk to a Mrs Holly Johnston please?'

'Who the fuck are you mate' came the gruff sounding reply, 'If you're bloody-well selling something you're wasting your bleeding time mate.'

'Hang on' I spluttered at this opening exchange of typical North-West language, 'I'm replying to a call from Mrs Johnston; it's the lady who wants to contact me.'

'Well why the hell didn't yer bloody-well say that in the first place mate,' followed by a loud... 'Olli, there's some bloke on the phone for you.' The gruff voice yelled.

After a slight delay, there was a rustle as Holly picked up the phone.

'Hello this is Holly Johnston here, manager of the Mount Newman Social Club, how may I help you?'

Well Robyn was right, Holly did have a beautiful English-speaking voice, crisp and clear, just like in the old British movies, but then did Robyn say something like that?

Trying to sound a little more up market, I opened with...

'Good morning madam, Niven Dallas here, Managing Director of Kimberley Electronics. I understand that you recently enquired after the advertised position of a radio technician for your husband?'

'Well yes, Andre is looking for some sort of new challenge. I noticed the position advertised in the West Australian and thought this would suit my dear Andre to a tee. And I must advise you Mister Dallas, that I have never been a "Madam" no matter what you may have heard to the contrary,' followed by a low chuckle.

This woman had a good, if not dry sense of humour, one of the most important qualifications for surviving in the remote North-West. On the other hand, was I mistaken in my interpretation of that last comment? I had best ignore the exchange for fear of being wrong.

'Well I didn't actually say all that much in the advert about the job,' letting my attempt at a proper accent slip down a bit.

'Ah but Andre has heard all about you Mr Dallas.'

'Really' I said, picking up my best voice again, 'I do hope it was all good things.' Then added a little trial joke 'you shouldn't believe all that you hear about me as I do have a number of very jealous and vocal competitors.' Holly came back with a stabbing dry reply.

'Yes, well we do know something of your Electronics servicing business in Kununurra,' then she got right down to business. 'When may we arrange for a job interview? Any time soon would be convenient for us.'

We... what is this "we, "and "us." I thought to myself, this lady is used to managing people, a bit heavy and a little forward so early, talking about an interview at this stage in the conversation. I had sensed that this woman was used to being the boss, a leader, and was now obviously setting down her own rules, conditions, and times. I must create some distance.

'I think I should speak to Andre first,' I said. 'I need to know what level of experience he has, especially in the kind of radio communication equipment that we service.'

I explained that my normal procedure is firstly with a phone interview, to get some background information, his qualifications, and suchlike.

This request for a one-on-one chat with Andre did not slow Holly down one bit, as Holly launched into a new higher level of small talk. With little effort, she managed to convince me that she could provide any, and all of the initial information that I needed.

'Do believe what I say Mr Dallas, I must advise you that Andre is a fully qualified and indentured Electronics technician, Andre works on the latest Philips and Motorola two-way radio equipment all day in his present job' came Holly's swift sharp reply.

'Where's that?' I gingerly enquired with reserved caution... realising this woman bites.

'Currently, Andre holds the position as the senior on site radio communications officer for Mount Newman Mining.'

Then a long pause as I was thinking as fast as I could.

'Are you still there?' Holly enquired. I had lapsed into one of my deep thought moments of. What a bit of luck, have I heard this woman right; her husband Andre holds a current position servicing similar radio equipment.

'Yes I'm still here, the line just went dead for a second, I should talk to Andre on the phone first, when will he be available for a chat, we can then arrange the best way for a job interview.'

This could be a stroke of good luck, I could not believe this; a senior communications man is he...? Then a senior thought suddenly hit me.

'By the way Holly, talking about senior, just how old is Andre?'

'My dear, Andre is a young, very fit forty-eight years old,' was the crisp reply. 'Plays tennis very well you know.'

The oh-so British social tea party comment went totally unheard as I launched into how I could arrange for an early interview.

'Holly I have to fly my small aircraft up to Kununurra tomorrow, if Andre can get up to Kununurra any time after that we can get together for the interview?'

'Well Niven, may I call you Niven,' (I thought it sounds better when Holly pronounces my name.)

'Why yes of course, by all means do,' there, I was trying to sound civilised again... Holly went on.

'Why don't you just land your little aeroplane at Port Hedland tomorrow and we will meet you there, after all you will be flying right past our door so to speak.'

This was a very smart woman indeed, why did I not think of that. I felt a little miffed about being brain snookered.

'Holly, can Andre be at the reception of the Walkabout Hotel which is directly opposite the Port Hedland airport at around midday tomorrow?'

'I know the Walkabout Hotel very well Niven. That should be fine, we will see you tomorrow at noon, until then, goodbye.' A click and Holly was gone.

I could tell that Holly liked to be in control down to having the very last word. Did Holly say "we" will see you at the Walkabout, this would then confirm that both Holly and Andre were coming to the interview?

***

The flight to Port Hedland was as they say in the flying world, uneventful. I was about one hour early for our meeting, so I relaxed in the Walkabout reception lounge, going over the questions I had carefully written down to ask Andre.

The chime clock on the Hotel reception wall was striking 12 noon. I looked up, and there standing in the double doorway, framed in the bright backlight from the sun were two unidentified human shapes. One large and one small, it was like watching a scene from an old western movie just before the twelve o'clock high-noon showdown. A familiar voice came from the duo, without doubt directed at the young receptionist who had just taken a large bite out of her messy lunch sandwich.

'I say there young lady, has a Mr Dallas by chance called in here?'

Err, 'over here,' I called out waving my hand furiously as if they could not see me, being the only other person in the large Hotel lounge.

The duo stepped forward out of the backlit entry door revealing themselves. Holly was indeed a big woman, around fifty-five years of age, well dressed and quite nimble on her feet. Our eyes locked-on as she marched forward across the lounge toward me.

'Come along' she chided Andre who had fallen a little behind like a small boy in a shopping mall. Hand outstretched Holly announced in a firm crisp voice.

'How do you do Niven, I am Holly Johnston, just call me Holly,' shaking hands vigorously like a man. Still holding eye contact, she cocked her head to one side and announced. 'This is Andre.'

Andre was a small man, about my size, except he looked closer to fifty-eight than forty-eight. He had thinning grey and brown hair with sad eyes, and a very grey completion. I thought to myself, I hope my staring was not obvious, as he did not look well at all; we then shook hands in a limp apologetic sort of way.

'I'm Andre' he said quietly as if to himself.

***

Is it not strange how some people, just introduced to you by their name, will then tell you their name again... almost as if you had not heard it correctly first time? Little was I to know that his name was the only thing Andre was to say at that meeting.

We sat down on the bulky leather lounges facing one another, with a small low table between us. Holly passed a large folder across to me declaring in a firm voice.

'Those my dear, are Andre's qualifications and letters of recommendation. I think you will find them all in order and to your satisfaction.'

I slowly opened the manila file and shuffled through the many official looking documents within. Andre and Holly looked on in silence; I looked up with a wrinkled brow, then in a confused voice...

'They're all in a foreign language.'

Holly was quick to point a relevant fact.

'Well my dear, Andre is after all Dutch.'

Holly announced this fact with a surprised look on her face as if I should have known. To this point, I had only ever heard Andre speak one word, his name.

It was then I noticed, when Andre leant forward to retrieve his glass of water, his Newman Mining site pass came into full view, clipped to the pocket flap of his shirt. It said; "Andre Bile Senior Radio Communications Officer" and had a small mug-shot picture of him in the corner that did not do him any photogenic favours.

An interesting point was observed by my keen eye and sharp mind; Andre's surname was "Mr Bile," this suggested to me that Andre may not be Holly's husband as she had led me to believe? Yet in my observation, Andre was acting the same as any well-educated and submissive long term married man. I made my next play in an attempt to engage Andre in conversation.

'How long have you been working at Mount Newman,' I asked Andre. Holly quickly replied.

'Almost two years now.' I tried addressing Andre again.

'Why do you wish to leave Mount Newman Mines, as you already have an excellent well-paying job?' Holly replied for Andre yet again.

'Andre needs a new challenge and he likes the Ord River Kununurra area, this offer came really as a blessing in disguise.'

212

I thought to myself, I don't remember having made any offer yet, have I? ... Holly was a very pushy woman indeed.

I continued looking through the file, which contained a number of impressive looking certificates, all in the name of Andre Bile, which were the only words I could read and understand. Holly accurately identified my problem.

'I can get those documents translated should you wish?'

'No need Holly, they look good enough to me,' then it somewhat just slipped out, 'What would you do in Kununurra...?'

Damn-it, hell, I have been snookered again, the gentle smile on Holly's face confirmed she had most certainly won this round. This was one hell of a woman I liked her style, and then she quickly took advantage of my weak negotiating position.

'Well I don't have much of a problem really, I have held a number of liquor licences managing Hotels, Pubs, and Clubs. Wherever people drink and wish to have a good time I will always find a job' then leaning forward and staring me in the eye Holly asked.

'Don't by chance know of any hospitality positions available in Kununurra do you?'

Then it happened again, my carefully planned interview with Andre was being hi-jacked to find a possible job for Holly... an answer to Holly's question just sort of popped out.

'Well as a matter of fact I think I do' I replied. 'The Ord River Sports Club has just thrown out the current manager for being drunk on-the-job, and for not collecting the tab money. The committee members are in there trying to run the place, but quite frankly I think the old manager they threw out was doing a far better job.'

Whoops, had I gone too far, I was now suggesting a possible position that would suit Holly. What had happened to my interview chat with Andre? That gentle "got you again" smile returned, this time with a fierce steady stare.

'Now that's my kind of challenge.' Holly declared firmly, 'I will soon have that mess sorted out, you mark my word. You will soon see my dear, I can tell you now with confidence

Niven; I have resolved this type of miss-management clean-up work many times before in my long management career.'

I did indeed mark her word, as Holly was right... and in time, she did fix all of the Ord River Sports Club problems.

Chapter Two:

New on the Job

Holly and Andre arrived in Kununurra six weeks later after giving the required notice at their old jobs. I accepted and respected that delay, as it was evidence to me that they were both responsible and caring employees. Andre proved to be a very capable electronics engineer. He was happy and at his best when he was at his bench working hard, refusing to turn away any repair challenge.

He was I suppose mainly a bench technician, as he liked to work in the comfort of an air-conditioned service workshop. This may well have been the reason for his lack of a suntan and his grey look.

Andre was a quiet spoken man; I have never heard him swear. He was not much on conversation, or for that matter drinking. The few times I got Andre down to the pub, he just sat quietly in the corner nursing a small beer, listening to the bar bullshit and chain smoking, as the Dutch do.

***

One day I arrived at work to find a large church organ unloaded into the mechanical workshop. The organ was dangling by ropes from the overhead gantry crane.

The electronics service workshop is within the mechanical workshop. The workshop area easily viewed through two large one metre by two metre-dividing wall windows.

Standing in the air-conditioned electronics workshop was Andre, waving his hands about through the large windows giving directions to the mechanical staff via the workshop intercom. 'Left a bit, down, watch-it.' It was a very amusing sight as I entered the electronics workshop.

'What the hell is all this' I enquired trying to conceal my anger. 'Do you realise that you can't get this organ into your electronics service area, it can't fit through the bloody electronics workshop door? Now the bloody thing has taken-up half the damn mechanical workshop floor space,' my anger was starting to show.

'Andre, we fix radio communication systems here not bleeding musical instruments.'

I could tell that Andre was not concerned at my ranting displeasure declaring.

'I'll have this organ going and out of here in a few days, I've repaired electronic organs many times before,' was Andre's soft reply. Curiosity got the better of me.

'Anyway, where did this thing come from?' I asked.

The organ was now sitting firmly on four of the mechanical workshops heavy, fuel-drum trolleys. When Andre was satisfied with the unloading, he quietly replied.

'The organ belongs to local Catholic Church. It has been broken down for some years now, but I will soon have going again.'

I was staring at the large organ being pushed to the side of the workshop by four of the staff and thinking we should be charging them storage for this huge organ.

'I've never seen that massive organ before. I never knew the Catholic Church had one.'

'Well, had you gone to Church you would have seen it,' Andre continued with a cheesy smile, adding. 'We will have to fumigate it before I start any work.'

Fumigate I thought to myself…why? Then another word came to mind beginning with F "freebee" and then Church. This all sounded like poor business was about to take place, asking the relevant question.

'Is this a freebee job Andre?'

Andre turned to me with a hurt look on his face, took two rapid puffs on his cigarette, and blew out a torrent of smoke then in his soft voice, launched into his organ story.

'The Catholic Church has been trying to raise money for years to fund a new organ. I had a good look at their old organ and convinced them to get the old one repaired. I told them that this organ was in its day, a very good and very expensive instrument. They then agreed to have the organ repaired.'

I stared at Andre in astonishment! This was the longest I had ever heard Andre speak, and could tell by his effort that this was a serious business for him, thinking he must be religious or something... then it slipped out...

'How much money have they collected so far?'

'A little over $5,000' replied Andre.

'Jesus' I gasped aloud, assessing that it was all starting to sound good again. Just then, there was a shrill scream like a little girl. Andre and I turned towards the window to see a burly mechanic flop back on his arse with about 15 to 20 small mice running all over him and the workshop floor. The mechanic had removed the back off the organ disturbing their nest.

'I see what you mean about fumigation' I laughed aloud. This was also the first time I had really heard Andre laugh aloud. We will have a hell of a job catching that lot I thought.

Then I decided the big old organ warranted a closer look. All the fancy woodwork was still in nice condition, other than that the organ was a total un-repairable mess, most of the keys on the three keyboards did not work or were scratchy. The register slide bars were stuck and the revolving Leslie speaker system belt-drive was gone, no doubt eaten by the hungry mice. I reported all this to Andre who raised a knowledgeable eyebrow saying.

'So you know something about electronic organs then?' he enquired,

'I have worked on a few in the past but played more, and I can tell you now Andre, this organ is fucked. I used to have an electrical and musical shop called Centralect in the main shopping strip back in 1972.' Andre interjected... another first for the super polite Andre.

'Well then, you're just the man to check the organ out and test everything is working okay when I finish fixing it.'

Trying to make my point, I continued, 'the keynote contacts are all stuffed' ...before I could finish Andre cut in again.

'The contacts on this type of organ are called "open gold wire." Overtime the key contact points rub the gold plating off and cause scratchy notes. The fix is quite easy, I just turn the gold key contact wire over and move the point up a little on the fixed contact bar creating a new gold contact switch.'

My jaw must have dropped as Andre gave me a strange look. This was the second long sentence from Andre since I had known him and both were well worth hearing, this man is defiantly no dill. I was starting to like and admire this quiet man.

True to his word, Andre had the organ finished in three days. Then we kept it for another two weeks as we all enjoyed a few beers and a sing along around the organ after work. A visit from the local Catholic Priest soon stopped our end-of-day singing drinks, and had the organ delivered back to the Catholic Church... they had received and paid the repair bill over a week ago!

***

Holly was quick off the mark, and was a joy to see in full business action. She snooped around the Ord River Sports Club, sort of casing the joint like an experienced burglar. She also drank with the locals and quizzed them on what was wrong with their club. I soon found out from a number of defeated drinking partners, that Holly could drink any of the old bar flies under the table with ease.

No doubt, this was a very useful qualification for a licensed premises manageress. It occurred to me that Andre was the exact opposite in character and in every other way from his wife. This confirming my often-touted theory down the pub that opposites really do attract and make lasting magnetic mates.

Holly compiled her submission for election to the position as Manager of the Ord River Sports Club like the hostile takeover of a big company. The standing committee members did not have an ice-creams chance in hell of opposing her well thought-out strategy. The vote to appoint her as Manageress of the Ord River Sports Club Inc. was carried unanimously.

***

Holly quickly settled in to her new role as the new Manager of the Ord River Sports Club. The job came with a nice little air-conditioned house within the Club grounds, so Andre and Holly lived on the Club premises. Holly was delighted with this, and the added advantage of always being close to the job. Then there was the plus of having no house overheads to pay each month.

Holly managed the Ord River Sports Club as a General runs a war. In the beginning, there was much blood everywhere, and many dead bodies from a short war with the old committee, while being systematically removed and buried.

She took no prisoners and showed no mercy to the old guard. The bar tab system was one of the first things to go. No form of credit ever again extended to anyone, much to the displeasure of the old members of the Sports Club.

Holly soon had the Ord River Sports Club trading figures back into the black and got the large debtors and creditor's lists under control. Holly sent the drunks home to their families and gained great respect and thanks from the many appreciative wives in the Town. She then introduced a menu of cheap quality food, and started a 16mm movie night, which brought back the local family nights to the Sports Club.

Everything in the world was going well for Andre and Holly. I had learnt a lot of very useful business strategy from Holly. She cherished hosting a good dinner party and loved people. You have to remember that a dinner party in the land of the bar-b-cue was something very different indeed.

Holly was not only a good boozer but also an excellent cook. This combination was the recipe for some of the most interesting times I have ever experienced, especially when invited to dine at the famous House of Holly.

***

'Dinner parties do have to have strict rules you know.' Holly announced one day, while looking me straight in the eyes with a quizzical look.

'Niven you alone are invited to my dinner party next Monday night providing you agree to abide by my four strict rules.'

Mondays was Holly's one-and-only day off, being the slackest day of the week at the Ord River Sports Club. I just had to know, and inquired with great interest.

'And what are these four strict rules Holly?' Holly responded in a serious voice, holding her stare.

***

'Rule number one: You must never tell anybody when invited to my dinner party, as doing so may offend those that are not invited. The reason being I can only host a dinner party for a total of twenty people at my table at any one time.'

I was astonished at this claim, as I had not considered that Holly's dinner parties were full sit-down affairs, this was a large table… and in such a small house.

***

'Rule number two: You do not bring anything or anyone with you. I will supply everything… everything needed for my guests to enjoy a good time.'

***

'Rule number three: Smoking, swearing, getting drunk, telling dirty jokes and the removing of ones clothes are all permitted, however; outright insults, fighting, spitting, and vomiting in my house are not accepted.'

I was about to ask if those rules applied to everyone or just me, then Holly quickly moved on to the last rule.

***

'Rule number four: and this is the most important rule. You must never discuss with anyone other than those who were at the same dinner party anything that was said, discussed, or done on that night.'

I scanned Holly's face for a hint of humour and found none, and then replied confidently.

'Sounds like one hell of a dinner party Holly, although the fighting, spitting, and vomiting bit does have me more than a little intrigued.'

Holly was not moved by my description of possible crude party behaviour. Holly knew this was not my scene, or liking, and then replied with a worldly air.

'Well that my dear, would all depend on who was at the party. I can however guarantee you this; you will most certainly enjoy the company Niven.' Holly followed that comment with a slow wink of her left eye.

***

Holly was correct yet again, her dinner guests were very different, made-up with a special choice of those in the Town who absolutely hated one another. The guests included arrogant-minded pompous government officials, Aboriginal activists, rough Station Managers, religious extremists, and right-wing small business owners... like me.

Holly would politely introduce each guest around the table by name and occupation. I could see and feel the seething hate as old enemies caught sight of each other. The booze was plentiful as she plied everyone with large amounts of all types of grog, and then Holly filled them up with a most gorgeous five-course meal.

It was not long before the local Magistrate was defending himself against the Station Manager who only last week was convicted in his court for not wearing a seat belt. Then pointing out that the man sitting next to him, who was a known Aboriginal activist had never worn a seat belt in his life, yet drove past the Police station 10 times a day.

Yes, Holly chooses her dinner guests with cunning precision, placing them around the dinner table with great care. I noticed that Holly always got the party going by winding people up on various tricky local issues, and then sat back, to observed her creation with much satisfaction and laughter.

Those memories are absolute gems, being some of the best dinner parties I have ever been to. Many a misunderstood comment or lie, or distorted story in the town was resolved, and many old enemies left as friends. These two, Andre and

Holly were lovely people, real personalities and in my opinion the very salt of this earth.

***

One Friday, as I had done so many times before, I asked Andre if he would like to have a drink with me. I jokingly suggested we should go to the Ord River Sports Club for a change as he lived there. To my surprise, Andre accepted this time.

Andre said he would go home and shower first, and would meet me there in the snug bar in about half an hour for a drink. I had decided I would stay in the office for that half hour to finish off some paperwork, mainly because had I gone home first, Lesley would not have allowed me out again to play.

Chapter Three:

Dead Unlucky

On the way over to the Ord River Sports Club, I decided to check the Post Office mailbox. As I turned into the car park, our one and only voluntary manned ambulance almost ran me off the road, sirens blaring and lights flashing. I resorted to yelling out of my window a range of selected abuse at the driver as he passed by.

This response was all quite normal in Kununurra, any excuse for the volunteer driver to drive the ambulance like a bloody lunatic. A dead cat reported on the side of the road could provoke the same sort of noisy emergency response.

My quick glance in the mailbox just confirmed the usual stack of bills. I was thinking who would be the lucky lotto bastard paid this month. As I pulled up at the Club, Holly ran out towards me, spilling out a torrent of words, she was obviously very distressed.

'Andre had fallen down in the shower, he was unconscious, but his eyes were still open. Holly was worried...

'I have no idea how long he was in there, the Club is all sorted out for tonight. I have gathered some of Andre's clothes, and was on my way to the Hospital?'

Holly looked frightened and confused. I was now also confused; this was not the strong Holly character, I had come to know.

I was regretting my earlier thoughtless remarks about the volunteer ambulance response. Hell, the ambulance must have been for Andre. Even with my limited medical knowledge, unconscious with his eyes open was not a good sign. Holly needed some assurance.

'Holly, I was on my way to have a drink with Andre, being a little early for a change. I doubt he would have been collapsed for more than a few minutes, what in the hell could have caused this to happen? Get into the car Holly and I will take you over to the hospital.'

At the hospital, the news was not good. Apparently, Andre had suffered a massive aneurism, a burst blood vessel in the brain, possibly the result of a tumour. The Doctor was not giving Andre much hope of surviving this ordeal. This was all happening too quickly for Holly and me to follow.

As we spoke, an emergency evacuation flight to Darwin had already been arranged, I was most impressed with how well organised, and how fast events were moving along... Then it started to sink in, this was a serious matter. The Kununurra Hospital staff had already stabilised and prepared Andre for the Darwin flight.

Within twenty minutes, Andre and Holly were in the air, on their way to Darwin Hospital some two-hundred and forty flying miles away.

As I drove back home, I started thinking how things had been going so good in recent times, and now two nice people were apparently facing a major health disaster... How quickly life events can change.

The flight is just over an hour and twenty minutes flight time in the RFDS Beach Baron twin to Darwin. Probably another two hours for the Hospital to work on poor Andre, and then Darwin is one and half-hours in time zone ahead of West Australian time. I thought to myself I will try to call the Darwin Hospital for any news on Andre at about 10:30pm Darwin time. Then a thought occurred to me; Holly would not know anybody in Darwin?

Then I remembered all the people important to me in Darwin; when in trouble always call Des and Dawn.

It was a Friday night in Darwin, so Deso and Dawn will be having a usual bar-b-cue party in their backyard, or someone else's backyard, as was normal.

Desmond Nudl was the owner of Port Darwin Motors, an icon of the Northern Territory motoring industry. I had known Deso and his wife Dawn for many years, in what now seems like a lifetime ago, beginning when I first purchased a few vehicles from him for the start of my Kununurra hire car fleet.

Des and Dawn were present at our wedding in Kununurra on 7th December 1974. When they returned to Darwin, only seventeen days later, they experienced the wrath of a massive cyclone called "Tracy" on Christmas Eve, escaping death by sheer good luck. Cyclone Tracy devastated Darwin on the night of 24th December 1974, snaking and passing over the city twice ripping the city apart, killing many people on that dark Christmas Eve... Lesley and I were married on seventh of December; only eighteen days before that horrendous event... this was one genuine hell of a wedding to remember.

This intense cyclone remains one of the most severe to ever make landfall in Australia. When my daughter Tracy came along, it seemed appropriate to name her after that memorable cyclone. I must admit it sure suits her. Des and Dawn are her Godparents. Yes, we do go back a long way and one could say are very good friends, although after this current request for help, readers would ever wonder why... I hesitated, and then gave Des and Dawn a phone call...

***

'Hi Des, am I glad I got hold of you.'

'Nibsey it's been a long-time no hear.' Deso's gravel voice rumbled down the phone. Nibsey is Deso's pet name for me, and we had last talked only yesterday, this was Deso's polite way of saying "what the hell do you want now?" Little did he know how different this request for help would be, I then launched into my sad story.

'Deso I have sad news, my radio tech Andre has just been emergency airlifted from the Kununurra hospital to Darwin with a serious problem believed to be a brain haemorrhage. His wife Holly is with him, and they do not know anybody in Darwin.'

I had hardly taken a breath to continue when...

'No worries Nibsey' assured Deso's gravel voice. 'Just give me their names and the hospital and I will go over and introduce myself to them.'

This was Des and Dawn's style; these people are the givers and helpers in this world and not takers or exploiters. I have never known people with so many friends. As time went by, these same people also became my friends. I soon realised that they were all thankful to Des and Dawn at some time in their lives. All receiving personal help that created a lasting lifelong bond of friendship and respect. They are the listeners, the rock solid counselling advisers, and the substitute Mother, and Father to so many who needed them in that remote City at the top of Australia.

When I looked back at my own situation with Des and Dawn, I soon realised that I was not that special, as they had helped numerous other people. We became just another addition to the many in Des and Dawn's extended family and friends.

This is a full story in its-self to tell later. Beautiful people still live on this planet, even if they do get a little grumpy, and become a pain in the arse from time to time. Nobody is perfect, we all live in the real world... including me.

***

I rang the Hospital in Darwin, enquiring about Andre at 10:30pm, and was advised that Andre was stable and in an induced coma. The Doctors had managed to reduce the pressure on his brain, and he was now responding well to medication. When Holly got on the phone, she was very excited. Andre was going to be all right, the Doctors expected a slow but steady recovery. I could hear the relief in Holly's voice, and had to butt into Holly's torrent of words.

'Holly I have some very good friends in Darwin, Desmond, and Dawn Nudl, and have asked them to get in touch with you so you will have someone to talk with in Darwin.'

'You are such a sweet man' crooned Holly.

I was chatting away with Holly, when Holly stopped abruptly as Des had found his way to Andre's hospital room.

'Oh I think your friend is here now' Holly whispered. I could hear Deso introducing himself to Holly in his gravel voice.

'Hi my names Desmond I'm a friend of Nibsey you must be Holly, Nibsey told me about Andre.' I could hear the exchange of conversation low but clear,

'Who is this Nibsey' Holly inquired.

'Oh that's just a pet name I call Niven just to stir him up a bit.' Replied Des.

'Desmond…' Holly started to say…

'Just call me Des like everybody else.' Deso interjected.

'I was going to say Niven is on the phone, would you like to talk to him?' Holly handed the phone to Deso.

'Hi Nibsey I have met up with Holly, I will ask her if there is anything I can do to help and will give her my address and contact details.'

'How's Andre going?' I asked hopefully.

'Well he looks like he's sleeping' replied Des; ' and he looks a bit bloody grey but then again, I don't know what he looked like before do I, since this is the first time I have ever seen him?'

Deso as always was right; it was not worth challenging such an exact statement of fact. However, the grey look of Andre was not all that bad news, as he does look like that all the time.

As was the normal with Des and Dawn, they offered that Holly should stay at their home while in Darwin. It was also normal for a Friday that Des had some of their many friends over that night for a bar-b-cue and a few drinks. The party was still going well when Des and Holly returned at about 11:30. As witnessed by those that were there. The night turned out to be a "9 plus on the party performance chart of 10."

Holly was so relieved at the news about Andre's good chance to pull through this sudden health challenge, that she really let her hair down. A reliable witness informed me that Holly was the evening's centre of attraction, being very drunk, and then swimming naked in Deso's pool. I am also reliably informed that it was a sight not to be forgotten… by anybody… ever.

The next day was a bright Darwin Saturday. Deso gave me a call to say that Holly was on her way back to Kununurra, would I pick her up from the airport. The Doctors had advised Holly that Andre was stable and slowly on the mend, advising this process will take a long time.

Being a dedicated businessperson Holly had decided to get back to the Ord River Sports Club, as there was nothing more she could do for Andre in Darwin... And so began the strangest and longest light aircraft flight in my life.

***

When I arrived at the Kununurra airport, the six o'clock evening jet flight was just landing. Apart from the normal drone of activity, the AWA (Airlines of Western Australia) ground staff was oddly excited about something. I was soon to find out why; all the AWA airline cabin staff were now officially on a no-flying strike. Apparently, this inbound jet was by all accounts the last AWA flight into Kununurra. Their union now grounded all of the normal scheduled flights until a bitter staff dispute was resolved.

I thought Holly was very fortunate to be on the very last flight into Kununurra, a little bit-o-luck... how wrong I was.

The AWA strike, I was later told was because of the overwhelming support of the entire airline cabin staff, and the flight attendants union. (I must admit that I did not know there was such a union.) The union and its members were all supporting the reinstatement of a silly, half-baked cabin staff attendant. Apparently, this irresponsible flight attendant was immediately sacked for not doing her job, simply to secure the bloody aircrafts main cabin door, prior to take-off.

The cabin door apparently blew open shortly after take-off. What an unbelievable aviation disaster for this young regional airline, and what poor safety procedures.

It is my opinion as a pilot; they should have sacked the Captain and the First Officer, as well as the flight attendant. There are bright warning lights, and a loud chime on the flight deck to advise the crew when the cabin door is secure and locked, and when the hull can be pressurised for flight.

The responsible blokes at the pointy end of an aircraft, being the Captain and First Officer, by normal operational rules must go through a pre-flight checklist, which includes a check if any of the hull doors not locked and secure for flight. It is also included again in the pre-flight take-off roll... Item four on the cabin check list, "Doors secured, armed and locked" to make sure the hull is secure before take-off.

Just what were the crew thinking off, I have sacked lowly charter pilots from my small air charter company for a much lesser deviation of the ANRs (Aeronautical Regulations) than this. The safety of your aircraft and passengers are always the first consideration of any proposed flight.

My angry thoughts on this silly AWA union strike were soon brought back to reality when a loud voice yelled out...

'DALLAS, someone wants you on the bloody phone. The call is on our private airline company unlisted phone number, so be quick.' I grabbed the phone. 'Hello,' it was Des, 'Hi Deso, how the hell did you get this special unlisted AWA phone number? I can tell you AWA are a bit pissed off about this.'

'You don't want to know that detail Nibsey,' announced the serious gravel voice down the phone, 'but I do have friends in all the right places. Listen Nibsey, Andre has taken a turn for the worst, the Doctors do not give him much of a chance, has Holly arrived there yet?'

I was watching through the window as the Darwin jet was just landing.

'Des there's been some sort of an AWA union crew strike, and all the flights in and out of here are now grounded,'

'I know that Nibsey.' Des broke in, 'listen, you will have to get Holly back up to Darwin, and fast... in that little bloody aircraft of yours.'

'Okay Deso, I will get the Cessna fuelled up, and will fly Holly back to Darwin as soon as she lands,' and then gently hung-up the phone.

***

Holly was all smiles, wafting down the aircraft stairs like a visiting film star. As she approached me, she could obviously see the serious look on my face.

'What is the matter dear lost your pocket-money again?'

Holly was always full of wise cracks; my reply soon changed that good mood.

'Holly, Deso has just phoned, Andre has taken a turn for the worst. We must get back up to Darwin. I have my Cessna fuelled and ready to fly you back up to Darwin.'

'I don't understand' Holly replied startled, 'I have just left Andre's bedside, a little over two hours ago, the Doctors said he was doing just fine. They said he was slowly recovering.'

I looked at Holly's confused face, offering little in the way of comfort with my reply.

'Apparently that's how things are with aneurisms Holly. They can continue bleeding causing further damage before the healing process can start to work.'

Holly followed me in silence into the flight service office. I lodged a flight plan for two people on-board the Cessna 182 TSX direct flight to Darwin. The Gestapo (flight service staff) knew all about Andre's medivac to Darwin yesterday, as they would have cleared the Royal Flying Doctor as an emergency flight. They also knew Andre was Holly's husband, as they were all members of the Ord River Sports Club, and knew that Holly was the club manager, who was now standing right next to me.

Knowing Holly had only just arrived from Darwin, the Flight Service officers put their simmering hates of me aside as they realised this was obviously another emergency. To the Gestapo's credit, they performed beyond their call of duty. They cleared my aircraft for a direct approach into Darwin's busy international airport and other such flight service magic. This most needed magic I was later to experience several times in this saga, as this light aircraft flight turned out to be very long, dark, and very interesting.

**

Cleared for immediate take off, we were soon on our way to Darwin. Holly was upset, and even more upset when I told her that I had just this minute received a relayed call direct to my aircraft from the flight control centre in Darwin. They advised that Andre was now in a critical condition, and not expected to live, they wanted my revised ETA (estimated time of arrival) for Darwin, I advised assuming a correct weather forecast, my ETA local time would be 10:15pm

The Darwin landing was a direct in approach to runway 36 slotted between two RAAF Caribou aircraft. Ground control gave me priority, and took us directly to where Des was waiting with the car engine running. I shut the aircraft down and opened the door, Deso blasted out.

'Stop farting about Nibsey we've got to get going.'

Holly and I quickly piled into the car and Des got us to the Hospital in record time. Standing in silence, all three of us stared down at poor Andre, hooked up to a large array of electronic monitoring equipment. I thought to myself, Andre would have loved to look at all this electronic gear. Then I noticed all the pipes and tubes going in and out of him and realised that Andre was on full life support. With this many pipes, he looked like a plumber's nightmare. The Doctor arrived to a chorus of enquiry.

'How is Andre doing?'

'Not that well at all I'm sorry to say.' Was the Doctors immediate reply; 'I am afraid the aneurism is large and deep, therefore inoperable. We have relieved some of the pressure on the brain but the blood supply has been reduced to certain areas, I am sorry it is only a short matter of time now.'

'How long do you think Doctor?' I asked.

'Could be a matter of hours, maybe a day or two no more,' replied the Doctor bluntly. Turning to Holly the Doctor continued with his bad news.

'Mrs Bile the hospital administration will require some personal details from you.' The busy Doctor then left as quickly as he came.

***

We stood in a row looking down at Andre when Holly broke the awkward silence in her crisp English accent.

'I must confess to you all, that I am not really Andre's wife you know. His wife is living in Perth somewhere, however I do have an address and a phone number. His wife's name is Marge and I believe they have two grown-up children.'

Des turned and rumbled in my ear. 'This could make things really complicated Nibsey', then to Holly. 'What are you are going to tell the Hospital administration, they will want some sort of proof of relationship?'

Holly said in a low slow steady voice…

'I will tell them the truth… the simple truth.'

Stunned at this quiet revelation from Holly, I croaked.

'I guess we will have to tell Andre's wife as soon as possible what has happened to her husband.'

Nobody was in a mood to reply to my suggestion. We then made our way down to the main Hospital administration where Holly in her crisp English voice delicately advised them of her matrimonial situation. The administration people were in plain fact not at all concerned, or showed any sign of interest in this matrimonial mismatch.

It occurred to me that this type of relationship problem is not all-that unusual around here. I just had to ask the question. As if by some unspoken sense, and without looking up from her form filling duties, the administration clerk replied to my un-asked question.

'Darwin is a very remote and transitional city; people come here from all over Australia and the world. Many have come here to hide from their financial and family problems, some to avoid the law.' The admin clerk quipped casually, 'we see this type of situation all the time, and it's not all that unusual.'

I could easily tell that Holly was not amused at this sanitized, cavalier, and blunt statement. Des lifted his eyes to the ceiling, pouted his lips, and added casually, while recalling grim times…

'After cyclone Tracy there were many hundreds of people killed; most were never identified. The government only released the total death figures for those formally identified. Consequently, only seventy-one people were officially reported as being dead, when in fact the true number of dead was in the many hundreds. The government couldn't trace their real family names or nationalities so they were all buried in pauper's graves.'

All were unexpectedly stunned by Deso's no doubt true version of the cyclone Tracy death figures… After all, he was there, being a well-respected businessman living and existing in Darwin right through that tragic event.

***

With all the required forms filled in, Holly glared back at the clerk who had just instructed her to wait. Advising she will be called shortly for a private chat with a senior administrator. This was enough bureaucracy for one day, Holly, then demanding to see this administrator immediately. Twenty minutes later Holly emerged from her meeting with a look of rage on her face... Des then asked the wrong question...

'Well how did it go Holly?'

I thought I had better change the subject again, and quickly.

'You know, I think we should all go back to Des and Dawn's bar and work out a plan to resolve this entire new situation.'

This time Holly was quick to see the advantage in my useful suggestion.

'Now that's an excellent idea' stated Holly with wide eyes replacing her thunderous look. 'After talking with that silly man, I could most certainly do with a good stiff drink.'

Chapter Four:

Tale of Two Wives

Back at Deso's house we all sat quietly looking at one another hoping someone would say something useful, then Dawn, Deso's wife asked the questions that Des and I were afraid to ask.

'Holly, have you ever met Andre's wife?' inquired Dawn with a pleasant but quizzical look, reserved only for woman's talk.

Holly took a sip of her drink and sighed a reply.

'Unfortunately no Dawn; to tell you the truth I have never even talked to her on the phone, or for that matter even seen a photograph of her. Andre never spoke of his wife at all. I have learnt in my life never to enquire of such matters in a relationship.'

Dawn had carefully identified an opening in this delicate conversation and continued.

'What have you told the Hospital administration people Holly, and what will they expect you to do now?'

Holly was quick to reply to the good female logic.

'Well, I have told them the truth. Andre has a wife named Marge, who lives in Perth, and that I do not have an address or contact number with me, but will get back to them tomorrow with that information. They said meanwhile they would get in touch with his employer in Kununurra.'

I was staring at the floor trying to think of something intelligent to say when I heard this.

'But I am Andre's employer?' I announced, 'didn't you tell them that?'

Holly gave me one of her silly little boy looks. I then realised there was more to come on this complicated topic. Holly explained the delicate problem in her crisp English.

'We cannot allow some junior Hospital administration clerk to just ring and announce to Andre's wife Marge that her husband is in a critical condition, possibly dying in a Darwin Hospital.' Holly continued,

'Also, I do not think it to be correct that I, as Andre's mistress should advise her of this terrible situation. I was hoping that maybe one of you two gentlemen would kindly make this important call?'

This made good clear sense to Des and me as all eyes then rested on me. It was obvious that I should be the one to make the call, as I was Andre's employer.

I mumbled 'what should I say, and by the way, it's now about 10:30pm in Perth.' Dawn broke the gloomy atmosphere with the obvious resolution.

'Niven, you will have to call Andre's wife right now, as it's the only way to get some idea of what she might want to do. For all we know she may never want to see, or hear of Andre again. We do not know how they ultimately parted. We will not know anything until you call her.'

Dawn was of course right, and Deso followed up with some obvious problems and useful suggestions.

'If Andre's wife wants to come up to Darwin we have another problem. As of this morning, there aren't any domestic airline flights in Western Australia, due to the AWA Hostess union strike, although I do have a good mate in AWA who may be able to help us.' Turning to me, Des said.

'Nibsey, you remember John McGowell. Well he is now the boss of Ansett operations in Karratha, remember John used to be in Darwin. You met him at a few of our bar-b-cues.'

'Yes Deso, I remember John well, I know he is a good bloke, but how the hell is John going to be of any help if the airline he works for is on strike?'

Deso, with a regal look of superior knowledge was quick to reply.

'Not all AWA jet aircraft are domestic flights, some are mining company charters, others are strictly for freight. As a pilot, you should know that sort of stuff Nibsey. I'll call John and see if he can do something, that's assuming Andre's wife wants to come up to Darwin; anyway you'd better get on the phone to her before she goes to bed.'

Des was right again, he called John who said that he could most likely get Mrs Bile on a charter flight to Karratha and maybe a Royal Mail flight to Broome. We should let him know as soon as possible as timing was critical to set things up.

***

The phone call to Andre's wife Marge was one of the hardest things I have ever had to do in my life. The phone was on open speaker so Holly, Des, and Dawn could listen in. The phone rang on and on and then a soft voice said.

'Hello this is Marge Bile.'

I took a deep breath and replied.

'Mrs Bile, my name is Niven Dallas; Andre works for me... before I could continue Marge burst in...

'Is Andre there, can I speak to him, is he all right. I have been so worried...' then it was my turn to but in...

'Mrs Bile.... Marge: may I call you Marge. I am afraid Andre is not well at all. I am calling you from Darwin, Andre is in Hospital here. Andre has unfortunately suffered a severe brain aneurism, and is presently in a coma. I am sorry to say that the doctors do not give him much hope. We are currently trying to arrange a flight for you to come up to Darwin. Will you come up to Darwin?' Marge burst into tears and sobbingly told her story.

'I haven't seen or heard from Andre in over two years. I reported him missing to the Police. They told me when they found him, and that he did not want to contact me. The Police said there was nothing they could do to make him call me. The Police told me Andre was working up north for some large mining company that is all I know. I don't know what to do now.'

Marge was very up-set and quietly sobbing when Deso whispered in my ear, a rumble that could be heard by all.

'Nibsey, John can get Marge up as far as Broome, if you could fly down and pick her up, Marge could, or should get to Darwin before Andre dies.'

That was the first time anyone had acknowledged that Andre was about to die. The Doctor had used words like, only a matter of time or days but not, he was going to die. I returned my attention back to Marge and I tried again for an answer.

'Marge, if it can be arranged, would you come up to Darwin? We know there is an airline strike on, but we can get you a seat on a mining company private charter flight, and then another charter flight to Broome. Once there, I can come and pick you up in my Cessna light aircraft.'

A soft haunting voice said, 'is Andre going to die?'

'I am sorry Marge, that's what the Doctors have told me. I will give you my phone number here in Darwin and the Hospital's phone number. They will also have your phone number by now, so you can expect a call.'

After some convincing words, Marge at last, agreed to come up to Darwin. Deso and I moved quickly into action, but the first action was a good night's sleep as it was now 1:30am on Sunday morning.

***

Sunday morning 8:30am, Holly rang the Darwin hospital and told them of the plan to get the real Mrs Bile up to Darwin as soon as possible. The Hospital administration advised that they had already been in touch with Andre's wife Marge Bile. The Hospital also advised us in true secret style (the privacy law) that they were not at liberty to divulge any part of the conversation they had had with Mrs Bile, as none of us lot were related to Mr Andre Bile.

A thought had occurred to me, I wonder if they would ever let us see Andre Bile again. My fleeting suspicion later confirmed, as we were never to see Andre in the flesh ever again after that last late Saturday night. Then again, I guess there was in fact nothing to see now.

***

On the way out to the airport, Des expressed his overall view on this sad situation, as only Des could. His gravel voice rose to a new higher pitch.

'What a fucking mess Nibsey. Now that Holly has gone and admitted to the hospital administration, she is not Andre's wife, and provided his wife's address and phone number... as far as they are concerned, we are out of his life... or what's left of it.'

The bizarre thought occurred to me. Deso was being all wound up over a bloke he had never seen or heard of only thirty hours ago. Deso continued.

'Do you know that without Andre's wife identifying him, and providing proof of their relationship, the bloody Hospital will never release Andre's body to Holly, for us to bury him?

There's another thing Nibsey; if you don't bring Andre's wife back, or if she doesn't claim the body, then poor Andre will be buried in a Darwin pauper's grave. Probably alongside those other poor bastards from cyclone Tracy.'

With this new grim view of the urgent situation firmly planted in my mind, I was even more determined to bring Andre's wife up to Darwin.

***

Deso stayed and watched me pre-flight the little Cessna. I crank her over. The engine burst into life on the second swing of the propeller, and then the radio crackled loud in my ears. "Cessna Tango Sierra X-ray clear to taxi."

I gave Deso a goodbye wave through the open window while thinking; shit, I could see things were now far worse than I had first imagined... I must try to get Marge up to Darwin as so many things now depended on it... a respectable burial for Andre was the least of them.

Chapter Five:

The Lost Wife

I departed Darwin in the Cessna 182RG at around 1:30 pm WST (Western Standard Time) to arrive in Kununurra at 3 pm. To my surprise flight service, Kununurra had arranged to have the refuelling truck waiting for my arrival.

Lesley was also waiting with a favourite sandwich and a soft drink. After a quick visit to the toilet I was back in the air within fifteen minutes, and on my way to Broome with a two-hour forty-five minute flight ahead of me.

About an hour's flying-time out from Broome, flight service on Darwin HF radio advised me that Andre had passed away and offered their condolences, they knew that my mission was now pointless.

I was surprised that the Darwin flight control people were taking such interest in my attempt to bring Andre's wife back to Darwin. I have since revised my thoughts that the Gestapo (flight service) do actually have a heart. I would from now on view these blokes in a much better light.

The landing at Broome airport was a little different from my normal Broome landings. Because of the union AWA strike, as such I had decided on pulling-up right in front of the main airport terminal, (since there was no domestic jet traffic about). A small crowd of people, stranded by the airline strike quickly, surrounded the Cessna all wanting a lift. Some wanted to go south others wanted to go north, whereas I just wanted to get over to the terminal.

I strutted out heading for the terminal entrance, with the jabbering crowd in tow. The daylight was all but gone with only the small arc of a moon. It was going to be a long dark flight back to Darwin. Once inside the terminal I looked around at the many stranded faces. Only then did it strike me, I did not know what Marge looked like. I was pondering over this difficulty when a familiar voice called out.

'Hi-there Neevan, well I'll be a monkey's uncle, am I sure glad to see you, yes-siree.'

I looked in the direction of the familiar voice and sure enough, as I had already guessed, it was Stu Skoglund with his unmistaken broad American accent.

Stuart bounded toward me through the crowd, his right arm swinging empty in a shirtsleeve tied with a knot, and his left arm outstretched ready for a thorough handshake.

Stu had lost his right arm in a very strange accident about a year earlier, and that will most certainly be another great, but sad story to tell.

The sad thing about the accident was Stu is a very experienced pilot, in both helicopter and fixed wing, a true pioneer of the new Australian aerial crop dusting and helicopter cattle-mustering era. This man was a living legend in his own time. Stu's flying career ended when he lost his right arm. You need both arms and legs to drive a helicopter. Stu was in Broome on business, and became stranded just like everybody else when the AWA union called their silly strike.

'Neevan, ya got a spare seat for an ol' flying buddy?'

'Christ what luck am I glad to see you Stu, you can fly the damn Cessna back to Kununurra I could do with a rest, I haven't had much sleep in the last three days.'

'Well siree yah'll know I haven't done much flying in a while, don't know if I can understand all them flash fandangles an stuff in these new type airplanes.'

I assured Stu that he would have no problems with "my little ol' airplane," mimicking his American accent, adding that I would trust his flying anytime. Then I had a thought, Stu might know something of Marge.

'Stu I came to Broome to pick-up a woman whose husband is in Darwin dying of a brain aneurism. I have been sent to get her up to Darwin as soon as possible; she might have mentioned her husband to someone?'

'Yes siree there was a woman who said she was on her way to Darwin to see her dying husband. Then she got this phone call from the hospital saying her husband had already gone, died. She left here in tears with a load of pot smoking flower power people, I'd reckon, maybe say about an hour ago.'

I knew that I must somehow find Marge; as she was still urgently needed in Darwin to resolve all the government paperwork. This being a standard bureaucratic requirement with her husband being dead or alive. I turned to Stu.

'Have you any idea where they might have gone?' I asked.

A loud voice from the crowd answered my question saying.

'She left with a load of no good, pissed-up junkies. They've gone down to Cable beach for a wake or something.'

'For a what,' I had to hear it again.

'A wake, you know, it's the sort of thing the local drugo's do for an excuse to get all tanked up. They light a big fire down on the beach, and dance around it like idiots until they pass out, with luck avoiding falling into the fire. When the tide comes in it puts the fire out, sobers them all up, and at the same time gives them a bath. Some crazy people live here in Broome mate.'

I had to agree. Yes, some people are very strange in Broome. Stu suggested that we should catch a cab down to Cable beach and bring her back.

***

We were very lucky, as just then, a taxi had dropped off another hopeful airline passenger at the airport and we both jumped in the taxi.

'Can you take us to Cable beach?'

'Why you wanna go to da beacha this timea night' the strong accent demanded to know.

'Only younga drugo an ol man perves go down there this time mate.'

I could tell Stu's normal laid-back composure was reaching its limit as he stared eyeball-to-eyeball, nose-to-nose with the taxi driver and said.

'How is it, that everywhere yah go Stateside or Australia, the goddamn cab drivers have so much ta say and always in some damn foreign-fucking Greek language?'

The taxi-driver then replied in a slow voice, to avoid any misunderstanding.

'I ama nota Greek, buta you musta be a Mexican one arma bandita yes?'

Stu then paused for a second; no doubt contemplating the current level of this possible insult. I took this opportunity to cut into this useless exchange of macho bravado, then pointing my finger at the cab driver.

'Your right, Stu is a cranky old bugger, and yes we are looking for a woman, but not in the way you think. I have just flown a light aircraft all the way from Darwin to pick-up a woman whose husband is in hospital dying. A bloke in the Broome terminal said she has gone to Cable beach, taken by a bunch of hippies for a wake. We must find her quickly, and fly her back up to Darwin, and we must leave within the hour.'

The taxi-driver listened carefully scratching the three-day-old stubble on his chin, then after a moment of careful consideration spoke.

'Whata isa wake? Some kinda booze eh? Theya go downa beach I booze or smokea pot and have a fu...'

'I quickly interjected, are you going to give us a bloody lift down there or not?'

This demand brought about a long angry stare, and then he softened a bit, hunched his shoulders as they do. Waving his arms around in the air for the maximum Croatian effect, the cabbie finally declared.

'Okay, Okay we go down there now.'

***

It was easy to find the wake. We could see the large fire on the beach long before we pulled into the small car park. The tide was out with the fire built some sixty metres or more from the shore.

Broome has a beautiful and safe beach with a firm sand base. Cable beach is a long stretch of fine white sand, creating a large very flat coastline in a gentle curve. The advantages are the water is not very deep. You can stand up in the water over fifty metres from the shore.

The disadvantage is the tides in the North are high. Broome has an eight-metre high tide. With this powerful combination, the tide comes in and out a long way, and extremely fast. I could well understand why the local Shire was tolerating such beach parties, as the party always ends when the tide comes in. Usually around midnight and it is probably the safest place to have a fire. With the tide, everything is eventually swept away by nature's most powerful cleaner, salt-seawater.

The time was 7:45pm, just after low tide Moonrise. In three more hours the wake, the fire, and the party will all be under water.

Stu and I strolled across the firm sand towards the fire and the party. I had given the taxi-driver a fifty-dollar note to wait for us; he took the fifty dollars. However, insisted that he come along to see what was going on. Stu and the taxi-driver were not talking to each other, and that suited me fine.

As it turned out, it was just as well the taxi-driver did come along. It was only ten minutes later he had to save us from being beaten-up by some very out-of-it, drugged-up, spaced-out ugly people.

As we approached, the party was in full swing. The large crowd were all sitting or standing in a large circle around the fire, which was burning fiercely. Two men turned around and were obviously having a piss when one noticed our approach, and in a raised voice.

'What the fuck do you lot want, this is a private wake so piss-off.'

By the time we were close enough for normal conversation there were about eight or nine others standing facing us, backlit by the bright fire. This was not looking good at all; we were at a disadvantage, as their faces were in the dark while the fire floodlighted us. However, the menacing way of their stance told me we were not welcome at all. Stu spoke first.

'Howdy there guys, wir looking fir a lady whose just lost her husband. We come all the ways from Darwin ta git her up to her husband's funeral, any yaw seen this fine lady?'

The broad American accent stunned them for a second. Just then, a loud wailing cry started from within the circle, and they all turned around to see what the noise was. That was the first time I had set eyes on Marge Bile.

She had heard Stu mention Andre's funeral and that had set her off crying. I called over to Marge advising that I was Andre's employer. The one who had talked to her on the phone, and could I talk with her for a moment. Just then, a very large hippie with a large threatening voice interrupted my plea.

'The woman don't want to go with you arsehole, she got a phone call and knows her husband's dead. She's having a wake right here, so piss off before we have to convince you to go.'

I looked over to Marge. She was a small slight built woman, sitting cross leg on the sand, holding what looked like a glass of booze in one hand and a large well-lit reefer in the other. Sobbing uncontrollably and was in no state to make any rational decisions. It was obvious these hippies were high, drugged on marijuana or something, and smoked up for a fight. Just then our taxi-driver spoke.

'Eh Violet you gotta listen to dees guys, whata you gonna do tomorrow when the tida commas in ana you all washada away again. This woman a gotta go, do da righta thing ana bury er husband, you understand, what a say Violet?'

I could not believe it. In a stunned immobile stupor, I must have stared at this bloke for a few seconds too long, thinking. Is this blundering big arsehole of a hippie's name really Violet? Stu grabbed my shirt collar, with a quick left hand, pulled my ear next to his mouth, and whispered.

'Now ah's knows what yer thinking Neevan, but ah reckons you should stay low on this gentleman's unfortunate name. Besides, the cab driver is doing real good fir a change.'

The taxi-driver appeared to have some magical influence on Violet, as he quietened down somewhat from bashing us all up. Then offered us a drink out of the bottle of Vodka he was holding. Stu and I declined this offer stating that we were flying, this brought about a strange but knowing look on Violet's face.

I think, he thought, we were advising him that we were high on hard drugs. (Apparently, hard drugs and hard booze do not mix too well; also, to be flying is when you were high.) This awkward moment was short lived as the taxi-driver grabbed the bottle from Violet's stalled outstretched hand, cleaned the neck against his footy shorts, and merrily started swigging down the free booze.

***

Marge was not very happy about going to Darwin; it took me some time to convince her that she should go, even if only out of respect to bury Andre. Both Stu and the Taxi driver looked at me in utter horror… What did I say wrong?

Apparently, I had just put my big foot in it again, as Marge suddenly ceased crying and wailing. Then with clenched fists and a look of rage, announcing loudly it was Andre who had deserted his family. What respect did he have for her?

With the considerable help of Violet, the taxi driver, and Stu, my insensitive damage was eventually repaired. Marge then gradually convinced to change her mind and fly to Darwin. We said our goodbyes to the hippies, hugging one another, shaking hands, and patting backs like old friends.

Back at the airport, a group of people who were trying hard to claim the spare fourth seat on the aircraft followed us across the tarmac hardstand to the Cessna like a flock of seagulls after my last greasy potato chip. The refuelling agent was standing next to the Cessna 182 with the fuel docket in his hand ready for me to sign.

'How did you know I wanted fuel and more to the point how much?' I asked, when the refuelling agent with a smile promptly replied.

'I was advised by flight service in Kununurra you will require fuel urgently and there will be only two people on-board. I waited as long as I could and then decided to fill your

Cessna to the maximum capacity, knowing the 182RG can carry three passengers and full fuel.'

I was amazed that someone at flight service had arranged all of this. They are not tin gods anymore they are indeed gods. Only thing now is with maximum fuel I cannot carry the fourth passenger. I had no problem now, as the very knowledgeable fuelling agent was carefully explaining all these flying limitations in detail to the unhappy group as we climbed aboard the aircraft.

***

We departed Broome at 8:15pm and climbed to nine thousand feet to get the best tail winds. Then setting up the autopilot I then handed over control to Stu who had no problems at all flying the Cessna with only one arm. His only concern was the altitude and the cold.

'God-damn Neevan, why-in-hell we got to fly so high? I've been flying choppers at no higher than three thousand feet for more than forty years; this is high for a little airplane. Another thang, it was twenty-six degrees on the ground at Broom. Up here it's a cold eight degrees outside, I'm freezing my balls off, and the heater don't work any too well.'

I let Stu ramble on without a reply until he just gave-up complaining, or thought I was asleep. We were getting the forecast twelve-knot tailwind at nine-thousand feet. Giving us better ground speed and fuel efficiency, which made it all worthwhile.

Stu was correct, with the cabin heater flap closed off, there was no hot air entering the cabin. I do not trust exhaust system cabin air heaters. One small undetectable leak and you could end-up dead from carbon monoxide poisoning. This was one of my pet light aircraft grumbles. I would rather be cold and alive, than warm and dead. Did I get that the right way around?

***

With about two hour's solid sleep, I felt a good deal better. Landing Kununurra at around 12:45am in the morning, this was now Monday. Flight service Kununurra had advised the refuelling truck would pull up to refuel on shut-down, all arranged again, and in the middle of the night. Stu and I shook hands as he thanked me for the ride, and then wished me luck for what was going on in Darwin. Lesley had arrived with more food and drinks, and shortly after Marge and I were back in the air again and on the way to Darwin.

The flight to Darwin was exceptionally smooth, I like flying at night as I find night flying very peaceful. I thought this was probably a good time to have a talk with Marge, who had quietened down after a long sleep. At least she had stopped crying.

'Marge I am very sorry about Andre, he had become a good friend and for a man of only forty-eight to die so young.' Marge looked confused.

'Andre is fifty-nine. He would have been sixty next month why do you say he's forty-eight?'

My look of startled surprise suddenly caught Marge's attention.

'Well that's what he had written down as his date of birth on his job application form.' I blundered, and thought to myself, hell, there is more secrets about this bloke than the KGB have in the Kremlin. What can happen next... is there more. Well I was soon to find out... there was.

I poked around with covert questions as to the possible reasons for Andre running away from his wife and family. Marge could not understand why he had left, and so suddenly. It would appear that in the beginning Andre was a loyal and faithful husband. A man who had always looked after his family, paid his bills, and always had a good job.

Apparently, Marge woke-up one morning, and he was... well, just gone. He left no note of goodbye, or telephoned later to explain things. The Police traced Andre to a mining company in the far north, where he advised them he did not want to have contact with his wife.

Further interrogation revealed another major looming problem. Without mentioning any names, my amateur detective questioning soon discovered that Marge had no idea about Holly, or that she even existed.

***

Was this some sort of male menopause or mid-life crisis thing? Do we blokes really go all funny at a certain age or time in our lives?

This was becoming a worrying thought to me, as I am in the radio communications business, and I am married, and I am a bloke. Could this matrimonial disaster happen to me? To one day to wake-up and just walk out of your home, your wife, your family's life, and your life-long friends.

At that time, this type of man behaviour was considered a bit unusual, or not talked about. However, in the years ahead I was to experience a few of my close friends go down this exact same path... Who will be next?

Intelligent people doing un-intelligent things in the expectation of a new life before it all became too late. On the other hand, perhaps a new attempt at...love; or just to get out of the steady painful daily family grind... Could this be the reason?

Possibly, the simple answer may be, that for a change somebody else was listening... taking an interest... offering a promise of another life... who knows. Well I do know this from experience, once these people start down the path of change; they never ever turn back to their old life and family.

***

I can hear you thinking. Yes, you know someone who has gone down this path... Well consider this... Just how long was Andre suffering with a brain tumour, the cause of his aneurism? Did Andre know he had a serious problem, and that it was most likely terminal? Was this his way to reduce his family's loss and stress? Was this his way to see a bit more of life before he left this life and present world... forever?

Chapter Six:

Two Wives Meet

I thought to myself Niven old boy, we have a disaster of major catastrophic proportions about to unfold before our very eyes. The real wife Marge is about to meet the pretend wife Holly, for the very first time in around twenty minutes time. Sadly over their deceased common interest, their man Andre. I spent that last short time prior to my landing in Darwin trying to think-up something intelligent to say, but nothing came to mind.

The landing at Darwin was as they say uneventful, I wish I could say the same for what was about to happen. Flight service as before had directed my aircraft to where Deso had a car waiting, it was now 3:45am in the morning Darwin local time, I could see Deso standing hunched over and grim, leaning on the front of his car. I craned my neck over the high instrument panel of my aircraft to see if Deso had brought Holly with him, to my relief Holly was not in sight.

I introduced Des to Marge; Deso offered his condolences, which started Marge off crying again. Des suggested that Marge should get into the car. I advised that I would go tie-down and lock-up the Cessna, and for the first time ever Des eagerly said he would give me a hand... I was naturally suspicious.

Walking across to the Cessna aircraft Des opened up with what was on his mind.

'I can tell you now Nibsey, you are in a right pile of shit, or should I say "we" are both in a right shit situation.' At that brief meeting with Marge, one thing was obvious to Deso, and he made the problem absolute and clear.

'Nibsey, when are you going to tell Marge about Holly? I figure you only have only about ten minutes to do it, because that's how long it's going to take us to drive back to my place. Oh and by the way Nibsey, Holly is totally pissed out of her mind again. This time on my gin.'

Des was right; this meeting was going to be something spectacular, I needed to come up with an answer. I then advised Des of my only plan.

'I have thought long and hard about this very moment Deso, and I must admit I don't have any real plan at all other than hoping that Holly can pull off one of her magnificent miracles.'

I could see Des was not impressed with this plan, adding.

'Well I must say Nibsey; this will certainly be worth watching. Holly is in mourning over Andre's death and has been drinking solid all day, I can tell you now she's totally pissed out of her mind. With a bit of luck Holly will be sound asleep by the time we get back to the house.'

That, I thought would give us about another eight hours or so before we had to face the two wives problem. I then mumbled barely audible.

'Deso, I most certainly hope you're right about Holly sleeping off the booze as I could do with some sleep myself.'

Des gripped the edge of the high Cessna wing with both hands, and then looked out over the massive Darwin airfield in some sort of subdued mood. He then opened his mind; again, rumbling on in his deep gravel voice.

'You know Nibsey; two days ago I was in my nice well-stocked bar at home, enjoying a quiet drink with myself. I was just minding my own business when I received a call from you for some help. Now my house is a hotel, filled with people I don't even know, visiting some bloke in hospital who has since died, who I don't know.

I have been a taxi service around the clock, then glancing at his watch, and I really do mean a full twenty-four hours.

Deso sighed with gloom; in about ten minute's time, this dead blokes two wives are going to meet up for the first time at my place. God knows what they are going to say to each other, or what they will do.' Deso paused and looked up at the bright tropical stars and sighed again...

'Oh and by the way Nibsey, I have just arranged Andre's funeral for 10am Tuesday morning, to be held at the Catholic Church burial ground. The service will be conducted by Father Tom, and another thing; I have paid for the lot because I just found out Holly is flat bloody broke.'

Des was right again, the world was using his good-natured friendship almost to the level of abuse. I had to offer some reassuring response to bolster his low mental mood.

'Deso, you know that this Catholic Priest Father Tom likes the booze, he's always pissed; a very nice guy but a bit unreliable... will he turn up to bury Andre?'

Des without a hint of surprise rumbled back a reply.

'I know that Nibsey, but he's also cheap, and he is the only Priest available at this short notice. Anyway,' he continued, 'if Father Tom has a drink with us on the Monday night, then we can be sure to get him to the Tuesday-morning funeral service on time.'

We both thought that a good idea and strolled over to the car in silence. We were deep in thought, with not another word spoken on the short trip back to Deso's house.

I was about to say something about being sorry to Des having placed him in such an odd situation. Paying for a funeral, for a bloke he never knew or had even met alive. Then remembering we did have to consider we had Marge in the car, Andre's real wife. Thinking it best to remain quiet, very shortly things were going to get difficult enough.

***

As we pulled into Deso's carport, I was surprised to see that Holly and Dawn were still up. In fact, they were sitting around the pool drinking and chatting like old friends discussing politics or the latest fashions. This was it, the moment we all dreaded. I introduced Marge to Dawn and then to Holly.

253

'Marge this is Dawn, Deso's wife, the lady who organises all the good parties around here, and this is Holly a very good friend of Andre.'

They all shook hands politely however, I did detect the fleeting exchange of eyes between Marge and Holly. The unmistakeable look of female suspicion was on Marge's face; a look that did not go undetected by Holly, who in true form saved the moment by announcing...

'Anyone for a drink,' then with a hint of a smile, 'I am sure that you have finished all your flying for today Niven, usual OP rum and coke?'

Then Deso slipped in a magnificent verbal manoeuvre to shift the centre of attention firmly back onto Holly.

'Nibsey and I will go get the drinks Holly; you girls just stay here and get to know each other.'

***

Braced at Deso's well stocked bar, being just a few steps away from the pool, we could clearly hear Holly move into her full crisp verbal swing.

'Marge, I would suppose that you are wondering what I have to do with Andre. Andre and I met in Mount Newman. At that time, I was the Newman Social Club manager, and Andre would come in for a drink every now and again. We were just two lonely people looking for some adult company.'

Deso whispered in my ear.

'That's a good one Nibsey, "two lonely people" and "adult company," haven't heard it put like that before? This is great; Holly's doing all right for someone who has been flat-out on the piss all day.'

Just then, Marge found some courage to speak up.

'Didn't Andre tell you he was married? He never wrote or called me, he must have said something to you?'

Holly smiled and reached out to hold Marge's hand, looking grief-stricken and sad, with a sorrowful look on her face, then with a passionate low voice Holly began.

'My dear Marge. In the northern mining towns, people do not enquire as to a person's past or background. You see my dear, it is not considered done, or for that matter the polite thing.

254

Yeah I thought to myself, Holly's spot-on right; ask any questions in a bar along those lines would normally get you a swift punch in the face. Not polite was an excellent description for Marge to get to grips with. Holly continued in her sorrowful voice.

'We have all suffered a great loss in the passing of Andre. I do not presume to imagine, the greater loss you have as Andre's dear wife, I offer you my deepest sympathy and condolences.'

That did it, Marge and Dawn burst out into tears. Holly was hugging Marge, looking over Marge's shoulder at Deso and I standing in the bar doorway with amazed looks on our faces, drinks un-touched in hand. Then Holly gave us both a knowing wink. What a woman, what a performance... what a day.

Deso made an audible sigh of relief, suggesting we should all get some sleep as it was now 5:30am on this Monday morning. Adding that the paperwork for Andre's funeral (which Deso had also arranged), must be sorted out long before the funeral time of 10am Tuesday morning.

Holly and I slept on camp stretcher beds (note: separate camp beds) in the downstairs bar area, while Marge got the spare bedroom upstairs. I could not get to sleep because of Holly's loud snoring, but finally did drift off in utter sleep deprived exhaustion, and an alcohol induced coma.

The sharp voice penetrated my brain like a knife. Holly who bright as a button, was demanding to know how many eggs I wanted for breakfast as she rudely awakened me.

As the bright light of day penetrated my eyes, and my head started to pound about last nights, or was it still today's intake of OP rum, I managed a squint at my watch. It was 11:30am. I then managed a feeble protest.

'Holly its 11:30, its lunchtime not breakfast, I was cut off in mid-sentence by Holly's rapier sharp tongue.

'Come along Niven, we will not wait all day, it is still am therefore breakfast is in order. Lunch will be at 2pm and that is a long way off.'

Holly proceeded to rip the sheet of me with one hand while offering me a welcome cold orange juice with other.

Just as well, I had my trusty Speedos on, not that it would have bothered Holly as she had already turned and was halfway out the door with a parting order.

'I will cook you two eggs, sunny side up. Do not keep everybody waiting.'

This last comment locked in my dull pounding brain. "Don't keep everybody waiting," were all the others up, and about? I did some simple mathematics using my fingers. We; or should I say I, had had about six hours sleep, less one hour because of Holly's snoring.

I was not very with it, or running on all cylinders when I climbed the stairs to the main house. Sitting at the table eating breakfast was a sad looking Marge. Deso and Dawn had already gone to work earlier, and apparently, Des was due back soon. I could tell that Marge was in about the same alcoholic withdrawal state as me. The only person who was un-affected and full of go was Holly, who had just placed in front of me a large plate of greasy bacon, eggs and sausage.

'Get that into you my dear, we have a full day of things to do. Desmond will be back soon, and I have promised him you will be ready. It would seem by Desmond's comments that he thinks you can never get to any place on time. According to Des you suffer from a profound punctuality deficiency.'

Not wishing to respond to that last comment, I struck up a conversation with Marge while poking the sausages around my plate, hoping Holly would not notice that her cooking effort was in vain.

'Did you get much sleep Marge? I had a hell of a time getting off to sleep myself; someone was chain sawing a tree near-by.'

'I slept very well; I was quite surprised, although I do have a terrible headache now. Holly has given me some Panadol.'

Marge was sounding OK, well better than she looked. Just then, Deso burst into the kitchen.

'Crikey you're up Nibsey, Holly and I have been up for hours. We have to get going; and be down at the Hospital within the next hour. Marge will need to identify Andre before they will release Andre's body to the funeral parlour.

We should get going right now. Marge you will need to bring all your documents, marriage certificate, and any other ID to claim Andre's remains.'

This was a bit too fast for Marge, and she burst out crying again. All this talk about funerals and identifying Andre's remains was just too much. Holly was comforting Marge as if she were old friend, when I distinctly and clearly heard among Marge's faint wet sobbing.

'I haven't brought my marriage certificate or anything else. Nobody told me I needed to bring them.'

Deso pulled me to one side and rumbled into my ear.

'She's fucking kidding, isn't she?'

I said I don't think so.

'This will really stuff things up; everything's been bloody-well arranged. The funeral parlour people are going to pick-up Andre's body from the Hospital at 2pm. That's less than two hours' time from now.'

***

All this dead body claim documentation and hospital protocol were well beyond me. I had never been at the other end-of-life funeral- arrangement stage before. On the other hand, Deso and Dawn had much experience in these sad matters. One might say the ultimate disadvantage in having such a large circle of old friends.

One thing I did know though; was that in dealing with government rules, regulations, and bureaucracy, there was always another way to get things done. I suggested that we continue with our existing plan and go talk to the Darwin Hospital administration. With a little luck, the Hospital people might just show some sympathy for this grim situation… well you never know it was worth a try.

Chapter Seven:

Getting the Body

For some unknown reason, the Hospital front desk was busy at midday, reminding me of a supermarket checkout, and just about as impersonal. We were in a small line of regular professional hospital queuers, shuffling along toward the reception desk. A voice called out...

'Next.' Deso, being a local tried to win over the only grumpy clerk behind the counter with his Northern Territory charm.

'We've come about Mr Andre Bile,' turning and indicating the small woman at his side. 'This is his wife Marge Bile, she has just arrived all the way from Perth, and'...

Deso was expertly interrupted by the no nonsense blunt desk clerk.

'How do you spell the surname?' asked the disinterested senior receptionist, staring at her computer screen. It became obvious to us all that Des had no idea how to spell Andre's surname. With fingers poised over the keyboard, the senior clerk was rapidly losing her patience. From alongside him a small voice said...

'B i l e' spelt out Marge.'

'What's his room number?' droned the receptionist.

Marge was lost; she had no idea what room number her husband was occupying.

'Room one, one, two my dear,' responded Holly in a firm businesslike manner.

'Not any longer, Mr Andre Bile is dead. It says here, that he is in the morgue, chiller-casket number thirty-seven. You will now need to go to the Hospital administration, Patient Discharge. The PD is down that corridor over there and then second door to your right.'

I thought to myself, that is interesting, these people still call dead people patients, and well... they even discharge them.

Marge started crying again as Holly put her arm around Marge's shoulders, we found our way down the long corridor to an office with a sign "Patient Discharge." The door was open, and led into a small waiting room with about six people sitting in the standard Hospital uncomfortable plastic chairs.

Two senior matron-like, no-nonsense looking ladies staffed the discharge desk. Behind the desk, as if to form some sort of no-go checkpoint were two, floor to ceiling, glass offices. I could see two slim weedy looking blokes sitting at desk's trying to look busy; Holly stepped up to the desk with Marge in tow, and in her crisp voice.

'We are here to claim the remains of Mr Andre Bile.'

'How do you spell the surname' asked the matron in a well-practiced business-like manner.'

'B i l e' spelt out Holly, and before you look into your silly computer and tell us that Mr Bile is dead and in your mortuary, I will advise you that we have come to take delivery of the remains within the hour.'

The matron looked steely into Holly's eyes, as a woman of position and power; she was not accustomed to being spoken down-to in this manner. Then in a firm tone, she demanded.

'Are you a relation of the deceased, as we will require full documented proof of the relationship, and then a physical identification of the deceased before releasing the remains, and then only to a registered undertaker.'

***

Holly was an easy match for this woman. Deso and I took a step back from the desk, Des folding his arms, turned his head, and whispered into my ear loud enough for everybody to hear.

'I told you this would happen Nibsey; Holly cut into Deso's loud whispering with a volley of crisp English to the matron.

'My dear madam, I have already introduced to you the wife of the deceased. Again, this distressed woman is Mrs Bile and we are here under extraordinary circumstances. Your assistance would be most appreciated in completing the release formalities for Mr Bile as soon as possible.'

My attention was on Holly's superb performance; I then noticed that one of the weedy looking office clerks was now standing up staring out of the glass office toward the reception desk. A big smile erupted across his face as he opened the office door.

'Well g'day, Desmond Nudl, I have not seen you in a while what are you doing at the Hospital Discharge desk commonly known as the rectum around here?'

All the office conversation and bickering instantly stopped. Deso tilted his head back at the required angle so that he could look through the right lens of his trifocal glasses to identify the figure, then in a gravel voice.

'Hi Bluey how long have you been working at the Hospital? I haven't seen you… oh, must be almost a year, well not since your wedding. Anyway how is Wendy, oh and we are here to pick-up a body, a dead body.'

We all looked at each other in horror; was there any other kind of body, it just somewhat just slipped out in Deso's laid-back, patter of conversation. However, it was more than enough to start Marge crying again. Bluey was quick to sum up the situation, and advised the now grim looking matron.

'Esmeralda I will look after this problem for you,' then waving his arms like windmills invited us all into his tiny glass office.

As I was entering the office, following behind Holly, the matron and I distinctly heard her say; "I once had a dog named Esmeralda, and she was a bitch too."

The two girls sat on tiny matching chairs in front of the small desk, as there was no room for any further chairs. Deso and I stood behind like footmen.

***

Bluey was a nice bloke, about thirty-four with a pleasant second-hand car dealer's manner. He was completely bald so I had assumed that having the name Bluey; came from a time when he did have hair, and it must have been red.

My fragile attention was riveted on his highly polished head. Then most fascinated by the habit of young blokes who are bald by choice, or natural events, to polish their baldhead with what I believe was... bee's wax. Yes that is right, bee's wax. This, I must admit did give Bluey a very distinct, polished bowling-ball type look.

With the introductions completed, Bluey took up a long-time no-see matey conversation with Des.

'Been a while mate, Wendy and I have been divorced almost a year now Des.' Deso butted in...

'Christ Bluey, you've only been married a bloody year?'

Still smiling, Bluey continued under full steam.

'It was all Wendy's fault Deso; you see she broke a major matrimonial vow, the most important one. She changed her mind in not allowing me to go out with my old girlfriends, ha ha ha.'

Nobody had joined him in his own silly laughter, his face rapidly slipped back to hospital business mode.

'Anyway what can I do to help you serious looking people?'

Holly and I looked at each other with the same thought, thinking this to be highly amusing, breaking into a quiet chuckle. Deso either missed the line or was not amused at Bluey's early matrimonial break-up.

Deso then went on and explained what had happened to poor Andre, delicately leaving out the bit about the two wives. He then reached the critical part that Marge did not have her marriage certificate with her to claim her husband's remains. Then Deso hit him with the immediate urgency, the funeral parlour would be collecting Andre's remains in around forty-five minute's time and that the funeral was booked for 10am sharp tomorrow morning.

Bluey listened politely then raised an eyebrow at Marge saying…

'You do I suppose have a driving license with you?'

Marge rummaged through her handbag and produced a West Australian driving license, passing the license over to Bluey who studied it for a moment.

'All we need to know, and hope for now; is can you find your marriage documents at home?' and then announced in a firm voice.

'Anyway, this will get us started. Now please listen to me carefully Mrs Bile, you should now phone someone at your home that can get access to your marriage documents.

The next step is to take the documents to the nearest Police station and have them photocopied and the copy signed and witnessed as a copy of the original. I will give you a fax number and my direct phone number so the Police can contact me.'

Bluey handed Marge the phone and a note pad with his details. Holly then helped Marge get things going. Marge rang her home in Perth and got down to quickly talking to someone at home.

I thought what a change in attitude and assistance, and then the old saying came to mind "It's not what you know; it's who you know that's important in this world." Then I thought that saying would no longer apply to poor Andre.

***

Deso proved that he has friends in all the right and high places. I was wondering just how high, as the next part of this story will be a call on God's business. These gloomy thoughts interrupted by Bluey talking very softly with practiced emotion to Marge.

'Mrs Bile, would you please come with me as we must carry out a formal identification of the deceased.'

Marge started crying again, Holly said she would go with her and they all stood up and followed Bluey out the door. Deso and I declined the offer to view Andre, and decided to stay in the office. We sat down on the vacant chairs and looked at each other. Deso had his grim face on again. I had thought that things were going well, for a change. Deso soon fixed that.

'Nibsey; the undertakers will be here at the Hospital in a few minutes to pick-up Andre's body, I don't think that even Bluey would be game enough to release the body without all the right documentation fixed-up. If they don't get the body now, there won't be a funeral tomorrow, and Marge will miss her flight back to Perth, it goes at mid-day, that's if the Hostess strike ends by tonight, as they agreed. It's all very messy Nibsey.'

Bluey and the wives were soon back, they could only have been gone ten minutes. Holly looked sad and Marge was still crying into a large handkerchief. I looked at Bluey, thinking, has he got any further information on the faxed marriage documents yet, and blurted out.

'Well how did it go?' enquiring had the documents arrived yet, to which Marge replied.

'Andre doesn't look very well at all.' Marge had totally miss-understood my meaning.

This was all too much, and too stupid for Holly to stay quiet.

'My dear Marge, what would one expect at this time, the man is after all well and truly fucking dead?'

I wished I had my camera and recorder. The look on Bluey's face, complete with dropped jaw, with the office fluoro lights reflecting off his very polished head was a sight to hold in my memory for some time. Bluey soon reclaimed his formal Hospital administration composure.

'Ladies please, have a little respect for the recently deceased; after all I'm sure that the funeral parlour can improve on Mr Bile's looks, they can work wonders, true artists you know, given the chance.

Now it was our turn to be startled. Deso was standing behind the wives and had a large smile spread across his face. He obviously knew Bluey far better than I thought; the man was having a gigantic "tongue in cheek" laugh at the situation. I then detected a small curl at the edges of Holly's mouth being the restrained effort not to smile. Marge continued to cry into her large handkerchief... I was starting too really like this Bluey bloke... he had a certain North Australian style about him.

With the critical moment of outright embarrassment now saved, as just then Esmeralda the large frumpy matron breezed into the office with a handful of fax sheets.

'I believe you are waiting on these.' placing the papers on the desk in front of Bluey, still eyeing daggers of hate at Holly. The matron continued.

'Oh by the way, there is an undertaker at the pick-up bay, requesting to claim the remains of Mr Andre Bile, what shall I do?'

Bluey scanned through the fax documents and announced that all was in good enough order. Looking up he said to Esmeralda.

'Would you please bring in the release note and the original death certificate and I will sign Mr Bile out.' Then turning to Marge,

'Well now, that was a close thing; I do hope this brings all your funeral arrangements back on track again.'

I noticed on hearing this comment Deso had decided to look at the ceiling with a clenched jaw look. Bluey had no idea that Deso had made all of the arrangements in regards to Andre, including paying for all his funeral costs.

Considering that Deso had never even spoken or even met Andre until two days ago, this must go down as some sort of funeral record. In fairness, Holly did agreed to, and eventually did repay Deso for all the funeral costs. Up to this point, all Marge had managed to do for Andre was cry.

Bluey stood up behind his desk, thus performing the standard bureaucratic sign that this matter was now finished. Then in a well-practiced move skirted around the desk and opened the door inviting us all to leave.

I had seen this cunning move many times before, mostly carried out by my Bank Manager when I was applying for a loan, he used it frequently. I figured they must all get the same exit training. We all trundled out the office, Deso was last to leave and I heard Bluey say as Deso went by.

'I assume there's going to be the usual wake, what time shall I get to your place Deso?'

Bluey knew the Darwin rules verbatim. Deso and Dawn were known for their good back-yard parties, and this situation did indeed give some form of legitimate excuse for holding such an event. Deso replied in a rumbling voice, after consulting his watch.

Christ! It's gone 2:30pm Bluey, I've missed my bloody lunch over this; we'll be starting the wake as soon as we get back. Call around my place after you knock off work.'

Deso dropped us all off at his home then went on to his work at Port Darwin Motors. Deso had not spent much time at work in the last few days; it was just as well he owned the company.

Chapter Eight:

The lonely Funeral

I thought this would be a great time to catch up on some sleep, and then a phone call from my Kununurra office soon threw that idea out. I spent the next two hours running around Darwin shopping for the office and sorting out my many business problems.

I had borrowed Dawn's car, backing out of the carport, I noticed the three girls were in deep discussion sitting around the pool. On my return, they were still in the same position except the mood was considerably merrier, and about six other people had arrived, it was obvious they had a good start on the wake.

Holly was up to her old tricks again. Avoid any bad news and unhappiness; her strategy was simple drink, be merry, and tell many funny stories. Holly firmly believed that time and laughter heals all troubles. One of her favourite sayings was, "You know my dear, time can fix anything. There are people out there in the world that now consider Hitler was not such a bad chappie after all. Then there was that Idi Amin fellow; well... now it appears he was just a misunderstood murdering tyrant."

Another Holly well-used saying was "Drink, eat, laugh, and fornicate today, for nobody knows what tomorrow may bring. After all, there is a chance we may all be dead." Holly, as ever, was correct about life's demanding trials and tribulations. As within eighteen months of this day, she too would be dead.

Holly was a victim of breast cancer. She had kept her cancer a close secret. I have calculated that Holly must have known she had breast cancer long before Andre's death. It is almost as if she knew what her future would be, then deciding to live what life she had left to the full... and she did.

***

As I pulled into the carport, Bluey stuck his head out of Deso's well stocked bar and yelled out.

'Your late mate, Holly told me you drink OP rum and coke, I had one sitting on the bar for a while waiting, so had to drink it, save it going off.'

By the look of Bluey, he had without doubt downed a few OP's being in good spirits, (excuse the pun.) Deso was cranking up the bar-b-cue as I looked at my watch it had gone 5pm, the light was fading fast; another tropical night had begun. I could see that this was going to be another long hard night... I must be getting old.

From what I can still recall, Andre's wake was from my early memories of the event, and as agreed by all, a total success. This was expected with a Des and Dawn show, I noticed that Deso had brought along to the wake Father Tom, the charming Irish Catholic Priest... all was going as planned.

However, his well-made plans were soon derailed. Father Tom being a very likable and very much in demand party guest, was soon quietly spirited away around 11pm to attend yet another boozy party... this was after all Darwin.

***

Holly was busy plying her skills as a fully qualified party host. She was in a deep meaningful discussion with Dawn and Bluey, and a small crowd of attentive listeners. They were discussing the merits and finer points of having a good wake.

Dawn had made the now obvious point, that you normally have a wake after the funeral not before. Holly soon put Dawn onto the right and correct thinking path.

'Dawn my dear, I have had a wake for people that were not even dead yet. Indeed, the person we were sending off was also at the party, enjoying themselves.'

Standing up and raising her glass, Holly then made a solemn toast to Andre.

'My new and beautiful friends, may we all hope that Andre will find a better life in the afterlife, which will no doubt be a hell of a job for whoever runs the pubs and party things up there?'

The party crowd broke into spontaneous clapping and cheers.

'Hear, hear, to Andre,' the party crowd chorused, all of whom had never even seen, or for that matter, heard of Andre Bile before this day. Holly still standing and I must add, still in full control of her alcoholic stance, declared that the wake was dying in the arse. Requiring a jolt of positive action to get the wake…, awake.

Holly then promptly stripped down to her bra and panties; took a bulging staggering run and bombed-dived into the pool, covering everybody looking on, frozen in amazement with volumes of water.

Deso, who was unfortunately was standing close by the pool was not quick enough to avoid the sudden drenching, rumbled something about a fifty five year old woman acting like an eighteen year old kid, and that he has just lost about thirty-dollars' worth of valuable chlorine water out his pool. Holly surfaced and advised that anybody found to be dry on both the inside and outside was a party pooper.

The wake went on at full steam ahead until the early hours of the morning, with everybody ending up in the pool. Surprisingly including Marge, whom I noticed had stopped crying; then again, just how would one know.

However, she was obviously enjoying the good company, and was now more than a little pissed and giggly long before the night ended. Observing all this I a thought, Holly can work her magic with anyone and everyone… even the grieving original wife of her lost, now deceased man.

***

This was going to be bad. I was smart enough to know that I should stay asleep until all the pain had gone. A sharp high-pitched voice was penetrating my sleeping safe world… I know that voice. There was no escape, being then rudely launched into the awakening world by a bright and chirpy Holly; fully dressed, complete with make-up, and looking like she was going out to dinner. Then I remembered... today is the day we bury Andre.

My head was pounding again, as Holly handed me two Panadol with a glass of water.

'Come along Niven, I have left you until last, it is now 8:50am. We are all due at the cemetery at ten minutes to ten, which is in less than an hour's time.'

A cold shower made little difference to the way I felt. The kitchen scene was grim, with everybody clutching a cup of strong black coffee, looking very hung-over except for some unknown reason Holly. Marge was in a bad way, looking like she was about to join Andre.

In a weak attempt at conversation, I asked Deso if Father Tom had called to confirm the arrangements were okay for today. Trying to keep a low key to my concerns that the priest may in fact not turn up for the funeral at all.

'Dunno Nibsey, Father Tom doesn't have a phone or a car; he's hard to get in touch with unless he is at the cloisters or the church... or the pub. We'll just have to turn up at the cemetery and hope for the best.'

Dawn decided to stay home and clean up the party mess. The drive to the cemetery was in silence mostly because we were all so hung-over. We all trundled into the small courtyard of the even smaller chapel.

To everyone's relief, Father Tom suddenly appeared in the doorway. Eyes screwed up against the bright tropical sun but smiling as usual. Then my relief turned to concern as Father Tom quickly reached out and grabbed the doorframe for support; Father Tom was still pissed, he could hardly stand up.

The priest looked like shit. His eyes now closed as if in prolonged prayer, he had been out all night on the booze. He needed a shower, and had a three-day-old beard. Deso walked up to Father Tom and had a quiet chat. We all leaned forward to listen to Deso's loud whispering.

'How should we do this Father? I don't think Andre was a Catholic and I haven't asked for a service of any sort.' Then he looked around adding in panicky surprise. 'And where the hell is Andre's casket?'

Father Tom's eyes flickered opened a little in the harsh light, replying in his soft Irish brogue with painful squinting eyes.

'Now don't you be worrying atall atall Desmond; every'ting has been taken care of. I had been to thinking you not having enough people for the bearers and all that, I had the boy's take the casket already ta the gravesite.'

Gathering some divine strength Father Tom then launched himself off the doorframe into the Chapel front yard, staggering a few steps… Then added a few late instructions.

'Now; if you will all be just taken ta following me behind about five yards, and I will lead you all ta the graveside.'

Father Tom went about his Godly business and prepared a holy gadget that I do not know the name of; but it is a metal caged ball on a short chain and filled with a smoky fire. The Priest set out down the road flanked by tombstones swinging the metal ball full of fire, smoke billowing out while he slowly walked chanting some sort of prayer in Latin.

We quickly fell in behind Father Tom at the regulation five yards as requested, the two wives walking ahead of Deso and me. None of us including the Priest wore a hat or thought to bring an umbrella. At this early hour of ten in the morning, the punishing tropical sun was determined to beat my hangover into submission. As we were strolling along the hot dusty path, Deso rumbled a few encouraging words into my ear.

'I don't know how were going to lower the casket Nibsey. The girls won't be much help, Tom's still pissed, and I got a bad back?'

I was thinking with my slick mathematics that only left just me. Trudging along in the heat, I was trying to figure out how I would lower Andre's casket.

We need not have worried, as when we reached the gravesite, the casket was already in the ground. I noticed two grinning Aboriginal gravediggers leaning on their shovels a discrete distance away under the shade of a large tree.

Father Tom took up his position at the head of the grave with Marge and me looking across the grave at Deso and Holly, it was now a little after 10am and the sun was blistering hot on my pounding head. The local temperature, I guessed was around thirty-two degrees. I could now understand why the two Aboriginal gravediggers were standing under a nice leafy shade tree.

Father Tom signalled the beginning with a stooping swoop to grab a handful of sand, and a steadying casting wave of the fireball. We all bowed our heads in respect, looking down on Andre's plain casket.

I was thinking to myself, the casket was obviously a budget model, no French polish or brass handles seen. This was difficult, looking down I was feeling a bit sad and sentimental as I had only known Andre only a short time and had grown to like him. This was a sad and very basic ending to a fine man's life.

Father Tom resumed his praying chant at the same time swinging his metal fireball which was billowing smoke quite nicely now. Then came the slow sad bit; with Tom scattering sand on Andre's coffin, while reciting "earth to earth, dust to dust."

Just then, a loud SHIT shattered my sombre thoughts! Then a clanking thud as Farther Tom's swinging ball of smoke left his grip. Falling apart, and tumbling down onto Andre's casket, spreading what looked like well alight bar-b-cue fire starters all over Andre. Everybody was startled with Father Tom running around cursing and wailing.

'Oh my be-Jesus, I only borrowed this, I have-ta get it back for a christening at two o'clock ta-day'

Marge burst out crying again; Deso, Holly, and I burst out into fits of uncontrollable laughter. The two Aboriginal gravediggers, who must have seen the lot, whooped in loud laughter and began rolling about the ground in stitches.

Father Tom saw the funny side of the situation and joined the infectious laughter with tears streaming down his face, then announced in his best sober Irish voice.

'Well I do hope Andre sees tis as a terrible error, and we're not at all trying to send him ta hell.'

With that comment, the entire side-splitting episode of laughter started all over again. Now everybody was crying, crying with laughter, which was most un-befitting at a funeral. I think Andre had set us all up; he was most likely having a good last laugh himself. Still laughing, Deso had found an old rusty star picket near-by with a bit of wire attached to the end.

We spent the next ten minutes fishing out all the bits of Father Tom's ball of fire from Andre's grave. Father Tom then reassembled his ball of fire with enough bits of smoking ash to provide the required holy smoke. He then proceeded with the funeral service amid restrained laughter and broad smiles.

It must have looked a sad lonely sight to Andre. His boss standing there looking across his grave at his mistress Holly, who was standing next to his real wife Marge. She was facing a man called Desmond, who she and her husband had never met or knew, existed. A man who had ultimately paid for everything, including his funeral conducted in mumbling Latin by a very nice, but very pissed Irish Catholic Priest.

We all said our last goodbyes to Andre and walked slowly back to the car, thanking Father Tom for his excellent and most memorable service.

Deso said it was a funeral service he would never forget and will always remember it to the end of his days, I must admit, I had to agree with him.

Nobody spoke on the way back to Deso's house. Marge had stopped crying and requested another Panadol she was still hung-over, and not fully recovered from the wake.

Back at the house, it was a time to reflect on all that had happened in such a short time. Marge had quickly learnt the rules, as she never did ask Holly any direct personal questions about her relationship with her husband. Holly, on the other hand never pursued any questions or details on why Andre left his family, or about his estranged relationship with his wife and children.

At Darwin airport, we all saw Marge off to Perth, (strangely, it was the first AWA jet flight out of Darwin since the beginning of the flight attendants strike.) Deso dropped Holly and me off at the light aircraft area. Departing Darwin in the Cessna back to Kununurra without saying a word during the ninety-minute flight.

That Darwin airport farewell was the last I ever saw or heard of Marge Bile, no one kept in touch with Andre's wife.

***

Many years later while in Darwin on business, I tried to find Andre's grave, unfortunately without success, nobody had left a marker... We are born, we live, and we die. Did we contribute something useful? Were we leaving behind a better world than when we arrived? Were we loved... will we be missed or remembered?

I still remember Andre and Holly... and now, so will you.

---- The End ----

Part Five: The curse of gold

Chapter One:

The bent Crucible

Since before recorded time, gold has been one of man's most desired collectibles. Murders have been committed and many wars waged over the possession of this yellow metal gold.

It has been often said and also written in the ancient scrolls, that gold has its own power over the possessor, the one who holds this yellow metal; a strange power never fully understood. Yet time and history has proved that a power of some unknown force may indeed exist.

These stories are about the mystical and terrifying power of gold and the consequence of this power for all humans that choose to seek and eventually possess this metal.

It is written in the earliest surviving scrolls that gold has had many owners, and no masters; and known to man as the first metal. Safe only when it remains undiscovered.

This first metal clearly describes gold as our human civilisations first interaction, and use with a metal.

As for many owners. That is simply the fact that gold is a highly valued collectible, changing hands and owners many times, as gold will always outlive man.

Then we move on to the most interesting anomaly of all, undiscovered gold. Could this be the very time, when gold has its strongest and mysterious powers? A time while gold is still deep within the earth, untouched for many millions of years.

What fortunes of good or bad luck may befall those who are the first to find and disturb this undiscovered gold, unlocking its first mystical powers.

Then we have the matter of stolen gold, is stolen gold embedded with its own unique curse, ready to be unleashed on a new and wrongful owner?

***

My first story starts in the year 1979; it was November, with an early wet season well underway settling down to regular afternoon tropical thunderstorms.

I had paused for a moment to look out of the window at the dark billowing clouds while having a short daydream about looking forward to the Christmas break. A nice pleasant six weeks in Perth with the family, and my new baby girl Tracy, born just a few days ago… then the phone rang.

'Eh it's me Dino'

I have no idea why my Italian friend with his obvious Italian accent should find it necessary to tell me who he was on the phone. Dino continued in his normal whispering, low secretive voice.

'Listen, I got some special business to talk; I'll be over in a minute.'

The phone went dead and Dino was on his way.

For some reason, most of Dino's normal everyday life seemed to be cloaked in drama and secret men's stuff.

I guess Dino was easily as good-looking as Dean Martian was, hence his nickname. However, he could not sing a note. That did not bother the girls who were seduced by his good looks and well-mannered Italian charm. The fact of the matter was that he spent a great deal of his time working hard on keeping the interested females and his second wife in very different places in his busy life.

Just then, Robyn my twenty-year-old office assistant stuck her head into my office.

'The bloody Mafia is here again, shall I send Caratti in?'

Robyn let out a little quip as Dino gave her a sharp smack on her cute little arse; she reacted quickly swinging the door open in the process. Dino stood at the threshold with a serious grin on his face and Robyn now standing behind him had a look of dark outrage.

Dino stepped into my office bringing his finger up to his lips in a sign of silence, firmly closing the door behind him, ignoring Robyn's (I will kill you) death look.

'Jesus Dino you took a bloody big risk there, last week Robyn clobbered a bloke down the pub with a bar stool for doing less than that, you certainly know how to stir-up the ladies, and I can't afford to lose Robyn.'

'C'mon, c'mon, she is a woman eh… they like that, they like being noticed it's the way of the world my friend, action and then reaction no.'

As Dino sat down opposite me, he drew his chair up close to talk secret style, I just knew that he was about to unfold one of his crazy plans. My only worry at that moment was what Robyn might be planning, as two of my guns were propped up against the wall in her office. Then I remembered, the ammo being all safely locked in my filing cabinet… or was it, then leaning forward to hear Dino's every word.

'What is this all about Dino, are you inviting me on another up-the-river duck hunting trip? Have you fixed that bloody great shotgun hole in your tinnie fishing boat?'

Dino did not show any concern at my disparaging comment about our last hunting trip, a terrifying incident when Bill, my mechanic accidentally discharged a shotgun creating a large hole in Dino's boat about ten kilometres up the croc-infested Ord River. We three blokes ended up sitting perched on the transom with the little outboard motor running flat-out; keeping the bow up high enough to clear the massive hole. This saved the day, and got us all back home in one piece.

**

'Niven I need your help; in return you will be rich my friend, but first I need your promise that you will keep what I say a secret.' He then had a quick look over his shoulder as if someone might hear, leant further forward and whispered, 'Omerta'

I could tell this was serious stuff. Keeping the Mafia code of silence was always serious stuff… but the Mafia were all crooks right? Then as usual, I should begin with a few questions.

'Is this plan, this thing, against the law in any way, as I am in enough trouble with the Bank and the taxman as it is? I can't go to jail right now; you know that Lesley and I have just had a new baby girl.'

Dino leant closer stared into my face and whispered softly...

'Gold my friend... lots of untraceable gold.'

We both stared at one another noses almost touching across my extra wide desk. I liked my desk; I had it especially made 8-foot long and 4-foot wide so I could spread-out my many WAC flying maps and mining survey maps. The size took-up almost a quarter of my entire office space, making a ridiculous statement in such a small office, however no more ridiculous than we must have looked that day stretched out across it, slightly raised from our chairs in a deep guarded conversation.

I knew Dino well; he cultivated the myth around town that he was a bad-boy Mafioso type. Nothing could be further from the truth. Dino, Gianni Caratti was one of the nicest people I have ever met in my life. The man gave far more than he ever received and was always available to help a friend or someone in need.

His one and uncontrollable weakness was his passion for women. He could not resist the challenge of a well... let me just say a female challenge. His code was not that of the Mafia but was that of a decent bloke, and maybe more than a little male chivalry. He was possibly a little old-fashioned, but quaint, and always a true gentleman.

When I look back this was possibly the very reason he got involved with this intriguing gold story, helping a friend in need. Mind you, this was only one of the many true fascinating stories about Dino.

In the interesting world of Dino, style and chivalry was always practiced. Women are there to be seduced, and men are there to be confidents in any exciting conquests or ventures... This I suspected was just another one of those (men only) business things that occupied Dino's busy day between pouring concrete and eying up the next potential conquest.

A few months back I had asked Dino why he was in the concrete business, as it was more than obvious to me, and most other people who knew him well, that he was an exceptionally smart man. This man could have quite easily turned his hand to just about anything and made a good living.

Dino hunched his shoulders as the Italians do and said the Romans invented concrete. The Colosseum was made with the stuff, and built seventy years before Christ was born, and still standing. What better way is there for an Italian to express himself other than in something that lasts forever? This man never failed to surprise me… Dino was indeed a deep thinker, maybe one who deserves listening to a little more, or as things later turned out… maybe not.

Dino placed his elbows on my desk then clasped his hands as if in prayer then launched into his story, dropping to a low voice so nobody could hear him in my especially constructed soundproof padded office.

'Niven do you remember the Croatian guy Andros, you know, he worked for me last year running the cement batching plant at VOC.'

'Nope can't say that I do, what about him.'

'Well, he left Kununurra and went travelling with another guy and they both ended up in Kalgoorlie working in a goldmine, the Super Pit. They eventually got a job at the Kalgoorlie gold smelting-plant that poured the gold bullion bars and…' I held up my hand to speak, interrupting Dino.

'That's a bit hard to believe as I know for a fact that they only let special, trusted and experienced people handle the gold at a smelter, a couple of half-baked Croatians would not get within arm's length of any gold. Another thing, the gold is not bullion at that stage of the process; it's called a (Dore bar) because it's a long way from being pure gold.'

Dino rolled his eyes and sighed at my obvious gold knowledge, from this I then suspected he knew all about Dore gold… Dino then became a bit frustrated.

'Christ, will you listen to me no… Do you want to be rich or not. I know the gold is still Dore, but what you don't know is that it's eighty-five percent gold, ten percent, copper and five percent nickel, making the Kalgoorlie Dore-bar one of the highest gold percentages in the world, good eh.'

'Your right Dino, I didn't know that. Therefore, what you are saying is that these two dumb blokes have stolen some gold from their last job, and they believe all the Mafia crap that you encourage, and now want you to fence the stuff for them… What am I supposed to do, be the get-away driver for you or maybe the armed bodyguard in a white suit with a stubby shotgun… a lupar?'

'No, no, will you listen to me, c'mon; c'mon the mine doesn't even know the gold is gone eh. These two guys were the only the ones who repaired and welded all the broken furnace stuff. They cleaned down and repaired all the crucibles after a pour. You're right they're not all that smart, they were just doing some labouring and odd welding jobs around the mine.'

'So how did they get their hands-on a few ounces of gold in a place that's guarded better than Fort Knox.'

Dino rolled his eyes at my negative response.

'Niven, it's not guarded after the gold pour is finished, that's when the maintenance guys go in to fix things up.'

Then looking around again as if someone might hear him, and whispering in a still lower voice.

'Anyway, who said they only had a few ounces of gold mio amico, (my friend)… they got forty-five kilos of the bloody stuff.'

My face must have registered a sudden look of shock, as Dino's head shot back a metre at my surprise, caused by his incredible statement. This was unbelievable. In the short silence that followed Dino had already read my mind and was about to provide the answer.

'It's like all good things amico, it all happened by accident eh. The day these two guys started at the gold foundry their first job was to weld-up all the crucible tilt pins and any lifting gantry damage. They noticed a two-ounce gold plug in the bottom of crucible number seven and took it with them… for well, you know, for safekeeping eh. Over the next few weeks they noticed the same crucible number seven always had a small bit of gold left in it… that's how it was done.'

I thought about this for a moment then pulled over my newly acquired electronic calculator and started keying in a few quick sums.

'These blokes are full of shit; I know for a fact that the Kalgoorlie smelter only has a pour every second week, to amass forty-five kilos of gold would have taken them at two ounces a time….'

Dino butted in with a big grin.

'Twenty-nine years, eh, c'mon they had a better idea than that, and for two stupid guys it was a real good one eh.'

I was always amazed at Dino and his fast sums, and that must have shown on my face again. He could calculate quantities and cubic metres of earth or concrete in his head with surprising accuracy and give a quote to a client right there on the spot.

'All right then I give up… how was it done?'

'These two guys figured out why it was, that crucible number seven always had a bit of gold left in it. The bloody thing had a bent tilt-pin which stopped the cast-iron crucible tilting to its full up position in the pour… they just changed all the fourteen other crucibles to the same pin angle so all fifteen of them held back a little gold… good idea no?'

I grabbed my calculator again and started to finger in the figures but Dino was well ahead of me.

'They were working there for just over a year. The local boys even put on a party for them when they left.' Then Dino went swiftly into the sums, 'Fifteen crucibles with the tilt adjusted to four ounces each, for twenty-six foundry pours, is 1560 ounces of gold or forty-four kilos, is about right no?'

He was spot-on as usual, but I was still unsure how they would have got away with this game. The mine security would have found out about this eventually. It's not rocket science the Dore-bar gold material is weighed and calculated to give a predicted end weight, someone would have eventually worked out there was a difference between what went into the melt and what came out. Dino had an answer to all of that… and more.

'The spoil factor is quite high with the type of slurry gold-extraction method used at the Kalgoorlie Super Pit. The impurities that are skimmed off the furnace-melt before the pour make it hard to be exact on weight, ten to fifteen percent is an accepted weight-loss factor on a normal pour... four ounces would never be missed... Remember this mine produces over 20 tonnes of Dore gold each year.'

I had four questions for Dino who politely waited for my delivery.

'Now that these two mad Croatians have gone somebody will find this gold left behind and report it, it's just a matter of time.'

'No, no my friend, they fixed all the crucible tilt-pins before they left, there will be no more gold left in the crucibles after a pour... smart eh.'

'Why did they leave this job if it was such a sure thing, this could have gone on for years?'

'Andros told me that his pal Branko has a bad lung problem, smokes, and drinks too much. The booze is killing him, he's spending a fair bit of time in hospital, they want to come up north again to the heat and get out of Kalgoorlie before Branko gets drunk and tells someone about the gold. That's why their workmates gave them a big send-off party; Branko was sick and needed to go up north to the heat.'

'Well Dino, this just leaves me two questions to be answered, where is the gold now, and what the hell do you need me for?'

Dino paused and glanced at my wall clock. Strangely, Dino never wore a watch in all the years I had known him. I had meant to ask him why, and will sometime, but now was not the time... another pun... maybe not. Dino had some other pressing matters.

'We have to go down the pub and talk to Andros before he gets into too much drink.'

'This Andros bloke is he here, in town right now?'

'Yes, I flew him up from Derby this morning, he will tell us where all the gold is but there is a small problem. First he needs to hire one of your Toyota Land Cruisers fitted out with full exploration equipment to go bush and get the gold and bring it back to Kununurra.'

There it was, the very reason Dino was talking to me. He wanted me to supply one of my fully equipped Toyota Landcruiser 4X4 vehicles to a mad Croatian bloke. A mad bloke who steals gold from one of the world's largest gold mines. Not just a few ounces mind you, but forty-five bloody kilos.

Chapter Two:

Do you believe me now?

The pub was surprisingly crowded for ten am on a Wednesday morning; I had never been to the Kununurra Hotel this early. My drinking and business time was always after work around six-thirty or maybe after three-thirty on a Friday for a late lunch if there was something worthwhile to talk about or celebrate.

On the other hand, Dino rarely frequented the pub other than at the occasional business meeting; he much preferred a wine at home. This important meeting was to be very quiet and covert, so he made straight for one of the little booths in the lounge.

'Where's this Andros bloke,' looking around, 'my bet is he will be in the front punch-up bar trying to sell his gold.'

Dino was not impressed at my cynicism and low interest in this gold thing, and walked off to find Andros. He was back within five minutes with a tall skinny man of about forty. I recognised him immediately from when he worked for Dino but he was much thinner now, in fact to me, Andros did not look very well at all.

Andros appeared pleasant enough in a sly sort of way although he would not look me in the eye, and I felt that I should not trust him… in anything. Dino advised me in a matter-of-fact way that Andros was flat broke; he had lost his

Land Rover and all his possessions, including his bank account details while being towed into Derby last week.

Seemingly, he and his friend Branko were trying to drive into Derby hospital because Branko had become ill again.

Their bad luck change to critical when the Land Rover they were travelling in became bogged down in the first heavy tropical storms. Two days later a truck came along and offered to tow them into Derby, but the Land Rover while under tow turned over on a road bend, about twenty-five kilometres from Derby… writing the vehicle off.

Branko was now in Derby hospital with a serious lung infection and three broken ribs from the Land Rover accident; he now had to get back down there to see him.

I asked Andros why he needed to hire a Toyota Landcruiser. With a look of surprise Andros turned to Dino as if I should have known something, then Dino casually provided the missing information.

'I didn't tell you before Niven because I wanted you to hear what Andros had to say first. When they first were bogged down on the main Great Northern Highway, they decided it best to bury the gold just off to the side of the road. Andros needs a good 4X4 vehicle to go down there and bring Branko and the gold back.'

Dino could see that I was faltering a bit in any support of this bizarre gold story, and told Andros to spell out his deal.

'Niven, my friend Branko he is very sick and I might need to get him back down to Perth for special medical help. Our plan was to come up to Kununurra with the gold and get Caratti to fix-up the purity to a hundred percent and then on-sell it for us.

Now with all this, I will share this gold between us if we can get a Toyota and some money to go to get the gold and bring it back.'

Dino did his thing and clasped his hands in front of him as if in prayer again and recited the numbers from the top of his head.

'Niven, at eighty-five percent pure gold of the forty-five kilos. This ends up as just a little more than thirty-eight kilos, which is close to 1360 ounces. The current US gold price is

US$258.00 an ounce; now that at a total of US$350,800.00 split four ways is US$87,000 each amigo (friend). Our Aussie dollar is just about at parity with the US dollar so that is about what you will get eh.'

I cocked my head to one side indicating to Dino that I wanted a private word with him away from Andros. He got the message and we walked over to another booth.

'What the fuck is this all about, you can't tell me that you really believe this slimy bastard do you? Anyway, what convinces you that he has this gold, and if he does, that the bloody gold-mine police are not already on his track wanting it back, this is assuming he does have any gold.

What's to say if this bloke is actually telling the truth that he would bring the gold back to Kununurra, he might just piss off… with my Toyota Landcruiser? And another thing, what do you know about purifying gold?'

'Steady down my friend, quietly, quietly, you'll have a heart attack no. I don't know anything about purifying gold but I know who does eh. C'mon lighten up a bit I know this guy; sure he thinks he's smart but he is in big trouble… come with me.'

We went straight back to the booth where Andros was sitting with a long miserable look on his face, then Dino announced with a majestic Italian wave of his hand.

'Show him…'

Andros pulled out a grubby wallet and fished out a tattered mining pit-pass with his photo on it for the Kalgoorlie Super Pit. He also produced a welder's certificate signed off for the foundry and a magnetic swipe card for the foundry access… Dino prompted him like an impatient schoolteacher.

'C'mon don't fuck about man, show him.'

Andros dug deep into his dirty shorts pocket and produced a half domed metal object and placed it on the table in front of me. I picked it up, and found it to be quite heavy for its size and brought it closer for inspection then Dino spoke.

'Do you believe me now eh;' nodding at the gold in my hand, 'that's one of the 340 crucible plugs he has, its four ounces of eighty-five percent pure gold…, untraceable and nobody is looking for it, because they don't even know this gold has gone.'

'I need to sleep on this one Dino; I will get back to you tomorrow if I decide to risk a Toyota 4X4 hire vehicle…'

'We will need an answer this afternoon Niven, Andros has got to get going before this wet season really starts to move in, things are starting to look a bit wet and muddy down there no.'

'Just then the background music stopped and the Hotel PA system cranked out a loud message…

'Niven Dallas your wife is at the Hospital with your new baby girl Tracy. Lesley wants' you up there quick smart to pick them up so get your bloody arse over there right now.'

There was no mistaking it. That was Big Bad Betty on the PA. She was one lady not to argue with, as she had the supreme power to expel you from the pub for as long as she saw fit… and this was after all about woman's business.

'See what I mean Dino, there are some things in my life that are more important than a pile of gold… I have to go pick-up Lesley and Tracy from hospital; they are ready to come home. I will get back to you both late this afternoon.'

Tracy was born on the Sunday the 4th just four days ago; this would be her first day at home. On the way to the hospital, I went over to the Cole's house first to pick-up Mark; my almost two-year-old boy thankfully looked after by Pam our good friend. He did not want to leave Pam and could not figure out what all the fuss was about… he was just about to find out why. Mark was no longer the only baby in the Dallas house.

Dino arrived back at my office for an answer, but my answer was no. I did not trust this slimy gold pinching bloke. Dino then launched into (convince him mode,) starting with, he had just checked out the Derby hospital and had confirmed that Branko was indeed very ill. He was in fact in intensive care.

Dino quickly followed up with a new plan. He would hire the Toyota Landcruiser for the three weeks thereby taking the responsibility for the vehicle. I considered this proposition as workable. Few hire vehicles went out during the wet season anyway, as such, the vehicle would be just sitting in the hire vehicle yard.

'Okay I'll do it, but this Andros bloke will have to be written on to the contract as a named driver... later this was proved to be the first of my many silly mistakes.

***

A full week passed without a word, I must admit both Dino and I were starting to get a bit concerned. Then Andros eventually rang Dino with an update, the news was not good.

Andros had spent the last six days trying to locate the spot where he had buried the two sacks of gold. The wet season was now well underway with the roads suffering heavy flooding. As is normal the MRD (Main Roads Department) had sent out all the available graders and front-end loaders to keep the roads open.

One of the standard road dewatering methods was to angle-cut many drains into the bush to take the floodwater away from the road. Andros was sure he knew the exact spot where the buried gold was, as he and Branko had driven into the ground two eight-foot long star pickets right next to the spot, with red survey tape tied to them as a marker.

He now suspected that a MRD grader might have made a road drain in the same place ripping out the markers. He had spent the last week frantically digging holes at every new drain he thought the markers might have been.

Andros was now back in Derby advising Dino not to worry as Branko had been a great help in describing the area and features close to the spot.

He was also waiting for the development of a roll of film from Branko's camera, which apparently had a picture of the exact position of the gold... oh and by-the-way Branko at only thirty-nine years of age had died late last night in Derby hospital of liver complications and chronic pneumonia.

I was thinking to myself; I wonder just what sort of conversation Andros would have had with his friend Branko, as he was for sure the last person ever to see him alive. I was not overjoyed at Dino's confident phone call.

'C'mon Niven you worry too much; I just sent Andros another thousand dollars to keep him going. He's driving back out there tomorrow to find the gold. Just relax my friend eh, everything will turn out okay… you'll see.'

***

Another two weeks passed, Andros rang Dino reverse charges this time from Port Hedland. All of the Great Northern Highway from the Goldsworthy turnoff all the way to the Derby turnoff, a distance of over 620 kilometres was flooded, now closed off by the MRD, and the government of Western Australia.

Andros had now been cut-off at the Goldsworthy end, with no way of getting through to the north. His new plan was to drive my Toyota Landcruiser down south through Kalgoorlie, Norseman, and across the Nullarbor to Port Augusta, then up the Stuart Highway through Alice Springs and Katherine to Kununurra.

In other words right around the vast bloody State of Western Australia, the idea was to resume his search for the gold after the wet season had ended, and could Dino send him another thousand dollars for the food and fuel? I nearly blew a gasket.

'For fucks sake Dino this gold thing is turning to crap, talk about the evils and bad-luck demons of gold. Tell that bastard to take my Toyota to the nearest local Avis hire car yard. Then you can fly the bastard back up to Kununurra to wait out the wet season. That will be a lot cheaper than running up nearly 9,000 kilometres on my bloody vehicle.'

There was a deep silence from Dino's end of the phone, I thought he had gone, and then he took a deep sad breathe and spoke.

'Niven I have already sent him the money, I never thought, I just wanted to get your Toyota back; he says he will be in Kununurra in about two or three weeks from now.'

I immediately reported the Toyota to the Police as stolen as the hire contract was now some two weeks overdue.

***

The Toyota Landcruiser never did come back. The last contact Andros made with Dino was from the famous opal-mining town of Coober Pedy in South Australia.

Could Dino send him another thousand dollars as he had run out of money again? Andros told Dino that he had on him the photo that showed the exact location of the gold with a good recognisable landmark in the background, confirming that the gold would be easy to find.

I do not know if Dino did send Andros the money, however, I did contact the local Kununurra Police telling them the last known location of my Toyota. The Kununurra Police contacted the Coober Pedy Police in South Australia who then questioned the driver Andros.

The local Police advised me that the South Australia Police had since let Andros go as he had a vehicle hire contract for the Toyota with his name on it. He had simply told them that he was annoyed and driving the thing back to Kununurra the long way because all the North-Western Australian roads were closed, which by all accounts was absolutely true.

So there it was, my smart idea of making sure that Andros was a named driver had come back to bite me. Another two weeks later, the Kununurra local Police advised me that my vehicle was now in a Police lock-up compound in Swan Hill in New South Wales. The driver Andros was in Police custody… in jail.

It was now obvious that Andros did not intend to return my Toyota; he was still heading east. Apparently, Andros was involved in a barroom brawl in which two young blokes ended up knifed; Andros was now being held in a Police lock-up for GBH (grievous bodily harm.)

***

Andros was not a man to give-up easily; his one legal phone call was to Dino... 'Help me, you know I can pay.'

Dino and I immediately jumped on a jet for Adelaide, then a light commuter plane to Mildura, and then in the freezing cold, a bus ride to Swan Hill arriving at five in the morning. The mighty plan was to drive my Toyota Landcruiser back up to Kununurra. This idea was soon totally dashed on first sight of the Toyota.

Everything that could be damaged or broken was. The front smashed in, the rear tray was hanging off, and the doors were missing along with the bonnet. All the tyres were bald and the rear tail shaft, along with the ripped off exhaust system was on the rear damaged tray back.

This vehicle was only one year old, now a total write off, presenting as a heartbreaking, grim and terminal sight. The local Swan Hill Toyota dealer, after much negotiation reluctantly paid $420.00 for the wreck.

I needed to know some answers why, and Dino needed to get that photo. Unfortunately, the un-corporative local Swan Hill Police Sergeant would not let us talk to Andros who was at the time in custody, held in the Sergeants lock-up cells. The reason being as we were not relatives or his legal counsel. Our long and expensive trip to Swan Hill was a total waste of time and money.

***

A month later, the local Kununurra Police Sergeant came to see me with some interesting news.

Over a cup of coffee the Sergeant told me that the bloke who had stolen my Toyota Landcruiser was dead, actually knifed to death in jail. Apparently, the fight being over something about a photo, the Sergeant adding, 'she must have been a bloody good-looking sort eh.'

I looked out of my office window watching as the Police Sergeant drove out the hire yard... if only he knew the truth about that photo. Then I started thinking, is there such a thing as a bad luck curse with gold. Everybody that I had known who had handled or touched easy gold, was dead, physically maimed... or now an utter psychological human wreck.

***

Now I am not talking about driving a truck working in a goldmine or maybe in a jeweller's shop selling the stuff. No, I am talking about the people who are caught-up in the greed for discovery and possession of gold, and the wealth that it may bring them. When they do eventually succeed, they are never happy people; in my experience, they eventually suffer the loss of health, family, and finally wealth.

....The End....

Chapter Three:

New Gold Curse

Susan stuck her head into my office; Stu Skoglund was down in the electronics workshop and wanted a job done urgently, could I go down and talk to him.

Stuart Skoglund was a living legend, a true aviation pioneer of the agricultural and cattle industries in the Kimberley.

Stu, an American, came to Kununurra on Anzac day 1965 after a good friend of his Chuck offered him a job flying choppers. The job was crop-spraying cotton on the new Ord River irrigation scheme, living in the newly established town of Kununurra in Western Australia.

Spraying cotton crops to control pests or to apply fertilisers and defoliants was a new method, and in its early days for Australia. However, most of the new Australian farmers on the Ord River who had farmed in many countries around the world were very much aware of the advantages of aerial spray applications; to them this was a well-proven new technology.

Stuart was an old school pilot; he had completed his flying training as a World War two fighter pilot and never did quite lose his style or preference for bold marginal flying. Crop spraying was perfect for Stu, and his style of flying.

***

Helicopter spray application was proving to have significant advantages to the health and quality of the early growing cotton crops; however, forcing the spray chemicals down through the crop had a major problem when nearing maturity and picking time. The helicopter blade downwash also blew the mature cotton heads off the trees... the farmers were not happy.

This prompted a new change of direction in crop spraying; the introduction of fixed-wing crop spraying. This smart move, resolved the crop loss problem but what was he to do with the idle Bell 47 helicopters.

Cattle mustering by fixed-wing aircraft was not new however, rotor-wing mustering was. Lang Hancock owner of Hamersley Station in Western Australia had carried out the first helicopter muster in 1966 using a Brantley B2 helicopter.

Stu thought helicopter mustering was the way to go and after much drinking and talking convinced Pat Shaw the manager of Ord River Station to agree to do a trial cattle muster. The rest is now history as helicopter mustering changed the cattle mustering industry in Australia forever.

Stu Skoglund was not the first to use helicopters and fixed wing aircraft for agricultural crop spraying and cattle mustering, however, he was the first to convince and prove the methods cost effective in the Kimberley and the Northern Territory.

I had never thought of Stu, as a dollar driven businessperson. My personal impression of him was that of an adventurer, my view of him later proved correct.

Most, if not all of Stu's good ideas and proven profitable flying activities, were quickly taken-up and copied by others who went on to make a great deal of money. Stu let many a good contract mustering opportunity slip through his fingers, and the first mustered cattle stations, which were owned by Vestey's and Hooker Pastoral quickly saw the advantages of aerial mustering, then after a trial muster promptly purchased their own helicopters.

As always nothing ever bothered Stu much at all, after a few gripes down at the pub to anyone who would listen, Stu just got on with life and flying.

Stu had reluctantly accepted the move from aerial spraying to helicopter mustering, now he was on the move again, this time to yet another bold flying adventure... gold prospecting.

***

'Hi Stu what is the urgent problem this time?'

It was immediately obvious what the problem was as Stu was holding one of his electronic metal detectors, or as Stu would call it a gold finder. We shook hands as all polite Americans do, then in his American drawl.

'I think the God-damn things broken a wire at the plug again Nev-en. I'm flying down ta Halls Creek ta meet up with the boys fir some gold prospecting. They're gonna need the chopper soon, it's pretty wet down there.'

I went about soldering up the broken wires again, as this had happened a few times before on this same detector, also on his other units. Stu was watching me every second so I thought this would be a good captive time to ask some prospecting questions... but I would have to be careful as Stu kept secrets, and did not appreciate people asking nosey questions.

'Do these things really work; I mean how can you tell the difference between a beer-can, an old horse-shoe, and a gold nugget?'

'Well Nev-en, if you kin git the fucker working again I'll give you a demonstration on how it works. It sorta needs some twaddling with these-here knobs and a bit of practice, but yeah you can tell if you got gold. We got four of em now, but this one's the best, it belongs to Jack Wightman, it's found more gold that all the others have together.'

I was surprised at this casual claim and had to hide my nosey curiosity. Found more gold than the others eh, maybe I should have a go at this gold detecting stuff; then again, I needed to know more.

'The overheads must be bloody high whizzing about in a Bell 47... choppers cost big money to operate?'

'Well Nev-en, Max's grader and front-end-loader cost a bit ta run, and then there's Jack's trucks... it all costs a few dollars, but we get by.'

I was thinking that's a fair bit of equipment, I wonder what Stu meant when he said, "we get by." My quick reckoning calculated that Stu's little gold prospecting venture must have been costing them many thousands of dollars a month.

'There you are Stu, we should give this gold finding machine a road test before I close-up the waterproof plug.'

Stu connected the handle to the main unit and then plugged in the repaired plug, but without assembling it. He then reached across and grabbed Steveo the electronic technicians can of coke and placed it on the floor. Then he grabbed Steve's small hammer and placed it about a metre from the can.

With the sound turned over to speaker, Stu started to twaddle and tune his gold detector machine, which was now giving off a whining pitch that meant nothing to the workshop staff and I, but did hold our attention in anticipation of something.

After a few minutes twaddling of the many knobs, Stu then did a sweep of the two objects. The coke can gave off a distinctive pitched noise and the steel hammerhead gave off a different noise. Steveo was not convinced so he placed an aluminium radio cover on the workshop floor and Stu swept it to give almost the same sound as the aluminium coke can.

Everyone was beaming with smiles at this convincing demonstration when John said with a technicians knowing smirk.

'It's supposed to detect gold isn't it, not coke cans and bloody hammers.'

Stu was not concerned at this quick sarcastic remark and reached into his pocket and placed a large teardrop shaped piece of gold on the workshop floor about one metre from the hammer head. That did it; Stu had everyone's attention as he tuned the machine to the gold teardrop. The gold detector head then passed over the three objects giving three distinct sounds. I could tell Stu was in his element here as he held our attention with childish wonderment, and then he played his ace card…

'Yah-all notice that the three different metals make three different sounds, now all ah do is switch off the metals ahs don't want like this…'

Now the sweeping gold detector head just sounded when it passed over the gold, Steveo said 'good one mate, very neat' and picked up his can of coke and started drinking it, john picked up the hammer and Stu picked up his gold and went about explaining how things worked.

'Friends, this here gold finder is a discriminator type. It kin rightly tell the difference between metals, and you kin just switch off the ones you don't want. The other gold detectors we have aint as smart as this one. It kin save a lot of time, and it kin find a lot of gold.'

I knew all about metal discriminator detectors, Stu was not the only one who had brought these gadgets in for repair. What I was more interested in was the large lump of gold that Stu was using as his reference. Where the hell did it come from? I asked Steveo to put the repaired and tested gold detector plug back together and offered Stu a cup of coffee, then we both headed up to my office.

Gold was all the talk down at the pub. Many new gold prospecting companies were dashing around out the back of Halls Creek in new Toyota Land Cruisers, and a few had hired my vehicles, so none of this activity was news to me. These prospectors were checking out all the old abandoned 120-year-old gold mines for a possible commercial gold venture.

The reason was simple, renewed gold interest now being driven by the highest ever market price for gold at US$420.00 per ounce, the reason for this hike being debated over many beers and long hours at the pub. Most agreed it was the fear created by the cold war. In the last year, all of the world's nuclear nations had detonated test nuclear devices; a new arms race had developed, and the cold war was heating-up rapidly. Still other knowledgeable drinkers bracing the bar were sure it was the fact that the Ayatollah Khomeini had declared a holy war, a Fatwa on America, confirming the USA as "The great Satan."

One thing I do know… it was all-good for my business.

'What's the big rush to get down to Halls Creek Stu, and why will the boys need your chopper when it's so wet?'

'Best time fir finding gold is when the ground's wet, we'd bin using Jacks road water binding trucks ta add some ground water, but this rain covers a bigger area. It's not hard ta figure out; damp ground with metal in it gives a much stronger gold detection signal than in dry ground.'

I could see that Stu did not like talking about his gold prospecting; however, I was fascinated at the amount of expensive resources that Stu and his partners were investing in this project, so I poked just a little bit further.

'Well I suppose the electrolysis reaction of water; metal and damp soil would give a better signal, but why use an expensive helicopter?'

'The most expensive part of prospecting is being in the wrong Goddamn place where there aint no fucking gold. After some heavy rain two of us fly the chopper out ta all the most likely gold spots and do a quick gold detection scan, ifin we gits some good signals we mark the spot fir future prospecting. We git faster an better results. It kin save a lot of time and money.'

Stu's manner was changing and I sensed that I was at Stu's limit of polite tolerance to my many nosey questions… but I had one more.

'Max is in the earthmoving and cattle breeding business, Jack is contracting his trucks out to the Main Roads, and you are in the helicopter flying business; can you guys find enough gold to cover costs and justify such a big change from your normal work?'

'Yeah we do all right and maybe a bit more, hell we've only bin at gold prospecting fir some seven months or so. The cattle business is low and there aint much MRD work around, much the same as there aint much chopper hire. Gold prospecting is paying some of the God-damn bills… hell it's better than sitting on yer ass at home, or drinking booze at a bar.'

With that last word Stu stood-up in his well-worn RM Williams boots, he then extended his right hand for a polite good-bye shake.

'Thanking you kindly fir fixing mah gold finder Nev-en.'

It was obvious to me that this matter was now closed to any further discussion and then Stu was gone out of the my office.

That handshake was to be the last time I was to ever shake that hand or for that matter see Stu with a right arm, as in four days' time the whole world would change for Stu... and his three gold prospecting partners.

***

The news came as a sudden shock to the town of Kununurra; Stuart Skoglund had been involved in a serious road accident while driving up from Halls Creek. He had collided with a road-train just the other side of the Dunham River Bridge, only fifteen kilometres from Kununurra. Stu was now on his way down to Perth where the surgeons will attempt to reattach his severed right arm.

***

Stu left my office and the half-drunk cup of coffee, driving straight to the airport. He then flew his Bell 47G-3B helicopter to his prospecting camp at Nuggetty Gully, just off the Old Halls Creek Road. The three partners, Max Lamoreaux, Jack Wightman, and a bloke call Nigel Dixon met Stu on landing at their camp.

The plan was simple enough and had proved most rewarding in the past. Stu would drop off a partner at different and likely prospecting spots then return in about an hour to relocate them to yet another likely spot. In this way, many good areas could be quickly identified for future close inspection, as such a considerable amount of potential gold bearing ground covered in a short time.

It was mid-December and building up to the start of an early wet season. The recent rains had worked there magic well. This rain helping in discovering a number of small gold nuggets, the prospecting group were quite pleased with their early good progress and worthwhile gold finds over the past four days.

Late on the fifth day 23rd December 1979, just after deciding to head back to the camp for the night. All of a sudden, Stu was astonished by one of the loudest signals he ever heard on his gold finder, or should that be Jack Wightman's gold detector. Two minutes of soft digging exposed a superb twenty-eight ounce, beautifully formed gold nugget, they had found the prospectors dream nugget... or had they.

***

As was the standard practice, this magnificent gold nugget find required the expected prospector's celebration.

Chasing last light Stu managed the two fifteen minute round trip helicopter flights from their camp into the Halls Creek airstrip. The last trip landing shortly after last light.

Halls Creek is the only town I know of in Australia that has a hotel and bar right next-door, within a short walking distance to the airstrip. By the time Stu arrived on his second trip from the camp, (The Bell 47G helicopter only has three seats) Jack and young Nigel, with the help of many locals were already well into celebrating their good fortune.

The word was out, soon the whole town was helping them celebrate; the time just slipped by all night and into the next day. Later reports from those that could still remember that boozy night and day, confirmed it was one hell of a party.

The old story began to circulate around Halls Creek about an almost identical nugget found ninety years ago. This important find remembered by the old prospectors who were bracing the bar that night. They were saying this is the twin to largest nugget ever found in the Halls Creek area.

Apparently, prospector Charlie Hall (whom Halls Creek named after) had also discovered a 28oz gold nugget on 23rd December 1885... yes the exact same day except ninety-four years earlier... also at the same place known as Old Hall's Creek. Just what were the odds of that?

***

Without doubt, this was to be a memorable occasion, however, not as memorable as what was about to happen over the next few weeks.

Christmas was just a few days away, and it had been a good year for Stu and the others in his prospecting group. A decision was made after they all sobered-up a little, to start winding things down for the end of this year. Jack lived in

Halls Creek and so would remain and keep an eye on the helicopter until Stu got back with his engineer to fix a bit that had broken. The other three decided at 3:00 am in the early morning to drive back to Kununurra some 358 kilometres with their large gold nugget, about a four-hour drive.

Just before the Ord River Diversion Dam Stu noticed a long string of lights in the dark, a road-train was on the single road over the Dunham River Bridge. A truck was heading towards them, and so he pulled over off the road a little, as is the way in the northwest (trucks are given right of way) to allow the truck to clear the bridge.

It had started to rain hard just as the road-train approached; Stu was tired but happy the hot humid drive to Kununurra was almost at an end. The other two were sound asleep next to Stu when the three-trailer road-train thundered by. Most passenger vehicles did not have air-conditioning and like most drivers in the hot northwest Stu had his arm hanging out of the window to catch some of the passing cool air… and then it happened.

***

As can happen with road-trains, especially after the tired driver has changed a wheel, if care is not taken to make sure that the wheel sits firmly and aligned on the spider hub, the wheel will run slightly buckled off track, causing the vehicle, or in this case the trailer to run out-of-track starting a swinging movement.

The last trailer was whipping across the slippery wet road in the dark and rain; timing its last swing just clipping the side of Stu's almost parked Toyota. The back of the trailer smashed hard into the side of Stu's vehicle with a tremendous flicking hammer blow, smashing the driver's door and windscreen then ripping Stu's right arm off in a split second of irreversible time throwing his dismembered arm far into the bush.

Helicopter pilots require both feet and both hands to fly. In that instant in time, Stuart Skoglund's long and remarkable flying career had come to an abrupt end.

If bad luck or providence wanted to cause the maximum amount of damage to this man while still remaining alive, then this was most certainly it.

In a strange twist of fate on that very same day at the other end of that same road some 100 kilometres away in Wyndham town, and at almost the same time of five-thirty am, a Wyndham Meat-works inspector lost a right arm in exactly the same type of road-train accident... Just what were the odds of that happening, on that day, at that same time?

It was touch and go for Stu's survival; he was placed into an induced coma for the long emergency flight, waking up in a Perth hospital to learn the devastating news of his horrendous injuries. However, this was just the start to this frightening story; there was far more bad news to come.

***

Two weeks later Stu's close friend and gold prospecting partner Max Lamoreaux, (another American Ord pioneer,) was discussing a cattle deal with a buyer while sitting astride his stock holding fence, (a corral in American speak.) The deal was going well that day to sell one of Max's prize young breeding bulls, when a sudden wind came up as was normal for this time of the year, and blew Max's all-American Stetson hat off, landing at his side in the muddy stockyard.

Max being a well-practiced man at retrieving wayward Stetsons from his long horse riding experience, just bent down to expertly scoop-up his treasured Stetson. Suddenly the frisky young bull, attracted by the floundering Stetson lunged at it, just as Max was picking it up. The result was devastating. The young bull's horn goring Max in the head tearing his left eye out of its socket.

The horn penetrated deep into Max's head breaking through and exposing the Dura matter of the brain sack... Max was in a critical condition... he was dying.

Max was American born, and a confirmed new Australian. He was a hard working quiet achiever with more than a few business problems on his mind... Max did survive this terrible trauma, but he was never to be the same man again... ever.

***

It was in late January when we all heard the unusual and tragic news about Jack Wightman, another of Stu's prospecting partners. Jack was a tough man, a strong man, which was just as well.

It was not unusual for Jack to repair three or four truck punctures in a day, all by himself. This was just normal truck driving in the northwest. Like all truck operators a man had to be a competent mechanic and a tyre fitter, a sort of Jack-Of-All-Trades (excuse the pun Jack.)

When problems surfaced; single handed, the ever resourceful truckie had to develop some smart ways to get the 80 kilo truck wheels off and back onto the truck spider during a repair. Most standard situations required the use of two long steel pipes, used to lift the heavy wheel off and onto the spider hub. This difficult job always accomplished with much swearing, buckets of sweat and a great deal of human strength. Jack could provide all of that, and more. The more bit comes from the fact that Jack was always seen with a nice looking girlie hitchhiker.

Jack was a practicing gentleman, always trying to be a perfect ladies man. For all his many faults; Jack, who was in his fifties, got into more pussy than most horny young males that I have known.

Jack was all of five foot four inches tall in the old scale, and just about the same in width. A powerful little man, a ball of muscle with boundless energy, and spare energy to pursue his favourite second pastime shagging. (First being drinking) I would say that this necessity for Jack always to have on hand something to fuck surely saved his life that unforgettable day.

***

Bartering is the common currency in the northwest, that's a two-beer cartoon job mate, or lend me you truck and I will lend you my grader. Can't pay your bar tab, work it off and don't slack; give good value for the good deed. You have to earn respect in the north-west, and a man's word is his bond.

Jack needed the use of a back-hoe to dig a septic tank hole in his little truck-yard plot in Halls Creek, and John the Motel owner had one. The only problem was the backhoe had a rear wheel puncture, no problem. Fixing a puncture was an everyday job for Jack. The deal consummated on a firm

Kimberley handshake and a beer; Jack would fix the puncture in exchange for four hours use of the backhoe… a done deal.

***

The tropical rain poured down hard that day, and it was a good thing as it cooled everything down. Nobody dashed for shelter in the tropics when it rained, it certainly did not bother Jack or his latest hitchhiker who was looking on as Jack went about fixing the puncture on the backhoe. Jack knew she was watching him as he strained in his rain-soaked thin worn footy shorts, going about the heavy task of dismantling the large tractor type wheel from the backhoe. He knew she would be turned-on by watching his muscular efforts… it had all happened before… it would end-up as an almighty fucking session after this work was done… he should save himself a little… he wasn't getting any younger.

It will not be long now as the puncture was now fixed, with a bit of luck he would be all finished in an hour. As per normal, he had attached the air compressor line to the tyres inflator nipple and turned the air compressor on. He was now getting ready to mount the massive tractor type wheel onto the eight wheel studs; the rain poured down… it was a cooling bliss.

The little air compressor on his truck rattled away filling the large tractor tyre with air as he struggled to mount the wheel on the eight studs. This was a bloody big wheel; it must weigh half as much again as one of his truck wheels. He was having trouble aligning the studs to the wheel holes, a problem he never had with his truck spider web hubs.

This was taking a bit of time in trying to align the studs to the wheel holes, the compressor continued to rattle on filling the massive tyre with air. Jack was straining with all his strength to pull-up the two long lifting pipes, raising the wheel to the hub. He had just yelled out to his new girl; could she kindly rotate the hub a little for him to align the wheel to the holes… and that's when it happened.

There was a tremendous ear splitting blast that shook the air. Jack felt himself propelled backwards as if by some Godly powerful, and mysterious force. He fleetingly caught the look

304

of terror on his frightened hitchhikers face as he rapidly blasted backwards past her.

Was this some sort of a dream, what was happening, then everything went blank for a long, long time? Jack was in a deep dark painful place... he must fight with all his strength to reach the surface.

It is simple to explain but hard to imagine. Jack being an experienced truck operator went about the repair of the tractor style wheel in exactly the same way, as he would have one of his truck wheels.

The only thing was, Jack not being aware of the method of inflation, and the power of compressed volume air.

Normally truck tyres are inflated to around 85-110 psi (pounds per square inch) depending on the vehicle load. Whereas Jack was unaware that tractor style balloon tyres normally inflated to no more than 12-15 psi.

The massive air volume size of the tractor tyre, and the added water lubrication by the rain, and of course Jacks unfortunate lack of knowledge, all helped to contribute to this horrific disaster.

As bad luck would have it. The inside of the tyre-wall blew off the wet rim first, forcing the 160 kilo wheel and tyre to propel itself outwards with a massive blast of air energy, collecting the startled Jack who was crouched, holding the huge wheel with two long steel pipes, and in the direct path.

Jack suffered two broken legs, a broken right arm, and a broken left wrist. Jack's chest was crushed suffering nine broken ribs, punctured lungs and a lacerated heart... any normal man would not have survived this horrendous accident.

It was touch and go for a while as Jack put-up a brave struggle to survive this ordeal. His chance to survive was only there because he had a little hitchhiker girlie hanging around to keep his man fluids moving after a hard day's work, she was quick to call for help.

Although those within the town said that the huge explosion alerted the Halls Creek hospital of a pending accident long before the little back-packer girl called for help. Jack spent five months in hospital, one in intensive care, he never did return to his old self... but he was alive.

This was the third catastrophic disaster within a month to befall the finders of this new gold, this twenty-eight ounce gold nugget… there was now only one of the four original prospectors left who had not yet fallen under the curse of this new gold…

Nigel Dixon was only twenty-six years old, and the youngest of the four gold prospectors. He had been following the tragic stories of his three prospecting pals, and was now quite terrified at what might befall him.

He had never contacted any of his prospector partners, not even when they were on their possible deathbeds from their various, and most unusual accidents.

Nigel had refused to accept any of the gold spoils or any money from the sale of the gold… he was terrified. He figured out that he had but one option, and that was to run. Then again, to where, how do you run from an omen… a curse.

Nigel was expected to spend an after Christmas holiday with his family in the Eastern States… he never did arrive home; some weeks later he was eventually reported as a missing person. The Police investigation proved his bank accounts were unused, and his personal belongings never claimed from storage. Friends in Halls Creek, still to this day hold Nigel's belongings.

Nigel Dixon had disappeared from the face of this earth.

***

As of the time of writing this story, Jack Wightman is the only known survivor of this gold curse.

Having previously suffered horrendous injury, I am pleased to inform you that Jack, now in his eighties is well, and living in Perth in peaceful retirement.

Jack never did receive any reward or part of that large gold nugget; in fact, he has no idea what happened to the gold. He is happy with his remarkably good health, and that he still has a clear memory of those strange and dark events.

….The End…

Chapter Four:

Alluvial Gold Fever

It was just after four as I waited at the bar for Greg to start talking. He had pulled me out of my office to have a quiet chat about something; apparently, it was important enough not to discuss in my office.

Just then I overheard Lofty the tall skinny bloke sitting across in the other the bar, 'that's him over there mate,' I was being identified by one of the locals, but to whom?

The man in the akubra asking was in no hurry to meet me, as he turned his back and continued talking to another man at the bar. I soon lost interest to continue my conversation with a Geologist, who had just hired one of my Toyota Land cruisers for three weeks. He was obviously going to do some serious off roadwork, as he had the vehicle fitted out for extended bush-work.

'Diamonds, silver-lead, oil, gas... maybe gold, what's your poison Greg. There has been a lot of interest down around Halls Creek over the last year or so. Now we have you guys; the big boys, sniffing around... something must have sparked your interest?'

Greg took a sip of his drink, and then replied.

'You know I can't say anything about my clients business Niven, who did you say was sniffing around in Halls Creek?'

'I didn't say anyone in particular Greg, it was just my general observation;' then with my drink raised in a salute, 'anyway you know that I have the same rules as you, I can't say anything about any of my client's business.'

Greg smiled a knowing smile, took another sip of his beer, timing his riveting admission, and then told me more than I had expected to hear.

'Okay, we're looking at small gold producing tenements. Around seventeen companies have compliant registered claims in the Halls Creek area for both alluvial gold and at least one underground gold mine.

We aim to check out what they have and if they do have something worthwhile, we will make them an offer... Okay I have given you some information, the least you can do is to give me a little info in return?'

Greg was trying the friendly guilty angle on me... so this was the big secret discussion eh. What a waste of time, smarter blokes than Greg had tried far more cunning and craftier methods that this and failed to get me to talk.

The truth of the matter was, this time I really had no idea, nor did I know anything about what was going on down at Halls Creek.

Everybody I knew in the gold business was saying nothing, being very guarded. All this silly secrecy had me a bit concerned; the attitude had tweaked my nosey probing curious antenna.

Had anybody actually found any gold? I had been living and running a business in the Kimberley town of Kununurra for over eighteen years... nobody could keep a secret for more than a week up here... Greg and his large company had me intrigued, could I get a little more out of him.

'I just told you that there were a lot of people and companies sniffing around down in and around the Halls Creek area. I also know they are interested in gold, so you heading down there would be an easy guess by anyone. Anyone who had half a brain that you are also interested in gold; so you really didn't tell me anything at all... did you.'

'Yes but what you didn't know is that we are only interested in buying any proven gold claims... that must be worth something?'

'Well you do have a point there Greg, so what I will do for you is I will pass on that information to my clients. Who will no doubt get in touch with you if they have something to sell or discuss... assuming that is you agree with me passing on your gold interest details?'

Greg looked a little miffed at my sanitised and disarming reply. He quickly finished his drink and offered his hand for a farewell shake.

'Sorry I have to go Niven. I have to be in Halls Creek by eight and as you know, it is a long four-hour drive. Yes, you can let your clients know that I am interested in looking at buying any producing gold claims... I will keep in touch.'

I was still going over in my head what Greg had just said and looked down the bar to locate the stranger who was enquiring about me... but he was gone.

My office was only a short stroll from the hotel, and most times, especially if I planned to go back to work. Walking to the pub was by far the simple and quickest answer for a private business meeting, or a quick refreshing drink. As I approached my office, I noticed a strange almost new Toyota in my hire yard, the sign writing on the door said only one word "Majeed."

I glanced up at the office window and sure enough, the same bloke who was enquiring about me in the hotel was talking to my office manager Sue.

The office door was open, and the man of about fifty turned to face me as I entered. He had previously removed his akubra in a polite response to his surroundings and was dressed as a typical geologist in khaki; however, this man had a tan-line on his forehead. This to me was an obvious giveaway… this man was a gold prospector.

An akubra will shade you from the direct sun; however, over the years, reflected sun from gold panning still directed enough UV rays to tan a man's face. I had learnt this much in the two seconds before he spoke. I wonder, what more I shall learn, then with my right arm outstretched…

'Hi I'm Niven Dallas, sorry about the hotel, I was tied up with somebody.'

'No harm done mate. The names Sam Hall, Majeed mine Halls Creek. I was heading over to your office for a chat and not particularly thrilled at meeting up with that Greg bloke.'

Thinking to myself, so these people know each other, I wonder what the story was behind all of that. I was later to find out that this Greg geologist was only interested in procuring gold prospecting tenements that he could prove had defaulted on their expenditure program; thus acquiring tenement land by default, grabbing the claim off the previous or sitting owner... for free.

***

Things were heating up again, the usual nasty business was in full swing, but this time it was over gold... I was already suspicious.

'Well Sam what can we do for you, can I get you a drink coffee maybe?'

This was always a good way to open a new client relationship. We were now sitting in my inner, timber decked, padded office; complete with a well-stocked bar.

Steve's eyes roved around the office with a look of interest then locked eyes on me ready to discuss business.

'Black coffee strong will do me fine thanks Niven.'

Most unusual, this Sam bloke did not want to get on the piss; this must indeed be serious business.

I had never heard of "Majeed," then again, that is nothing new. These old gold mines and leases around Halls Creek had changed hands so many times over the years, although from what I remember, all normally kept their original founding name. The history of these old gold mines was just as important to attract investors, as was any possible gold found on them.

My thoughts drifted to just who was the new owner of this gold mine, and what man would disregarded this prime advantage. My thoughtful questions were soon answered.

'I am the mine manager at Majeed gold lease, near Halls Creek.' I quickly interjected. 'I have never heard of the Majeed gold mine. Is this a new mine?'

Sam gave a sigh as he continued, so I guessed that this same question had been asked many times.

'No, it's not a new mine but an old alluvial gold lease with a new name. It's a complicated story mate, but basically, a bloke called the Jah; he's an Indian Prince living in Perth. He bought one of the old gold leases in the Baily Range and renamed it after his Turkish Grandfather, why I don't bloody know or care. What I do know is this bloke is loaded, he's a billionaire and is willing to spend big money to bring this old alluvial gold lease back into production.'

I thought to myself how odd, as the only thing going for those old gold mines around Halls Creek was their famous 120-year-old names. Certainly not for the gold potential, or out-put, as none of them to my knowledge had ever become a commercial proposition over that long period.

This was proving to be most interesting; especially as I had never known one of these old mines to employ a proper licensed mine manager. Had they discovered a commercial amount of gold? I must hear more.

'Sam can I ask what brings you to see me?'

As with all people who have something they cannot see without a mirror, Sam looked quite funny sitting on the other side of my desk; akubra parked on the desk holding a cup of coffee while sporting a pronounced suntan-line across the middle of his forehead.

His coffee cup rattled a bit as he placed it back on the desk alongside his well-used akubra, he then launched into business. This cup observation put me on high alert... this man might have a small drinking problem.

'Your company offers a number of services that our new mine will need. Firstly, you have a mechanical workshop specialising in the service and repair of off-road vehicles and a Toyota 4X4 hire service. Second, you have a Codan HF radio communications, service, sales, and repair workshop. Thirdly you have a light aircraft available to service your client's remote and urgent problems, and you know the Kimberley area well.' He then added matter-of-factually...

'We will of course require you to sign a confidentially agreement, after which, Majeed Pty Ltd will open a line of credit with your company. We will pay promptly on statements tendered the twenty-fifth of each month.'

311

Sam had stopped talking, there was a strained extended lull as we both looked at each other; someone should say something. I could tell by his expression Sam wanted an answer, and right now, but that was not my style.

***

I could say without a doubt that I am an old hand at this type of offer. Prospectors usually have lots of secrets and little money, or being a little blunt; they just had no bloody money at all, and were full of bullshit. Even the so-called larger exploration companies and new ASX mining floats appeared to have great difficulty in paying their bills... I had distinctly heard Sam say, "They will open a line of credit," thinking what about if I refuse. I wonder had he considered that.

If I managed to collect just fifty cents in every dollar, lost in trusting these weird gold people, I would not have my current large overdraft problem, and would have a much happier bank manager... Then again, an Indian Prince who is loaded, well maybe that is worth a go.

I had a distinct feeling, the juicy lure and hook was for me... yet again. With the potential sniff of some good future business, I was always an easy catch knowing greed has no true master, just like gold. However, this time I had a plan to reduce my usual exposure to financial pain and ruin, well so I had thought.

'Okay I am interested. I will of course sign your confidentially agreement; but firstly we will need to start off quite small. I would suggest we start with a simple payment on delivery or completion of a service, and then see how we go. Have you any immediate service we can offer as a sort of trial prior to possibly opening a full monthly account?'

Sam's eyes eyelids flickered rapidly in surprise; I do not think this was quite what he had in mind. It was obvious he expected me to be somewhat overwhelmed by this Prince Jah person, but the truth of this matter was... I had no idea who this Jah bloke was.

Sam looked down at my desk, and with a sigh tried again. I could almost read his very thoughts. This man was not dumb; however, names and powerful rich owners had little

312

impact on this ignorant bush businessman. How then could he gain some measure of trust, then choosing his words carefully.

'Well the first thing we will need is communications. At this time, we have to drive over fifty minutes into Halls Creek to make a phone call. There are nine full-time workers at the mine; as such, we are required to have a RFDS (Royal Flying Doctors Service) radio at the site in case of an emergency.

This is our first priority; can your company supply and install this radio equipment?'

'When do you want this radio system installed?'

Sam snapped back with assurance…

'We would prefer as soon as possible.'

'All right then, I will fly the radio equipment and a technician down to Halls Creek early tomorrow morning if that is convenient enough for you.'

The man looked stunned.

'Niven, that would great. However, I would much prefer if you could land at the Ruby Plains Station strip. The tenement is only twenty minutes from there, and we do have permission from the manager of Ruby station.

I am surprised that you can both supply and install an RFDS radio system at such short notice. I had thought it will take time applying for the required radio licence for a new company channel, and we will also need radio operator's certificate. Then we have to register Majeed with the RFDS.'

Sam obviously knew the complex bureaucratic procedures in these matters, which was good. This man was not a city slicker and understood the challenge.

'No problems Sam, I will sort out all the licensing details. Initially you will have the use of three of my company private HF channels while we apply and wait for your own.

You will initially have to use our call sign until we install your assigned frequency, we will also train your radio operator to the required standard.

Another advantage is, we have available a radiophone hook-up service, just the same as the RFDS open phone system. It is not very private but it works on our own company frequency, and it is available from 6am to 6pm, all day. This service is far better compared to the RFDS, one-hour morning, and afternoon session on a five-day week, Monday to Friday.'

Sam again stared at me in silence... I could almost read his mind. Other radio systems quotes could not match this for a next-day service, but the equipment might cost him less... but at what overall delay cost?

During this short silence, I had completed my sums and now ready to provide an answer to Sam's doubtful thoughts.

'For the supply and install on site of a Codan 7727 transceiver, battery powered; with long-wire antenna system, travel cost and labour, a total off... $1,980.00.'

This was still a considerable sum of money; the ball was in Sam's court... did he still want to play?

The silence continued as Sam scribbled down some numbers in his mine-managers notebook, ripped out a page, and handed it to me.

'Those are the ground co-ordinates of Majeed gold mine. Make one low flyover and I will drive over to Ruby Station and pick you up.'

I was just about to remind Sam of my first condition when Sam casually pulled out a well-worn chequebook and proceeded to fill out a cheque for the full required payment. Now I was stunned into silence.

Sam stood up, retrieved his battered akubra from my desk, and then fitted it to his head with meticulous precision right down to the suntan line. He extended his hand and we shook the deal done in true Kimberley fashion, and then he said his last few words before departing my office.

'I will see you early tomorrow morning at the Ruby station strip.'

Little was I to know that this was only the very beginning of a long, hectic new business relationship. It was a time and a place involving some shady people, and some well-known colourful mining and prospecting characters.

Chapter Five:

The Majeed gold mine

All was ready; the radio equipment channelled out, and antenna system built to suit the Majeed gold lease. Stevo my radio technician had everything packed for our first light departure tomorrow morning.

The flyover of the Majeed alluvial gold mine revealed very little activity on the ground as the position was thick with trees, giving us only a glimpse of the odd vehicle and a green tin roof.

Landing at Ruby station, the station manager drove over in his Toyota to meet us. He was not impressed when I told him we were waiting on Majeed. I could tell that Sam had not advised this man of our intended landing at his airstrip… this was not the correct bush etiquette… this was not a good start.

The manager explained that he had some issues with the Majeed lot, and were not on talking terms. I apologised for landing on his strip without his direct permission, he softened a little and said he understood it was not my fault offering his hand. Then just before the Majeed Toyota pulled-up, the station manager quickly drove off.

The guy in the Majeed Toyota was not Sam; he looked around thirty-five, and dressed in typical khaki geologists gear, long sleeved shirt, and long pants.

'Hi I'm Gary from Majeed, you must be Niven Dallas. Put your gear in the back and I will take you over to the Majeed mine.'

I introduced Gary to my radio tech Steveo who grunted his acknowledgement. Steveo was a man of little words and a great fear of flying. It will take Steveo another two hours before he will get over the flight out to Ruby plains station... Then there was the flight back to worry about, such are the challenges of a technician working in the remote north-west.

With our gear loaded and on our way, I thought this might be the best time to find out why the Ruby station manager was not happy with our arrival. Then there was the other question... where was Sam?

'What's with all the agro with the station manager, he almost threw us off the station strip. I was told by Sam I had clearance to land at Ruby... and Sam said he was going to pick us up?'

Gary had this silly almost jovial attitude to my question that caused me to glance at Steveo who I knew had the same opinion... this bloke was strange. Gary burst-forth with...

'Sam is on another mine site, he is the mine manager to around six mines in this area alone and many more in the Northern Territory.

As for that Ruby manager bloke, he thinks that since the Majeed mine is on his station property, he should get a piece of the action. Anyway we are building our own airstrip, right next to the mine, which should shut him up.'

Gary drove his Toyota like a maniac down a rough bush track, a track cut through thick bush and mature trees. Strangely, from the air this area did not look that heavy with foliage, or that hilly. All this secrecy had me a little concerned; have they really discovered a viable, commercial goldmine? Then again, Halls Creek has a long history of gold prospecting and mining, however, nothing that ever provided a real long-term sustained commercial mine.

We were obviously following and crossing a well-defined riverbed. Then another thought came to mind, just where, and how would they build this airstrip around here? Well, why not ask this and other questions, starting with...

'I thought a mine manager had to remain on site during a working day?'

***

Between the violent back-wrenching dips in the track, it was hard to hold a conversation. However, Gary who had a firm grip on the steering wheel was okay, with a wicked grin gave his answer.

'You only require a fulltime, on-site mine manager with a full production mine, we are nowhere near that yet… but will be soon. We need a qualified mine manager in place for when things start moving.'

With welcome relief to my back, Gary slowed down. I thought we must have arrived at the mine. Through the thick bush, I had noticed a number of mining camp transportable buildings, and heavy earthmoving and mining equipment.

I started to think this was quite a big mining operation. We then slowly drove past this lot and continued up to the top of a small hill. From this small hilltop position, I could see the mine site about half a kilometre away. One very large 12X12 metre, almost new; corrugated tin shed, built close to a well-defined running creek bed.

Steveo came to life again and grunted. 'No wonder we could not see the bloody mine from the air, the fucking mine-shed is the same colour as the bush.'

As we pulled up at the side of the shed, it was only then I noticed setback in the bush were three olive green transportable camp buildings. A silly thought came to mind, were they trying to conceal this mine?

Gary stamped on the brake bringing the Toyota to a sudden stop and shut the diesel down, parking behind one of the transportable buildings. Steveo and I pealed our fingers off the grab handles above the doors, happy that this ordeal was over.

A small generator chugged away somewhere close by, with a musical complement of the Seekers "I'll never find another you." These sounds drowned by a very vocal argument that was taking place just the other side of the camp building. We paused in our tracks to listen.

***

'Yer a bloody liar, we had a deal shithead. You lot cover all the costs of fuel and maintenance fir the plant, and we git all living provisions and twenty-five percent of the gold outa this here mine. We reckon that you're ripping us lot orf. I warned you before mate, somebody could end-up bloody dead.'

Just then, a sort off rough female voice pipe-up in her broad Queensland accent.

'You lot should know by now we don't take no shit. Mat and mah boys are gittin mighty toey fir an answer. We agreed ta do all the mine earth works, but that don't include a fucking airstrip. I thinks yer pushing yer luck… mate.'

The response was just as shattering to hear. A very proper upper-crust clipped English voice took to the floor and answered the tough threatening Queenslanders.

'My dear chaps, might I impose on your limited intelligence to consider the facts. You must accept that many matters are much beyond your meagre understanding. However, we must progress in the correct order to achieve our aim. The proposed airstrip will ultimately become vital to the success of our gold operation.

I might also add that others are interested in our efforts, if they do indeed succeed; we will then have little or nothing to do with the control or operation of this gold claim. In such an event we will all loose.'

It was just about then Steveo and I came around the end of the transportable, bringing the argumentative group into view. Three people were sitting at what looked like a card table; they were facing three others, standing with a look of astonishment on their faces. A stunned silence filled the air.

It was obvious that they were having problems understanding the gravity of what the very British voice said. This short silence was soon interrupted, suddenly the rough looking woman who belonged to the rough voice, noticed our presence and demanded.

'Who the fuck are you lot?'

The movements were quick like a cornered wild animal. The old man wearing a battered bush hat, rough Ned Kelly beard, and slit eyes swung around to face us with an evil grin.

He had his hand firmly around the butt of a well-cared-for Glock nine millimetre automatic. Thankfully, the gun remained rammed into the front of his dirty jeans.

My eyes were beginning to reach saucer-size. A quick eyeball swivel confirmed that Steveo with his mouth open at the quiet scream position had missed nothing.

The young man covered in many tattoos standing next to Ned Kelly had a powerful looking cross-bow strapped across his bare back, but with lightning speed had un-holstered a beautiful all stainless-steel 44 magnum revolver.

My fear ramped up a notch when this young man cocked the weapon as he pointed it… at me.

In panic, I thought it was lucky I had completed my ablutions prior to departing Kununurra, failing which I would most certainly have shit my pants. A sudden powerful smell advised me that Stevo might have released to this terror in the bush… Flying back home in a light aircraft was no longer his main concern; this present situation had him thinking about his immediate future term of life.

The three men sitting at the table had little or no interest in the display of weapons. They were waiting like the others for our answer. The tense moment rapidly averted as Gary stepped out from behind us.

'Hi guys, don't shoot these blokes, they are here to install our new RFDS radio system. Shoot them after it's up and running. Ha ha ha.'

The older man at the table broke into a wide smile as he added some mortifying humour.

'Fuck that was lucky mate; Young Mervyn here was keen to blow somebody away again. I reckon his old man would have sent us a bill for the back-hoe time to bury em in the bush.'

The young man reluctantly holstered his big gun, displaying a disappointed glum face that matched that of his Mum. These people were a rough looking lot that would have made Jed Clampett and Granny of the Hillbillies look tame. I was soon to find out they more closely resembled the inbred characters portrayed in the movie Deliverance.

What the hell did we get ourselves into this time? Suddenly Ned Kelly turned to the three at the table and announced…

'We're outa here, an don't forget what a said yah hear. We want what's due to us, and bloody soon but.'

The hillbillies moved on, leaving the meeting and us to ponder the next move. Just then, I distinctly heard the shssh of a beer can opening and the man sitting at the card table raised his can and announced in a very upper crust British accent.

'I say chaps, if I am not mistaken those Neanderthals were seemingly threatening us. We should remind them they are not the only ones around here with weapons… anyone for a beer?'

A beer, I glanced at my watch, it was only a little after seven-thirty in the morning. Now standing at the table was a sun burnt slim-built man, wearing only a pair of dirty well-worn football shorts and well-travelled rubber thongs on his dirty feet. His hair was long and matted, in keeping with his week-old grunge beard and the large unkempt moustache… I thought; was this the same man who spoke in the cultured British accent. This matter was soon resolved when he spoke again.

'Now settle down there chaps, the bad men are gone, no harm done.' With a radiant smile, he then courteously extended his arm for a civil response.

'I am David Michaels. I over-see matters around here on behalf of the Majeed mining tenement owner, Mukarram Jah, the Eighth Nizam of Hyderabad. This is our esteemed geologist Bill and this chap is the well-known local identity Jack Whiteman, tenement caretaker.'

***

With the introductions out of the way, Gary suggested that Bill and Jack should come along and help Steveo install the new radio system in the other transportable. The boys grabbed a beer each and followed Greg. This left me chatting to David Michaels, offering a good time to ask a few questions, and I did have a few.

'If you don't mind me saying Dave, you don't sound like you come from around here. However I notice that you have taken-up some of the local habits.' Nodding at the beer firmly clasped in his hand. David looked a little disturbed, if not embarrassed at my observation, and then added.

'Well I must admit Niven; this is not really my normal employment function. My position is as secretary to the Jah, attending to his daily business matters as instructed. The Nizam has purchased this gold lease, and I am here to see his instructions are carried out.'

This odd man fascinated me; I also had a secretary, but she didn't look or sound anything like this bloke. David continued.

'As you have no doubt realised, I am British. I have been to Australia many times as the representative to Her Majesty's service, being a Queens Guard, and with the British Foreign Office.

My last assignment prior to my resignation from my command and the British government. I had applied for a permanent residency in Australia, taking the position as aide de camp to the West Australian Governor Sir Douglas Kendrew.

I met the Jah many years ago while at Sandhurst, and had renewed our acquaintance when attending a Perth Government function on foreign trade.

So you would see this gold mining line of occupation is somewhat out of character for me.'

Listening to this bloke talk, he sounded to me just like Captain Mannering in the old TV series "Are you being served." This was soon to be Michael's nickname; I was to find out over the coming weeks that Captain Mannering had an extensive, odd and chequered past.

This man had seemingly crossed swards with more than a practice opponent in the Queens Guards, but with some of the most powerful men in Australia, and later in the UK.

Being a resident in one of Australia's remotest places, along with most others living in this area, I had given up on trying to stay current with the Perth and world news. Unknown to me, this man's affairs had been all over the news headlines during the past year.

As personal assistant to the Jah, the Jah had placed great trust and responsibility with David Michael in managing his day-to-day business matters... matters that were later to take a sudden and unfortunate financial turn for the Mukarram Jah, the Eighth Nizam of Hyderabad. This present situation had me wondering, why was David Michael way up here in the remote Kimberley.

I was later to discover that this was David Michaels second term of employment with the Jah. On receiving the resignation letter, the Jah was said to have replied to Michaels, "I see you are leaving the tent of a Prince to lead the camels of a merchant, possibly a wise move."

Soon Michaels would yet again head for a high place, as in late 1985, some ten months after our first meeting. David Michael then resigned his PA position with the Jah to take a similar position with Alan Bond, who had offered the added aloof position as (The director of toys,) based in the Bond Tower in St Georges Terrace Perth.

Some eighteen months later in early January 1987, I was in Perth, having just enjoyed a much-needed Christmas break with the family when my new, on loan Philips PC105T mobile phone rang. I had earlier telexed my new mobile number to Captain Mannering in Perth, and he was the first to call that new phone. David arranged for a meeting and a City lunch for the next day; I was to meet him at his office in the Bond Tower at midday.

Captain Mannering was waiting at the security desk to escort me in the private Dallhold lift up to his office. The fast lift opened at the Alan Bond Dallhold headquarters, occupying the forty-ninth floor. This was a man, who had indeed reached high places.

The first item to be seen on the lift doors opening was the famous painting by Vincent van Gogh, Irises. Captain Mannering with a sweeping hand and a broad smile announced boldly in his crisp English, 'what do you think of that Niven?' My answer must have come as a dim shock to this sophisticated social climbing man.

'I really don't have a thing for paintings of flowers, and well... this painting is in my view not a very good artist impression of any real flowers.'

With eyebrows raised and jaw dropped, Captain Mannering was not amused at my artistic ignorance, or lack of being impressed by this faded old painting.

'By the great hanging balls of Hector and Alexander; Niven old chap, this famous painting is the one and only Irises created by no other than Vincent Van Gogh. It is distinguished throughout the world as a fucking masterpiece and cost our Chairman Alan Bond a mind-blowing fifty-four million American Dollars.'

I had suddenly realised at this point that I had pressed the wrong social etiquette button. Now my mind was racing; how could repair this verbal mess, bearing in mind that Captain Mannering was just about to take me out to a slap-up boozy lunch... an urgent diversion was needed.

'David, you will have to make a large allowance for my low intelligence and lack of artistic knowledge, especially in matters of paintings. Remember I am from the outback, and quite dumb about these important things. I can tell you now; even the Kimberley Aboriginals give me a strange look when I refuse to accept that twenty million red, white and black dots arranged into childish shapes of lizards and snakes is actually art.

Why don't you tell me all about the important things you do each day for your Company Chairman Mr. Bond?'

Captain Mannering stepped out the lift, turning sharp right into a small office, advising he worked from what was originally a small stationary storeroom, hastily converted into his office. This small office had no windows being next to the lift shaft and very noisy when the lift was travelling. I was quickly drawn to what was covering his desk, a large-scale model of a Boeing 707

'What's this' I enquired picking up the model, and noting the many texture markings on the hull.'

Captain Mannering replied with obvious pride.

'This Boeing 707, when rebuilt will be our Chairman's flagship, the aircraft is currently in Israel undergoing extensive engine power upgrades and many other modifications such as increased fuel-load and the latest electronics.'

This was a long way out of my flying experience and league, I was impressed... this was serious money. The only concern I had was Captain Mannering appeared to be in control of this large project, and I knew for a fact he knew nothing about aircraft or flying. I remember asking why he choose an old expensive to run and maintain four-engine airliner; Captain Mannering was quick to reply...

'Safety is our main concern Niven; four engines are much safer than two. We will not compromise on the safety of our Chairman.'

I looked Captain Mannering in the eye, and noted the flicker doubt. David knew I had previously owned an air charter business with four single engine and two twin-engine aircraft. Captain Mannering realised that the Bond Company bullshit line will not work with me... this time it was he who diverted the line of conversation.

'I say Niven, look at the time we are running late; lunch at Coco's has been booked for one-thirty, we may miss the best of the fresh oysters, and that will not do.'

Over a splendid and extended lunch, Captain Mannering eased his tension a little, as we reminisced over old times at the Majeed gold mine. Clearly, something was bothering him, and I ventured to take the risk and ask what... David replied in a low guarded voice.

'Things are not all what they would seem Niven; you obviously do not follow the media. Our Company and Chairman are under great pressure and threat from outside business forces.'

On the way back to the Bond Tower, Captain Mannering remained silent in deep thoughts. I took this opportunity to change the subject back to the Irises painting.

'One thing that I thought was a bit odd David, why was a fifty-four million dollar painting hanging in the lift foyer reception area? It should be hanging on a wall in Alan Bonds house.'

David perked up a little, replying...

'That is only a temporary position; the Irises will hang in the boardroom when the current renovations are finished.'

During our nice lunch, David admitted to his Perth nickname of "The toy man" given to him by Alan Bonds wife Eileen. His main job was to arrange all the travel documentation, company private jet flights and all the parties. We agreed that I would be included on the next party list... sadly that was to be the last time I was ever to talk with David Michaels/Captain Mannering. History and media records show David Michaels had much more important matters to answer. It was eight months later again leaving the Bond camel merchant and taking up his old position in the tent his previous Prince.

***

Back to 1985 and the Majeed gold mine.

The thought later crossed my mind; could there be the reason for the low mining profile and camouflaged buildings? Was this man hiding?

Nonetheless, right now, I did not know what to believe, and was very worried about the gun tooting Neanderthals. More questions and more answers were required.

'Who the hell were those gun-happy idiots; we only came here to install an RFDS radio and were nearly blown away. I can tell you now I am not financially secure enough to die right now. My wife and kids would have been a bit pissed off.'

Captain Mannering took a long draw on his beer and sighed...

'I must confess old chap we do have a small problem to resolve with the Neanderthals. They think mining for gold is easy, and splitting the profits is like after robbing a bank. We do indeed have a major situation to resolve... and quite soon.'

I was lost. Why would anybody demand or threaten anything, especially a contractor?

In my business, we have little or no conflict with our contractors. Before accepting a service, we always agree on a firm price for the service required, and when to be completed. The same business rules apply when I am the contractor... end of story. However, I was soon to learn, this was not how the Jah conducted his business.

I could learn something here, maybe not to enter into business with the Jah. I was soon to find out, the Jah was innocent, and had no idea what was going on at his gold lease… nor for that matter did he care.

Other devious skulduggery was in play, together with other financial and legal matters. Matters that would bring about the end to the Jah's happy gold mining days, but not before someone attempted to make a great deal of money.

With a small amount of verbal coaxing, Captain Mannering spilt the beans and told me all about the Neanderthals.

Apparently, these people were taking up a whole truck rest-bay just outside of Halls Creek. The local Shire had given them orders to move on, as they had been there for over a week. The local truckies were complaining about five big semi-trailers with Queensland plates, loaded with earthmoving plant, who appeared to have set-up a permanent camp in the local truck-bay.

As the story goes, Jack Whiteman being a nosey bastard pulled in for a chat. He discovered over a few rum's that they were a family of Mum, Dad, three boys and an uncle. They were in the earth moving business in Townsville when the work and money ran out.

The Bank of Queensland had foreclosed on their loans, so they just loaded everything up and hit the road north-west. Now they had another problem, they had run out of fuel and cash.

Jack had an answer to all their problems… hide in the bush. Then he suggested a true bushman's carrot deal; In return for carrying out the earth works at the gold mine, they would get a percentage of the recovered gold. The hillbillies slipped in their demands, it was only a deal if the gold mine included all living and equipment running costs.

Grandma hillbilly and Jack spat on their hands and then shook hands. The deal then concluded by drinking few litre bottles of over-proof Queensland rum.

Jack never did admit to what the hillbillies claimed the deal was. Frankly, I doubt after all that rum, any of them remembered the details. Never the less, this was the basis of all the tension at the gold mine. Tension that had now apparently escalated to direct threats of violence.

'David is this a new gold lease; and how long has it been active? I ask this because in the twenty years I have lived in the Kimberley, nobody has ever turned a profit out of gold mining in this area.'

Captain Mannering shrugged his shoulders the way the French do. Then with a voice of caution and narrowed eyes, gave his reserved reply.

'The Jah bought this gold lease some two years ago. I do believe it has been around for over one hundred and twenty-three years. It was part of the old Ruby mine, having a considerable history of producing gold. I have no idea if it were ever profitable.'

At this point, I could tell I was close to my limit in poking around in his business. They do say that it was curiosity, which really did kill the cat.

'If you don't mind my nosey interest, the last question is; why the hell did this bloke the Jah buy the bloody place?'

'Simple old chap, the Jah is very fond of gold. However, he likes the idea of owning a gold mine even more.

You must understand Niven; the Jah has no need for profits. In addition, the Jah's prime interest in this place is it is extremely remote. Here he can carry out his greatest passion. Driving bulldozers.'

He then looked me straight in the eye with a smile; my face must have reflected volumes of doubt that required clarification.

'Some wealthy people do like their sailing or golf. However, the Jah prefers charging around the place in his bulldozer. He is quite good at it you know.

As for the gold part; my employment brief is to make this mine at least self-supporting.' Captain Mannering stood-up and finished his beer in one gulp. 'Come along Niven, I shall show you how gold is recovered.'

We travelled at a more stately speed. Following the narrow creek to a small pool, where a man on his knees in a wide brim hat was inspecting a panning dish.

Captain Mannering asked Bill, the same bloke I had met at the gun drama to demonstrate how they find gold. Bill called out.

'Come take a look mate.'

I positioned myself looking over his shoulders, watching him expertly move the panning dish in a typical prospector's cyclic motion. Within twenty seconds, I could clearly see two minuscule specks of gold. Bill expertly picked both up with his wet finger, placing them onto a clean plastic lid.

'There yer are mate… gold, Mother Nature's reward for hard bloody work.'

This was amazing; I had never seen gold panned from a creek bed, it was the stuff of movies. Captain Mannering and Bill were beaming wide smiles of proof, and no doubt future wealth. This was when I asked the wrong question. What was the value of the gold specks on the plastic jar-lid? Captain Mannering replied with bubbling enthusiasm...

'You must understand Niven; gold is the world international currency. I do not know todays London gold bullion market, however, three days ago it was trading four hundred and thirty-two dollars US an ounce. All indications are it would seem gold will exceed seven hundred dollars an ounce by November this year.'

I asked again.

'What are those two gold specks worth?'

The smiles dropped off their faces as Bill replied.

'I would fink if yer had a scale small enough to weigh em, say a couple-a-bucks.' Then realising my point quickly added.

'Mate, we only use the panning for testing for a good spot. Then we use the HPC gravity spiral separator.' He then nodded toward a small barrel machine on wheels. 'If we're lucky and find a good spot we can separate around half to one ounce of gold a day, not bad eh?'

These figures did not impress me at all, especially when I discovered they only had one spiral barrel machine. Five or six hundred Australian dollars a day would go nowhere near the cost of running this mine. Again, I had my doubts challenged before I spoke. This time Captain Mannering attempted to resolve my obvious doubts.

'We must be going; I do have urgent business to attend to. Do understand these alluvial gold tests are in line with our geological expectations. The plan is to build a sixty ton per hour, as you say… barrel.

Our existing system can only process five ton, so using Bill's numbers we should recover around eighteen ounces of gold each day.

At today's market price that should equate to around seven thousand, seven hundred and forty dollars a day, or two hundred and thirty two thousand dollars a month. Considering our early plans, this is not such a bad return for the effort old chap. You see, we just need to find someone who can build us a larger machine.'

I was in shock mood again, that was quite a bit of money. Then thinking, if they ran the proposed new plant on three shifts, they would stand to turnover seven hundred thousand dollars a month… However, what would all this cost, and would this Jah bloke cough up the development money?

I came out of my mathematical daze as Captain Mannering had pulled into the large green shed. The contents came as another big surprise.

Standing there in all its glory was a Fiat-Allis HD 41 bulldozer, at that time this would have been the largest available bulldozer in the world. Next to the dozer was a nice 12E Caterpillar grader. Behind the huge dozer were two diesel powered generators, one large and one smaller with all the required power cables and control cabinets.

The remainder of this shed almost full with building materials and mobile fuel tanks; a thought came to mind. This mine was well equipped for something, and by the choice of earthmoving plant, it was not gold mining.

Being inquisitive, as well as nosey is a problem I have lived with all my life. I just had to ask the question.

'This earth-moving plant is a bit on the huge side for a small alluvial gold mine. Is all this equipment belonging to those gun mad Queensland Hillbillies?'

I could see Captain Mannering was reacting well to my new-surprised look, and eager to tell me more.

'No, no Niven, all this plant, and equipment are owned by the Majeed mine. The HD 41 is the Jah's personal favourite toy. When the Jah is at the mine he spends most of his time, driving that monster making roads.'

'Well I hope this Jah bloke didn't make the road into this place, it's a bloody mess.' Captain Mannering was quick to respond.

'The Jah prefers to leave the mine entry road as it is, rough. You see, Jah is a very private man, he will not have a perfect two-lane highway into his mine, and he much prefers to stay out of the lime-light as it were.'

Captain Mannering slipped into a nostalgic mood, while staring passionately at the Cat 12E grader, and opened up his mind.

'We would start working at first light, taking a small packed breakfast and lunch, with a few bottles of water. The Jah, a being Muslim takes no alcohol, so I had to make do with warm water and rum.

We worked all day in the hot sun, building new roads until last light. Jah would bulldoze the roadway, and I would follow-up with Cat grader touching up things. I would say to date we have made many kilometres of perfectly straight roads that go to nowhere. If the Jah thought the new road had a kink in it, we would have to redo the bent part.'

I was starting to get that creepy feeling again; kinky and bent were words that fitted well with my assessment of this place and the people. Captain Mannering noting my confused look was well ahead of my thoughts again... adding.

'As I have said earlier the Jah has no need for profits, he just likes remote areas, and making roads with his HD 41 bulldozer. Niven, I am the one who is trying to make this mine profitable.

I have brought you here, to show you the yet to be installed diesel power generators. The reason being, can you recommend someone local who we can contract to install our mine power system?'

***

I was in captive mode again. The lure of future dollars was creating a powerful attraction, overpowering and rejecting my natural restraint, screaming out a call for immediate caution... too late, I had opened my mouth.

'I can do better than that Captain Mann... err David. I can recommend to you two men who are not only qualified Australian commercial electricians; but one also holds a shipwright ticket. John Varga and John Caratti are owners of VOC, a company that has all the qualifications and resources to build your sixty ton spiral separator, and can install your diesel generators and electrical equipment.'

***

Little was I to know this was just the start, to my unwittingly trusting involvement. I could feel myself drawn childishly into events with the Majeed gold mine... and the interesting Captain Mannering.

I was soon to learn there is no difference between a gold prospector, a nutcase adventurer, an underhanded gold salting crook, or for that matter an idiot. You can guess who the idiot was... me.

Chapter Six:

There is gold here

It was only about a week later when I called around to John Varga and the VOC workshops. However, Sam from Majeed had already been in contact with the VOC boys. In fact, both Johns had already been down to Halls Creek by road and inspected the required Majeed work.

Varga had two electricians working on the mine power generators as we spoke. This was fast work, Varga was not happy to discuss the contract to build the spiral gravity gold separator, it was not normal for John to be secretive. However, he did confirm that he was going to build it.

I was thinking this is strange; from our odd conversation, the two Johns had no idea I was the one who had suggested them for the job. I would have preferred to tell them all about my shooting scare by the family of gun slinging hillbillies. What would they have thought about the strange bulldozer road-making habits of the mine owner, this Indian Jah Prince bloke?

I wondered would they have taken the job if I had. Then there was another thing; the Jah had owned the mine for almost two years. What was the big hurry to start mining development all about? I was soon to find out.

***

The two Johns were very smart businessmen, always on the lookout for a good deal and a way to make money. They had both heard of the recent gold mining activity down in Halls Creek, and had considered getting into the action. This was just the right opportunity.

I had nothing to worry about when Caratti later told me they had done a deal with Captain Mannering. Apparently, Majeed were not about to pay cash for the new sixty ton spiral gravity gold separator. Majeed were looking for a goldmine partner to offset the cost.

The two Johns had sniffed a number of odd problems with deal. Nonetheless, they did eventually agree to build and operate the gold separator. The deal was they pay Majeed twenty percent of any gold recovered on the Majeed gold claim. I was later to discover that this deal was then offered to other small gold leaseholders in the area.

***

For the record, a few years later, I had a long chat with the two Johns about this exciting time. They advised me they regretted ever getting involved with gold mining. The sixty-ton spiral separator cost them a huge amount of money and time to build, the cost was by far more than they ever recovered in gold. They went on to say, what little gold they did recover never actually covered the expense of just running the plant. With luck, they later sold the plant to another hopeful gold prospector.

***

There was very little gold recovered from the Majeed gold lease. The two Johns were becoming suspicious about all the gold recovery talked about down at the Halls Creek pub. Talk they both knew to be lies… but why spread all these lies?

***

Some months later I received a call on the company HF radio from the Majeed mine, they had decided to take up my option of hiring a radiophone interface. Would I come down to the Majeed mine and install the equipment as soon as possible.

On reflection I should have sent someone else; however, I was flying to Port Hedland in the next few days to deliver some documents and sort out a small problem with the radios on my old Piper Aztec aircraft, an aircraft I had sold some six weeks ago. I would simply call into the Majeed mine on the way down. This would be a chance to inspect the new Majeed airstrip, and check if they were they building airstrip to ALA (authorised landing area) standards.

***

My business activities were now taking on another important turn. With the workload increasing, something must go, my decision was regretfully difficult to make, and I now admit I had made a mistake. However, in my overworked mind, now was the time to put Kimberley Air Charter (K-Air) on the market for sale... before Lesley or I went mad.

Chapter Seven:

K-Air Sold then Ruined

My business life had taken a hectic turn. I had just entered into a complicated deal to sell my air charter business Kimberley Air Charter. The deal was proving very difficult as the lending bank; Commonwealth kept changing their lending security requirements for the purchaser.

As with all banks, their dealings with the client is confidential, even though I was a party to the lending deal being the vender.

The purchaser, I shall call him Mr Bull Dozer. Mr Dozer being a keen buyer, and having a life-long interest in flying. He responded to my Australia wide advertisement for the sale of K-Air (Kimberley Air Charter.)

Around twelve other people responded to my advert, these enquiries kept me busy answering their many requests for detailed information.

Having sold many small businesses in the past, I pride myself in quickly detecting and separating opposition business operators, and nosey sticky-beaks from the genuine buyers. One name stood out, an eastern states charter operator with a South African accent. I had met this man a while ago in Kununurra, he was sniffing around talking to everyone in the air charter business.

In his first contact, he demanded to know who my direct opposition were, and what the future prospects were. No mention made regarding the financials and other important information, my danger sensors were on full alert. I returned a reply advising the business as sold. Unfortunately, this was not the last I would hear from this man.

***

Mr Bull Dozer sounded to me that he was well out of his depth. After noting his flying experience was limited and his charter flying experience was zero, along with his business experience. I then advised this keen buyer to work in the industry for a year or two before buying into this hornet's nest. One week later Dozer decided on a face-to-face meeting with me, arriving with little notice in Kununurra... well I had to admit he was keen.

Dozer was a strong pushy type of a bloke, hence the new surname, and Bull being a perfect description for a first name, as his attitude was all wrong, and level of knowledge low. The word "no" was not in his vocabulary. This man had made up his mind to get into the flying charter business. He had advised me he was considering two other similar business deals, Dozer wanted to look over my charter operation before deciding on which to buy.

In twenty minutes I had, what I thought was the full story. Mr Bull Dozer was on twelve weeks long-service leave from his government job of twenty-three years. His intent was to resign his senior government position prior to the end of his leave, thus determined to buy and run his own flying business.

This was a basket case; it became obvious to me Mr Dozer was trying to live out his business fantasy. I tried to explain that being a boss of sixty people in a government office was a very different matter to running a private business venture.

The taxpayer pays for all business leasing premises, the wages and costs for the government employees. Whereas in the private business world, the business must stump up all the costs. You must run a very profitable business to cover all the bloody costs... and it is not easy.

What was easy to do, is make a quick, and wrong decision, causing you and your business great pain. In other words, display a lack of experience and judgment. I can recall that I too had this same can-do attitude when first trying my hand at running a small business. Dozer was firmly committed, this being the first qualification on the narrow bumpy road to success. He was determined to try his hand at business.

Eventually we struck a compromise deal, whereby I would sell all the business and chattels for a lump sum. Dozer would then refinance the Cessna 402 at the current debt, (being well below the current value,) he could then continue to cross-hire the Piper Lance from Darwin.

I then offered to cross-hire to him my Cessna 207, and Cessna 182RG. This offer brought down the cost of buying the complete business by around half, while still providing him with a working fleet of aircraft.

I introduced Dozer to my Commonwealth bank manager who was interested in transferring the Cessna 402 finance to the new Kimberley Air Charter owner. The bank then agreed to fund and continue business with K-Air and the new owner. The sale of K-Air now confirmed with a deposit taken and a settlement date set. All was looking good for a normal settlement and handover… or was it.

***

Bull Dozer and his family arrived in Kununurra about three weeks prior to the settlement. He had sold his house quickly, and decided to take up my offer in learning a bit about the air charter business.

Dozer was a quick learner; however, he had his own way of running a business and getting things done, which had me a little concerned. Then the first of many bombs fell.

Two days prior to the settlement, the bank had called Dozer in for a meeting. I was later to find out that the bank had demanded further security on the already agreed and signed business deal. This new demand was a requirement for the sale to proceed. Dozer was mad at the bank; this was to him, after all, an approved done deal. However, the bank had other nasty things in mind.

With the additional bank security, eventually provided by me, the sale now back on track. At the settlement held in the bank office, the bank manager made another change to our

339

agreement. At the last minute, the bank insisted that I personally cover a $50,000 security on the Cessna 402 lease.

This was bank extortion and manipulation at its worst, a move to further reduce and spread their lending risk.

Bull Dozer had given up his job, sold his house, and moved his family away from relations and old friends. This family had given up everything to buy a business, and a new life in Kununurra... The focus and decision of any future sale now lay firmly placed with me.

I had never experienced in my long business career this level of bank extortion. At this eleventh hour, I had little choice but to concede to the banks demand. I did however have a few conditions that both the Bank and Dozer were willingly agreed to.

I would sign the security if the bank and Dozer agreed to keep me informed of any possible default on the aircraft lease payments. In the event of a default and any suggested repossession, I should have first claim on purchasing the aircraft and or the business. A document then signed in accepting these conditions.

At that meeting, I made known to all parties that I would be available to offer any advice to help the business until Dozer felt confident. Unfortunately, this offer of help was never once called on.

Around ten months later Bull Dozer was starting to throw a track. He had managed to cause problems with his chief pilot Paul. Paul Roberts was a well-experienced professional pilot, being the best chief pilot K-Air ever had.

He was a well-respected man in his profession, over qualified for this small air charter job. I was happy that Paul had decided to remain as chief pilot, but just like me, he was a stickler for air safety and aviation rules that matter. The new owner Mr Dozer being made aware of this. He was also aware of the company motto, drilled into every new pilots head. "When in doubt don't." I might add a company motto that in the past has saved lives and possible aircraft damage.

***

The aircraft maintenance was slipping; the unpaid fuel bills were mounting, then the aircraft cross-hire accounts were unpaid, and urgent mandatory D of A paperwork not kept current... all were bad signs. Now heard on the town business gossip, Dozer was considering a business partnership with that same South African bloke I had seen around town last year. I tried to contact Dozer and warn him, but unfortunately, it was too late.

***

Lesley and I had months before planned our first real holiday in ten years. We had decided to visit our relations in the UK, to show them our children. On returning to Kununurra after seven weeks holiday, I was suddenly confronted with a huge shock... Kimberley Air Charter had failed. The company had become bankrupt, and the Cessna 402 sold off by the bank... The company I had created from nothing into the greatest and best air charter company in the Kimberley was gone.

Then the ultimate shock, on emptying my mailbox. There was a letter from the Commonwealth bank.

***

Dear Sir

We advise this bank is calling on the security given to the bank on ... as a lease security in the purchase of Cessna 402. We require you to deposit a sum of $50,000 into this bank account within one week from today's date to honour your commitment.

Sincerely

Your trusted Bank Manager

***

I was stunned. I rang the bank. The phone was immediately answered by some new young guy, who did not know who I was. While waiting to talk to the manager I tried some fishing, asking if the bank was now in the aircraft sales business. The young bank teller laughed, and then spilt out the current town gossip story.

The bank had repossessed a large aircraft from a company called Kimberley Air Charter, and then sold it to people in Darwin who at the time were servicing it. Apparently, the Darwin Company had refused to let the aircraft go until the repair bill paid in full.

341

My bank manager was indifferent about the current situation, not in the least interested in the fact that we had a binding agreement covering such an event. This matter was now in the hands of the banks debt recovery people; and due process will continue. I asked what the bank recovered from the sale, as by my reckoning the aircraft value should have easily cleared the debt.

I was advised that information was confidential, and a matter of bank business. However, he then quickly assured me my agreed security on the aircraft lease would most likely cover the shortfall.

A phone call to the Darwin aircraft company who ended up with the aircraft was to say the least, enlightening. I knew this company and owners well, having had considerable aircraft service work carried out there. Therefor this company were aware that K-Air had new owners. My enquiry was simple, did they wish to sell the Cessna 402, and if so for what price?

The casual reply blew me away.

Before accepting the banks offer to buy Cessna 402, they had already on-sold the aircraft to a flying school in Alice Springs, taking a quick profit of twenty-six thousand dollars.

I then phoned the flying school who knew all about the demise of K-Air, and reminding me the Cessna 402 still had the Kimberley Air Charter colours and insignia.

Just try to imagine my surprise when this flying school advised me the aircraft sold four days ago to an aircraft dealer in Adelaide. Apparently, this Adelaide dealer was looking for a cheap, large eight place aircraft for a parachute jumping school in Brisbane.

In the space of three weeks, this aircraft had sold four times, with a profit on each sale… and all the buyers were happy to pay. I advised the bank of this; however, their answer was firm. Pay the $50,000 security debt, failing which the bank will immediately initiate recovery action. The bank had immediately closed ranks, denying all responsibility.

***

The $50,000 security problem was eventually resolved some months later at a special meeting in Kununurra with the Commonwealth State manager for the bank. This was a stressful time; I had to prove the aircraft sold by the bank at well below the current market value. Also that this aircraft, as per the normal practice was not offered to the highest bidder. In addition, as per my agreement with the bank, I was not offered the first right of refusal in the event of a sale. Again as per our written agreement, the bank did not keep me informed on any defaults with the K-Air leasing payments of the Cessna 402

Giving this man Bull Dozer a chance to realise his dream was my huge and expensive error. I have since discovered you cannot help someone who does not wish to listen to basic well-proven business advice.

Unfortunately, this would not be the last time I would fall into this self-made trap. A trap causing a large money handling institution to latch-on in a face-saving, come hell or total destruction legal battle. This type of action obviously taken in an attempt to justify their poor employee decisions, then coming after your blood as they already have all your money, and want more. Seemingly, these institutions prefer to close ranks against common sense in some sort of bent way, to defend their stupid actions and wrong business decisions.

Beware the self-important person given a power that can personally affect your pocket and future lifestyle. A power that cost them nothing but time waiting on (dead men's boots promotion.) They take no responsibility for their actions, are poor advisors and are tormentors of the business world. Some are silly enough to think they can understand, and actually run a business... until they try.

Meanwhile I had no option but to take the massive loss of more than I had received for the sale of Kimberley Air Charter... and the disgrace that I was the creator of this now failed business.

***

You win some and you lose some. In any event, I will still have my memories, and personal experiences of those great times. Just remember the priorities in this your only life.

Your family, your friends, and your health are far more important than money. It just annoys me how easily I manage to keep losing my hard-earned money, and how easily others manage to get their bloody hands on it.

...Back to the Gold Mine...

Chapter Eight:

Back to the Gold Mine

The landing was to be at Ruby Station again as the Majeed strip was still not finished. Talking to Captain Mannering on the HF radio, he advised the station manager had approved the landing and all was in order, assuring me there will not be a repeat of my last visit.

This time Captain Mannering came to pick me up in person, still in his old footy shorts and thongs, but this time he had on additional dress code, a dirty wife-beater blue singlet.

I was trying to imagine this grubby bloke in the Queens Guard, polished boots, bright red tunic, and polished brass buttons, with a busby on his head.

As he stepped down from his Toyota to greet me, I was again trying to visualise him sitting on an immaculate black horse at attention with sabre drawn.

In the previous two weeks since my last visit to Majeed, it appeared to me that Captain Mannering had washed neither his clothes nor himself, and his grunge stubble was now almost a full beard.

'Hello Niven, so awfully nice to see you again, we have some proposals to offer you.'

Mannering greeted me like an old friend, again my alert antenna was shouting; beware those who come offering gifts.

On the way to the Majeed mine, Captain Mannering added a new aspect to our business relationship. His proposal was a bit odd, but sounded better delivered in his crisp upper-class British accent.

'Niven I was wondering, would you consider your charter company being the official confidential carriers for the Majeed gold mine.'

This sounded to me like a charter contract. Then remembering what equipment they had to extract gold, and the type people who work there. I was suspicious, how could this mine afford a regular air charter service, hell, were they into drugs. If so, I do not want any part of this. I should ask more questions.

'Please excuse my Australian bush ignorance, but what is an "official confidential carrier." What would this job entail?'

Captain Mannering reduced the speed of the Toyota to a crawl, a move to give him time to implant his plan into my slow brain well before arriving at the mine.

'We will require regular flights in and out of the gold mine. The destinations will be Darwin, Kununurra, Halls Creek, Broome, and Port Hedland. Also, and most important Niven, these flights will need to be most confidential.'

My attitude and disinterested look on my face caused Mannering to pull over under a shady tree. This was obviously going to take some time and effort to make me understand the complexities of his "official confidential carrier" proposal.

I was thinking; this secret crap was not my style. Anyway, I had more than enough of this childish stuff in my West Coast Surveys diamond claim pegging days.

This may be a good time to let Captain Mannering know about the Kimberley Air Charter sale. Mannering appeared quite surprised, as I gave him a full updated account on the settlement and contact details of the new owner.

'Do I understand correctly old chap; you have sold your air charter business, so you no longer own an aircraft.'

'Well not quite, as I still own two aircraft, which are contracted to the new owner as a cross hire. I will still have their use to service my hire fleet and radio clients. However, the sale contract prohibits me from entering into any commercial air charter work.'

I could see this man was in deep thought. I think that somehow I had managed to throw a large spanner into his well-planned game, whatever it was.

Last week, in my casual phone calls to business friends in and around Perth. I asked everyone and anyone if they knew, or had heard of a David Michael's. The response had me more than a little alarmed. Even my mother-in-law knew of his name from newspapers. What was he doing up here? Apart from hiding, I soon found out he had another important agenda... to sell the Majeed gold lease at a vast profit.

***

'David, I can no longer offer you a flight for payment. I am no longer an air charter operator. From now on, my flying will only be a means to service my distant clients.

I have advised the new owner to get in touch with you by radio. Right now we should continue into the mine and install this radio-phone gear, as I must be leaving soon.'

Forty minutes later the Majeed mine was connect by HF radiophone to the world. Mannering and the others watching were impressed as I demonstrated how the phone worked.

I must admit it was one of my better installations, or was it, as this was the ideal time-of-the-year for best HF radio reception. I sensed that Mannering had something to say, and sure enough...

'Niven, I understand you are flying on to Port Hedland on business. Would you mind taking our man Gary with you, assuming you have a spare seat? Gary will have with him around fifty kilos of mine samples for Perth analysis.'

Samples eh, he was having samples analysed maybe they have struck gold... that was interesting.

'That will be okay I have plenty of room, but we will have to get going soon as I want to get back to Kununurra before last light. Also I would like to have a look at your new Majeed airstrip.'

***

The new airstrip was right alongside the mine, and it looked good. The only thing was; someone had decided to build it in the middle of the only patch of thick bush around... why?

I paced the strip out, it was over eight-hundred metres, around two-thousand seven hundred feet long. There was no doubt; it was certainly long enough, but it was around three metres too narrow for a registered ALA.

In addition, the approaches, both ends needed some trees topped or knocked down. However, the most important thing was; they had built it facing the wrong bloody direction, by not considering the prevailing local winds... This airstrip effort could never be a registered airstrip, an ALA (Authorised landing area.)

I just had to ask Mannering why he had built this strip this way, against all the information I had supplied.

'I had no say in the matter Niven. The Jah made the final decision on everything. He wanted the airstrip hidden, best as possible from the air. The matter was final.'

Shit, why try to hide an airstrip? This airstrip was now limited in its use, not being an ALA. Commercial flights cannot land their aircraft, as the aircraft insurance companies will not accept this risk... I thought, why build an airstrip at all.

Mannering soon provided an answer.

'The way I have been told, is this airstrip can still be used. The only matter is it will not be a registered airstrip. Even if it did meet all the requirements, the Jah would not want it registered. In addition, there have already been two small aircraft in and out of this strip in the last few days. Now you have had a look, would you use this strip?'

What was going on? I could see the strip was usable enough, just that with a little or no extra effort, they could have made it into a normal approved ALA. Captain Mannering obviously knew that... I was again suspicious.

'The Jah's bulldozer work and your grader skills have turned out a nice flat strip. If you could just trim the trees a little at each end, and provide a windsock. Yes, I would land here; I have landed on far worse.

Anyway, why build a strip that is hard to see alongside a gold mine? Another thing is assured; this new Majeed airstrip will still be plotted onto all the WAC maps for all pilots to see and consider.'

***

On the long flight to Port Hedland Gary never stopped talking. A time when I regret forgetting my noise-cancelling headphones, I let the drone of the aircraft and the drone of Gary's nonstop talking drift into the background. With the weather calm and the autopilot set, I was lulled into a reflective state, admiring the magnificent view while thinking of things.

The last words of Mannering still had me confused. When I explained everyone would know of his airstrip, as it must have a name. He wanted the new Majeed airstrip named Concert, and could I kindly attend to that matter when text time I lodged a flight plan to the mine.

Captain Mannering might be a little grubby and in need of a shower. However, it was obvious the Captain remained well informed on current flight rules. As such, it would appear he is no dill when it came to conforming to bureaucracy. I could hear a distant voice...

'Are you listening to me, I said why are we flying North-West to the coast. We should be flying almost due West.'

Gary was breaking into my deep and suspicious thoughts; provoking an instant response...I was angry at this intrusion and the diversion from my suspicious thoughts. I tersely responded.

'Do you think I am lost? I have seen enough of the Great Sandy Desert in my years up here. I am aware it is a little longer this way but I much prefer to fly down the coast on a beautiful day like this... Anyway this is my flight; you are here travelling as my guest.'

Thinking that should shut him up; then again, this bloke was getting on my tits with his continual banter all about himself. I must admit though, Gary does have a well-developed sense of direction, even if he does have a lot to say.

This ability was later to prove most useful, as his hobby was finding things... odd things.

I sensed that Gary got my drift; I was not interested in his chatter or hobbies. Then as chatty people like Gary often do... he hiked the interest level up a few notches.

The next time he opened his mouth was to drop a bombshell… several bombshells.

'Niven, do you know that right now we are on a gold production run, the sixth one I have done in three months. Here let me show you last week's alluvial mining effort.'

With that, he quickly reached into one of the two large cardboard boxes on the rear seats, held in with the seatbelt harnesses. Then produced what looked like a cigar box. He held the box under my nose and flipped open the lid.

The bloody box was almost full of gold particles of all sizes. He then placed the box in my hand; no doubt to convince me with what I guessed was over two kilos in weight of gold.

By my slick calculation, at today's price of about four-hundred and thirty dollars an ounce. What I was holding was worth about thirty- thousand dollars.

Gary had played his hand well; I was gob-smacked. A glance out the aircraft window confirmed I had overflown the Northern coast of Australia. I was now about ten miles on my way to Indonesia.

Casually reaching out, I turned the heading bug on the autopilot to regain my intended flight track; the Cessna immediately executed a perfect rate one turn. Gary acted swiftly at this sudden movement and grabbed the box of gold from my hand.

'Shit man; be careful, we don't want this gold spread all over the floor of this aircraft. We would probably lose a couple of grand in the cracks.'

'What bloody cracks?' I responded with anger. 'There are no cracks in my aeroplane mate.'

What is this bloody idiot of a person on about? This statement to me almost amounted to an insult. A suitable and immediate response was called for.

'I can assure you of this Gary, there are no cracks in my aircraft for things to fall through. However, the same could not be said of this strange Majeed bloody gold mine, since it is full of cracks. Nothing to me adds up.

This Jah bloke has owned the place for almost three years, apparently using the location as his personal bulldozer play sandbox. Then this old mine, has suddenly after one-hundred and twenty-three years struck commercial quantities gold! Then we have the large contingent of expert personnel who just appeared from out of nowhere that now work there… including you.'

***

Gary had shut up, it was almost like silence. There was only the sound of the droning aircraft engine and the wind slipping past the hull.

I could see in his eyes that my simple observation of the Majeed events were a mighty concern. In fact, I feared that I had opened a Pandora's Box. Gary was searching for a believable and acceptable answer, no doubt this time to shut me up.

'If I tell you, you must promise not to pass this information on to anyone. You must also remain quiet about your thoughts and views on the Majeed gold mine.'

'Okay, if it's not illegal or can harm someone, then I agree.'

What followed next was another bomb of exploding interest. Gary advised me the Majeed mine was for sale, and what's more, they had a possible buyer.

We both sat there looking at each other, Gary was expecting some sort of an answer.

My mind snapped back about five months to that sly geo Greg, who in Kununurra had hired one of my Toyota's and then headed down to Halls Creek. From memory, this bloke was looking to buy producing gold tenements… The other thing was old Sam the mine manager knew him, and did not like Greg. Then there was the fact that from what I could gather, Sam was no longer working at the Majeed mine.

My bet is this Greg bloke was the possible buyer. Should I divulge this snippet of knowledge to Gary, maybe not? At least Gary may now understand about my nosey interest in all the recent Majeed activity. Even so, I must first try to find out what all the activity is about, for what purpose, and why? I was soon to find out.

***

On landing at Port Hedland, I taxied over to the avionics service building. Gary asked me how long I would stay adding he might need a lift back to Majeed. I told him I would be flying back within two hours and headed for the terminal. The new owner of my Piper Aztec met me at the terminal. He was busy apologising that the aircraft was not there being still on a charter, but due back soon. He suggested that I go have a chat with the avionics repair people to sort out the reported problem.

The avionics service was small, owned and run by Fred, his wife, and their two sons. I had quite a bit of radio work carried out by them over the years, and knew them well.

'Hi Fred, I have come down from Kununurra to sort out a problem on my old Piper Aztec RYR, apparently both the VHF radios only work when they feel like it. Also I will pay you for any work done to date.'

'No worries mate, that problem was fixed early this morning when I cut the pilots headset cord into six inch bits and handed it all bloody back to him. I lent him another headset that works just fine' I don't know what that bigheaded shit of a pilot is going to tell his boss when he gets back? Looks like you came all the way down here for nothing.'

Oh dear I thought, this must be another example of "pilot error" or basic stupidity. You know I have always said that the most useful asset a person can have, and not just by a pilot, I mean by anybody, is common sense. Those that are fortunate to have this gift know you have to be born with it. Unfortunately, common sense can't be taught, and taught answers and rules do not resolve all of life's tricky problems.

'Looks like I have a couple of hours to burn before I fly back to Kununurra. Fred, I have a problem with my Cessna 182RG for you. Have you ever come across a piece of radio or navigation equipment that time and again, works okay in a bench test then fails again shortly after it's installed in the aircraft? I would like to get my Cessna ADF (automatic direction finder) performing as it used to... any ideas.

'Here' handing me a long thin Philips screwdriver. 'Pull the bastard out and I'll have a look at it.'

Three minutes later, it was in Fred's hands. I could tell Fred was an old time avionics technician, the first thing he did was smell the ADF. Next, he shook the thing aggressively and listened for any loose bits. Then he gestured me to follow him into his workshop. Everything was as expected, except all the test equipment was old ex-military surplus AWA vintage, except for the strange gadget he reached for.

I had seen and used this instrument many times; it was for inspecting engine cylinder bores through sparkplug holes. It was a flexible bore scope. Fred had attached a bore scope to a pair of modified goggles, and was inspecting in magnified detail the circuit board edge connecter, and then he gave out a well-used ah ha, followed by...

'There's your problem mate, the bloody edge connector contacts are all worn and fucked. I've seen this a few times before. Tell me, was that Cessna 182RG of yours built between 1978 and 1981? Cause if it was, they had a heap of em with this same problem.'

He then removed his homemade gadget and gave his accurate diagnosis.

'I'm betting my left knacker the radio stack connector socket is crimped up too tight and the edge socket can't move with the ADF unit. You'll need to loosen off the frame connector bolts a bit to let her float about. Just solder-tin the worn edge connector on the ADF for now to get you going, fix it proper later on.'

That is just what I did; I was then rewarded with the best performing ADF I have ever had on this aircraft. It was just as well, as I would shortly need a fully functioning ADF. I am now convinced that a good nose, ear, and eye with lashings of common sense can fix almost anything.

***

Gary turned up just as I was testing my newly fixed ADF; I was a bit cheerful now that my long flight had proved worthwhile. Gary was a little excited... I was suspicious. He then rummaged around in a backpack I had never seen before, and pulled out a folder of documents held together with an old elastic band.

He handed me the first of several faded black and white crumpled photos. It was a typical world-war two snapshot, a young Aussie digger in army tropical uniform posing with a wide grin. What was in the background was obviously the point of interest, being two spitfire mark four aircraft. The most interesting point was the huge armoured hanger doors set into the rock face behind the aircraft. The first photo had a note scrawled on the back, Great Sandy Desert 1942.

Seven photographs showed various angles of this obviously secret 1942 WW2 aerodrome. One photo that took my interest was a photo of a stripped down spitfire in a wooden crate, apparently mothballed. The photos showed huge amounts of armaments and ammunition stacked in wooden MoD boxes.

'How the hell did you get a hold of these, and where is the location?'

Gary was enjoying the moment, soaking up the sensation effect, creating a mode of want and intrigue. This was not my scene; I do not like playing guessing games. If this bloke had something to say, then he should say it. For some reason I suspected his plan included me, I then handed back the photos.

'Right let's go; the Cessna is fuelled up and the flight plan in. If you are still coming along… jump in.'

The confused look on Gary's face was worth my effort as Gary opened up immediately.

'Okay, I got the photos off an old digger in the pub last month; the old bloke was a good mate of my dad. He knew I liked the bush and searching for things, he thought I might like them, especially when he told me that he was the bloke in the pictures.'

Gary told me a great story about the old digger's wartime activities in the top end of Australia. Apparently, at that time, the Australian Labor party favoured a capitulation, defeatist plan called the "Brisbane line." Sitting on the coast were Truscott and Darwin, at that time, the only two known large operational RAAF air bases in the north.

Within the agreed capitulation plan; the Australian government decided, these bases would fall to the Japanese. The old digger was part of a special forward detachment of engineers given the task of preparing a hidden catchment of fighting equipment, fuel, and provisions to fight a future rear-guard guerrilla action against the Japanese occupation of Northern Australia.

The old digger had no idea where the base was, except it was north of Percival lakes in the Great Sandy Desert. However, Gary had carried out some detailed research and had taken clues from the old photos, zeroing in on a likely location. From the map he unfolded on the front seat of the Cessna, the likely location calculated at only some fifty miles off my intended track up to Halls Creek.

***

Here we go again; drawn into another crazy adventure, there was no thought of refusal. Especially when Gary listed all the equipment secretly buried at this wartime location. We could be rich, just imagine owning a new Mark four spitfire?

Gary was good with maps, and offered to navigate to the location, which just happened to be in the middle of the Great Sandy Desert. This is when I thanked the Gods for a fully functioning ADF. From this vast lonely desert position, I will have strong signals from Port Hedland, Broome, Derby, and Halls Creek. With a few lines on my map and some simple sums, I knew my exact position to within half a mile.

At the plotted location, and flying slow and low at five hundred feet, we then decided on flying a grid search pattern. I had no idea what I should look for, and just followed Gary's instructions. There were no roads or tracks to see, and I came to thinking this would have been a perfect spot to hide from any Japs.

After nearly two hours flying low grids and many with photo taken, I advised Gary that fuel determined we must continue on to Halls Creek. About an hour later, I dropped Gary off at the Halls Creek airstrip, his parting comment was "better luck next time," I had no idea he was serious. It was only a week later I found out that Gary no longer worked for the Majeed mine, then never hearing anything again from Gary until around two years later.

I accidently bumped into Gary again in the Travelodge bar in Darwin. Gary was just the same talkative bloke, except he was involved in a new exciting adventure. This time it was a wartime Japanese sub, sunk about one hundred miles off Darwin. As the story goes, this sub was one of two Jap sub's laying mines at the entry to Darwin harbor. As with most vessels at that time, they carried tradable valuables, in this case it was believed to be one hundred kilos of gold, and mercury to use as currency for when in trouble in foreign waters.

He showed me a crisp new aerial photo of a distinct submarine shape laying in about seventy metres of clear water. Apparently, this was the second Jap sub; thought to be the sister sub the L-123 sank in January 1942, and never found, or had returned to its base. Was I interested in flying some survey work and time for twenty-five percent of the gains? It was a simple and short answer...no.

In 2011, the Darwin NT News reported the discovery of this second sub; the article mentioned that our Australian Navy divers were not the first to visit this site. The exact location now kept secret as the site now declared as a war gravesite.

Did Gary get there first... who would know... maybe...?

Chapter Nine:

Was that gunfire?

About two weeks after dropping Gary off in Halls Creek, I had an office radio call from Captain Mannering at the Majeed gold mine. He had heard that I was flying down to Broome, then anticipating my next question. He added, he was simply placing an order for refreshments at the Hotel Kununurra, and overheard that I was flying down to Broome tomorrow on some Tropicana Hotel business.

Would I be so kind and pick-up a geologist from Broome and fly him to the Majeed mine, landing at the Concert mine strip. While there, could I resolve a small problem with the radio/phone thing?

I agreed providing that the Concert strip had the approach trees at both ends trimmed as previously explained, he assured me this had already been done.

I guess this would be a good time to explain why the Tropicana in Broome needed my services. Well, as the story goes at that time there was no TV in Broome.

The Tropicana being only recently built offering new hotel accommodation with everything except TV. Frank the owner demanded an urgent quote for installing cable TV to all the rooms. My trimmed down quote was explosively received with Frank's rapid puff panic smoking, and a bout of popeyed coughing.

'Fuck you Dallas, that's almost what it cost me to build the damn place; there must be a cheaper way, what did you charge Weymouth for his TV on VRD station?'

'That was a cattle station in the middle of nowhere Frank; you can get away with things in the bush. Your pub is in a coastal tourist town.'

I was wasting my time explaining anything. If TV could be installed a cheaper way, then Frank wanted it done that way. Therefore, bending to popular demand, and a few extra dollars, the TV system I had used on VRD station, but somewhat modified, being eventually installed at the Tropicana.

As it happened, there was now there was a big big problem brewing in Broome. Ninety-five percent of the Broome residents were mad and complaining. They were complaining that they could not get any TV, the other five percent were very happy... except for the quality.

You see, the Tropicana TV I installed was simply created by running 300 Ohm TV antenna ribbon cable through the hotel roof-space. This antenna cable then connected to a modified TV channel modulator and a reversed TV antenna booster. The result was a neat low power transmitted TV signal... simple eh.

Not so simple; apparently my TV handiwork was so good that people three streets away from the Tropicana suddenly found they could get two channels of reasonable quality TV.

Then the trouble started. You see all those people in Broome who could not get TV, (about 98%) and the ones who received poor TV complained to the ABC, that's right The Australian Broadcasting Corporation.

It was easy for them to figure out who was transmitting the TV in the town. Frank then accused of unlawfully transmitting TV without a broadcasters licence. This was the reason why I had to fly down to Broome... to turn the bloody thing off before we all ended up in jail.

***

It was easy to spot Denis the geologist; he was sitting all alone in the Tropicana cave bar, dressed in the usual geo uniform, khaki shirt, long pants, and desert boots. This time I noted well used indicating the man had been around a bit. He was in his early thirties, very tall, with scholarly glasses. I introduced myself, offering to replace his small beer, which looked warm.

Denis was an easy-going young man of few words, nodding an okay; he then noted my soft drink and asked if I would like to have a drink. This bloke was checking me out, I got the distinct impression he thought I was a wowser, or a religious abstainer.

'No, no I will have my usual OP rum and coke when I get back home. I still have to face a long journey back to Kununurra.'

Denis mumbled that he was willing to do his bit with the driving, I then realised that something was wrong; he had no idea we were flying directly to the Majeed gold mine. I said we should go after these drinks as I had completed my work in Broome. A quick word with the manager, who then offered us a lift to the airport.

Denis heard the offer and now looked worried... no terrified. What little he said previously now reduced to an uncomfortable hush.

***

When Denis first caught sight of the Cessna, I knew then he was fearful of flying in a small aircraft. This was a two and a half hour flight, and Denis was a big bloke. I needed to sort this problem out on the ground, and not in the air.

I have had some bad experiences with fear of flying passengers; I would say that every pilot has seen this phobia in their passengers at some time or other.

It is all about how you as the pilot handle the escalating situation, or how good the passenger is at hiding it. Some people try hard to cover their fear, and get through the ordeal. Others do not make it, for example, these are a few true stories I have experienced with this problem.

***

On this particular occasion, I had to pick up two new hire fleet Toyota Landcruisers from Darwin needing the help of a second driver. Big Cecil, all six foot three of him agreed to drive the trade-in up and the new vehicle back. I then by chance, in a sudden change of plan I sold both trade-in vehicles locally. Cecil was a very good refrigeration engineer but I was soon to find out also a terrified flyer.

Like most Australian males of his vintage it was not manly to admit fear, so what is a man to do; that's right, simply get drunk as a skunk before boarding the plane.

On the short forty-five minute jet flight to Darwin, Cecil was supposed to sit next to me; however, he became very loud and kept walking up and down the aircraft aisle.

In fear, he consumed a further two full large bottles of the free promotional bubbly, which caused him to exit the Fokker Fellowship in Darwin by falling down the exit stairs. Cecil was then taken to the Darwin passenger terminal unconscious in a wheelchair. There we met up with my good, but confused friend Des Nudl who had arrived to give us a lift to back his place

Cecil had just come-to, then realising that he was now safe on the ground, headed straight to the bar to celebrate his safe arrival in Darwin.

***

On another occasion, I had a passenger in a total out of total control situation. This time it was Gary; Frank's spoilt know-it-all seventeen-year-old son. This idiot lost it during a difficult landing, creating a very dangerous problem.

Frank, his son, and his hotel manager Greg joined me on a business trip to Argyle diamond mine in my Cessna RG. Gary was keen to sit in the right hand co-pilot seat telling me during the flight out all about his great knowledge of flying.

Unfortunately, we had stayed thirty minutes longer than intended at the Argyle mine. Then receiving a poor weather forecast of a tropical front building quickly at the Kununurra end, we needed to depart Argyle immediately. There was another problem. Greg the Hotel manager was due to catch the mid-day Darwin flight and by my calculation, I had planned to land Kununurra around ten minutes before the Jet's departure.

The Kununurra ATIS (automatic terminal information service) was favouring runway 30 with a twelve-knot crosswind gusting to eighteen knots. Entering the circuit, I noticed the Jet turning on the hardstand and radioed the jet pilot advising I had a passenger for his Darwin flight. The jet pilot confirmed that he was departing a little early, as a weather front was heading this way, but agreed to hold for a few minutes.

On the final approach to runway 30 the wind started gusting a little as expected; however, everything was under control. To me this was just another chance to get in some crosswind practice, and the only chance to get Greg on that Jet.

Just before rudder kicking the aircraft straight for a normal touchdown, Gary started shouting, 'you idiot, you're not in line with the airstrip'... and then grabbed the control column. While I was fighting to regain control from the strong young man, the first wave of squalling rain started sweeping the airfield in a torrential thunderous downpour, adding to the drama.

I yelled out at the top of my lungs, (get this fucking shithead off the controls, or we are all dead, unless you think he can fly this aircraft better than I can?)'

That did it Greg the manager sitting directly behind Gary put him in a firm half-nelson left-arm choke while using his right hand to prise one hand off the control column. Frank, sitting behind me had seized-up in terror with Greg yelling, 'Frank, get his other hand of the fucking steering wheel.'

Correcting this messy landing was a miracle of my brilliant flying ability, or possibly you might wish to believe it could have been just good luck. Greg did catch his Darwin flight and Gary in some form of reduced embarrassment told the town how crappy a pilot I was.

Looking up at the six foot six inch Denis, I concluded it was time we had a few pre-flight words.

'Denis, you don't look comfortable about flying in a small aircraft? I on the other hand having had previous experience in these matters do not like to fly with someone with such a fear condition.'

Denis stared at me in silence with a blank look on his face. I was wondering what was going through his mind at this very moment... I did not have long to wait.

'Niven, I must get to the Majeed mine today; it's now a matter of urgency. I am not afraid of flying; I just don't like small places I can't get out of when I want to. In addition, I don't like to be in situations that I have no form of control. Lastly, I would have preferred some time to prepare for this light aircraft flight.'

I was thinking; this bloke does not know the definition that describes, fear of flying. Denis was obviously a man of measured trust and self-control; I guess the point now, was how much control he had over his own fear of flying... I decided to give Denis a quick test.

'Denis, I will be departing within ten minutes, so if you wish to come along, you will need to convince me that you can keep yourself under control. As the pilot in command, I have over two thousand hours hands-on flying experience in the Kimberley with small aircraft... and never had a crash.

I admit there have been a few incidents and narrow escapes in my flying career. Incidents that have served to remind me that nothing is perfect or should be left to chance; as such, I have learned much from these few experiences, staying alive by resolving any potential problems on the ground... just like we are discussing right now.

Any human leaving the ground for sustained flight is in an un-natural state. Therefore, is subject to a higher level of stress than if they just remained on the ground or in bed.

However, it is a fact that in this world, far more humans die in bus related road traffic accidents each year, than in all known aircraft crashes. Then again, I suppose riding to work on a bus is also un-natural, and yet you still trust the bus driver.'

Without so much as a smile, Denis threw his backpack on the rear seat and climbed into the co-pilot seat, so he must have formed a convincing reply..., which was.

'Niven, I can get off a bus anytime I want, and the bloody bus is on the ground. Okay, I will trust you.' He then firmly replied, 'and I promise not to go berserk in the air, just let me know what you are about to do first, and no surprises... okay.'

'Right then Denis, let's go. Nonetheless, you must agree to tell me if you get the urge to go outside. I will need to put all my aviation maps away first, I only have one good set and can't have them blow away, sucked out of an open door..'

***

We roared off into the beautiful blue sky with Denis sitting bolt upright and ridged, looking straight ahead through the windscreen. He was terrified, and so was I, a feeling fully justified a little later on in this peaceful flight.

For two long hours, Denis had said nothing and just stared ahead. I was careful not to make any quick moves, flying the Cessna RG in as cool a manner as I could, cruising along in steady flight at a brisk one-hundred and forty-five knots maintaining an altitude of seven-thousand feet...

At that point in the flight, we were only some twenty-two minutes out from Majeed, and I must start my decent soon for a smooth approach into the new Majeed mine airstrip called Concert.

I slowly reduced engine power for the decent; this action stirred Denis into a sudden vocal reaction.

'What was that is the engine okay? The noise has changed.'

Well howdy know, so this was his pent-up flying terror... the landing. Well I am good at landing the Cessna RG, I've done it over six-hundred times on this same aircraft, and I told Denis that.

Quick as a flash, he wanted to know how many times I had landed at the Majeed mine. That was a tricky question; a question I was not about to answer, as this was going be my first.

I rapidly changed the conversation drift, confirming we were now on a controlled decent, about eighteen minutes out from the Concert airstrip, then asking if he would like to feel the controls.

I was quite surprised when Denis accepted my offer taking the control yoke with both hands; even more surprised how gentle he was.

He was convinced that I was somehow steering the aircraft, then added the autopilot must be doing the steering. I then held my hands in the air, pointing to the autopilot

363

disconnect flag, and assured him he had full control of the aircraft.

Then it happened, I had witnessed this same experience a few times in the past. Denis then developed a huge grin from ear-to-ear; he was experiencing that special first moment.

The amazing feeling of being in control of an aircraft, and loved it… Had I ignited a new passion in his life… was this the end of his fear of flying, would he someday wish to become a pilot?

Wrong… as I pointed out over the nose of the aircraft to the small dirt airstrip called Concert, and suddenly sensed and smelt the odour of fear. A quick glance at Denis with hands balled into fists of white knuckles had me more than a little concerned. I must get this aircraft on the ground, and quickly.

Captain Mannering answered my radio call to the Majeed mine instantly with a staccato of questions.

'By Jove Niven are we happy to hear from you, things are a little hot down here; is the geologist with you, how far away are you, when will you arrive, over.'

'Affirmative, Denis the geologist is on-board and our ETA is ten minutes to landing Concert. What is the wind direction and ground temperature? err over old chap.'

'I do believe the wind is coming from the east old chap; I did as you asked and placed bright orange survey ribbons in a tree. The temperature on the ground it is rather hot, but we can handle it, oh, I see what you mean… it is about twenty-eight degrees Celsius… over.'

I was a bit suspicious, but had other things on my mind. A quick glance at Denis confirmed he had reduced his borderline terror, down to basic fear; I must somehow keep this situation under control.

The normal procedure was to fly a circuit, checking the strip prior to landing. However, I had previously walked the airstrip and knew Kimberley Air Charter had recently landed at the new Majeed Concert strip. Deciding in view of this increasing urgency to fly a direct in landing.

Gently descending on final approach I reminded Denis that he promised not to go berserk, and expected him to keep his word. There was no reply but a glance at him had me more than worried. His eyes were all but bulging from his head. This man was fighting for control of his own fear.

The landing was one of my better arrivals, complemented by a few loud random pops, thought to be from the engine. I taxied to the side apron and shut the engine down.

Denis was elated, and a beaming smile flashed across his sweaty face. A volley of loud cracks instantly disrupted his look of utter relief. I thought that's odd, nevertheless always, a good sign, happy the noise was not related to my aircraft.

***

With both aircraft doors open we then stepped out; I started looking around for the greeting party... just then I heard a distinctive posh voice call in a loud whisper.

'Niven, over this way old chap, I looked towards the voice and picked-out Captain Mannering hiding behind a bush. 'Hurry the Neanderthals are shooting at us.'

Mannering wearing only a pair of dirty footy shorts and rubber thongs, then instantly dropped out of sight as three high-powered shots rang out. The volley of bullets then slammed into a tree, splintering the bark next to where Mannering was previously standing.

I took two steps towards Mannering then realising that's where the mad Queenslanders were aiming and stopped.

Looking around, I noted Denis frozen to the spot. His arms were in the air in a gesture of surrender, eyes bulging, and a large dark stain began spreading in his crotch area of his khaki geo pants.

I had a fleetingly thought... now we both have something to be terrified about, the tense situation quickly saved by Mannering shouting at hillbillies in his crisp British accent...

'Steady on there you lot, this tall chap here is our promised geologist; this man is bringing the assay results for the mine, information proving the gold mine is indeed viable, that is to say for you not so smart types. The mine produces reasonable amounts of gold.

We should stop this childish action and all go to the camp to discuss this matter over a few OP rums like decent human beings.' Then like talking to a child. 'We have all had our playtime; now there is a good chappie do put away your big guns.'

The response was quick and clear, and came in a shrill reply from Grannie Neanderthal, and she spoke plainly, shouting across the airstrip.

'You bullshit pommy bastard, you git that geo bloke to talk to us about how much gold is out here... we will give you lot one bloody hour, then we're coming over, yah hear?'

There was a hiss, and an arrow imbedded itself into a tree, not a foot from Mannering's head. Then Grannie had the last word.

'Okay we'll put our guns away... for now. Another thing, git that plane outa here, it's fucking up our aim, and be sure that geo bloke stays put here.'

With the threat of death subsided for now, I walked over to Mannering as Denis ran past me into the bush. I was furious; this was all about their problems with the hillbillies and nothing to do with me.

'What the hell was that all about David? I will tell you right now if my aircraft ends up grounded by a bullet-hole, you can expect a large bill. Just as that old hillbilly woman has ordered, I am out of here.'

Mannering was grinning, no he was laughing at me; he was winding me up. I looked around for Denis, or any sign of the hillbillies but there was nobody to see, they had all disappeared.

'You have nothing to fear Niven; our shots went into the air only to let the Neanderthals know that we too were armed. Had those idiots wanted us dead we would most certainly be dead by now. They are all excellent marksmen; even the old grannie can shoot better than I can.'

Unlike Captain Mannering, I was not impressed with this silly game of macho action. Turning I headed for the Cessna to inspect for any damage and happy to find there was none. I then taxied back down the runway turned and departed the Concert Majeed airstrip never to return... ever.

***

One week later Lesley, the children and I went on our first ever trip back to the UK for a seven-week family reunion.

For me, it had been twenty-one years since leaving old England for Australia. My departure caused by the British Labour government increasing the cost of a pint of beer 25% to two bob a pint. At that time, you might describe that as an impulsive move. Nevertheless, one I have never regretted, being one of my better life decisions.

***

On my return to Kununurra, so many things had changed forever, including who now owned the Majeed goldmine in Halls Creek.

Another change was the story as previously told; that during my UK holiday, Kimberley Air Charter had failed, with the assets sold off by the bank. However, there were many more shockwaves to endure.

Greg the geo who at the start of this story was looking for promising gold leases to buy, was in fact the same interested party that Gary had mentioned on our flight to Port Hedland.

Although unknown to Gary, Greg was working for Peter B, the original owner of the Majeed gold lease, who had sold the mine to the Jah.

Peter, being a man not known around town as a fool in any sort of business transaction, went about acquiring his old gold claim back in another way. He simply contested the rights to the Majeed lease in the Wardens court, stating a powerful case for forfeiture… and won.

This matter was heard before Warden D.J. Reynolds on hearing number 17/88 folio 8 "*The matter is of sufficient gravity to justify forfeiture.*"

The Jah had lost his much-loved Majeed gold mine. However, the Jah had other larger and far more important matters of concern; he was just about to lose a far greater asset, his much-loved Murchison sheep Station.

Other things were starting to look bad. Apparently, further testing of the Majeed gold samples proved the previous gold assay tests were heavily salted to produce elevated gold sample returns. The Wardens Court were looking very closely at the people involved with the day-to-day running of the Majeed mine, including David Michaels (Captain Mannering.)

Sometime later, I thought about all of this complicated attempted sham. The only person who saved this whole matter from leading to a full police investigation was Peter B. He had for some time been working on acquiring the Majeed mine back, supposably not knowing about or relying on the false gold assay… did he know?

***

You have read this interesting story thus far, and now want to know how it relates to the "curse of gold" I will tell you. This story is odd in itself that no gold, other than a few alluvial grams ever found. The curse is in relation to the name of gold taken in vain, and the manipulation of our human greed for gold.

The elaborate plan, as to the existence of any gold at the Majeed mine, was a figment of David Michael's most active imagination… He should have been a fiction writer.

Old Sam the mine manager disappeared early in the plan, my guess is he would not have anything to do with this goldmine deception.

***

As for Gary, well he was an adventurer seeking anything that involved a possible treasure and a good story, especially if someone was paying the bills. Then we have Denis the geologist. I do not think Denis knew what was going on; he was just a manipulated messenger, ending up as a very frightened geologist messenger.

All of the gold displayed was to tempt a buyer; we think it came from the melting of Jah's gold trinkets. My involvement was a mess; a poor attempt to carefully groom me to provide a regular air service and pass-on gossip about fictitious gold shipments out of the Majeed gold mine.

***

In my view, the two Johns were drawn into the same elaborate plan to show a massive development at the mine with the arrival of a sixty-ton spiral gravity gold separator.

I guess we blokes from the bush were just too stupid to swallow the bait… probably a bit too complicated for us simple bush blokes to grasp.

***

All the Jah wanted, was to be the owner of a gold mine. He had no need for gold, thus becoming an innocent victim, ultimately leading to the loss of his Majeed gold mine. Other people in his employ were busy salting his mine samples in an attempt to raise the sale value... all for their own personal gain.

They had also taken great advantage by not advising the Jah that he must maintain a simple expenditure program to keep his mining lease. This was the beginning to the end of the Jah's love affair with Australia... The Jah is now living in a type of voluntary exile, and resides in Turkey... I wish him good health, and a long peaceful life.

***

As for the Queensland family of earthmoving hillbillies, who Captain Mannering affectionately described as the "Neanderthals" The Western Australian Police arrested the entire family. Their equipment and plant being firmly repossessed, and the family extradited to face a Queensland a court for stealing and possession of illegal firearms. Some say this was a smart move on Captain Mannering's part, otherwise he would have ran out of Band-Aids to cover his many future bullet holes.

***

Peter B had been involved with investing in small gold mines for many years. Peter had originally sold the mining lease to the Jah prior to becoming a target and eventually an unlucky victim of the blame someone Australian governments (bottom of the harbour) resolve.

His head then firmly placed on a government pike as a bad boy example. Peter acquired the gold lease back again; shortly after his release from an eight-month stint in jail for so-called tax evasion. For all his trouble, the mine lease contained the same amount of gold as when he first owned it... nil.

***

Jack Whiteman was involved with the Jah's Majeed mine as the caretaker, and mentioned in Folio 8 17/88, being the Warden's summery on the mines forfeiture as a reliable witness... The again witness for who?

In an earlier part of this book, at a time some two years later, Jack after finding a large gold nugget in the Halls Creek area, Jack was involved in a horrific accident, almost claiming his life… was this his fate, set for the future.

***

With the demise of Mukarram Jah, brought down partly by his own employees, in both Australia and Hyderabad India, this was a sad Australian ending for a great man.

All the Jah wanted was what he thought was a normal life. He did not want the power or extraordinary wealth he was born into, or to assume the expected position as the last Nizam of Hyderabad. Mukarram Jah just wanted to be a humble Australian sheep farmer. Sadly, events took that modest dream away from him.

***

David Michaels (Captain Mannering,) eventually went back working for Alan Bond as (The Toy Man.) I had David's mobile number for years and did have a few long chats about the old days at the Majeed gold mine.

I found that he had become increasingly suspicious about everything and everyone. His activities, and outrageous claims were difficult to follow, more so, when he eventually returned to England. However, he still described himself as some sort of ex-MI5 and SAS undercover agent, or spy.

In 2010, David Michaels was sadly found dead in his London flat. He had supposably fallen over in the bath, hitting his head and drowning… Was he really a secret agent, a spy? Did he know too much? What a miserable ending to the life of a most interesting man.

***

In this strange story of gold, everyone had lost something. For some, it was their health, while for others it was their time, name, and lifestyle. Then some had lost rational for reasoning, and finally their sanity, and for a few their life. With others, it was their dream of great wealth that was lost in a vast sea of hope.

We should all be careful. The curse of gold may be in just the name, and the wanting of this yellow metal. Then we must consider; does gold have a dark soul to keep?

Now do you believe that gold has no master?

***

Greed has much to say when opportunity listens, lifting its evil head to consider the succulent temptation of an easy gain.

In the end, who will eventually claim to be the rightful owner of this yellow metal?

Many may claim it, and many will ultimately hold this metal; however, nobody will ever be the master of gold.

….The Very End….

About the Author

I was born in Edinburgh Scotland, this making me a true Scotsman with rights to wear the Dallas Clan tartan.

My working background covers a number of trades and disciplines, with many years based in the north west of Australia. There I worked, owned, and operated; as the founder of a number of small, but varying types of business ventures. These ventures included a long career in RF communication systems, mining claim pegging, contracting to the mining industry, electrical and musical retail, aviation air charter, vehicle hire, and automotive sales and service.

After twenty odd years of ten hour days, and seven day working weeks. The family and I moved down to Perth Western Australia. There becoming a director/owner of yet another radio-systems sales and service company, "Communications Australia Pty Ltd." This new venture was promptly followed by a classic and vintage vehicles sales business. "The Toyshop." Then for some unknown reason, I drifted into the herbs and spice wholesale business, "Whittington's," and then into owning a Mexican restaurant "Zapata's."… Why, I really don't know.

I remain as planned, happily married with beautiful children, who have now given us beautiful grandchildren.
My hands-on diverse business background has provided me with a long list of interesting true-life experiences to write this, and other novels.

I am fortunate in having a wide range of odd life experiences. They go, well together with my sound technical input, and a wild and cynical imagination. This combination also offers me endless material to write another genre I have called. Convincing, modern, realistic fiction.

For those that are interested, yes, Dallas is a real Scottish name. Moreover, there is indeed a Dallas tartan, and there is a Dallas Scottish clan. Would you believe, there is also a town of Dallas near Forres in Scotland, and we do have a family crest (coat of arms.)

There is also a Niven Scottish clan, but not so flash, or having as much fame. Unless you count David Niven the well-known actor as a credit, being the author of, "The Moons a Balloon" and "Bring on the Empty Horses."

Strange as it may be, remembering the many odd things in my life that just sort-of happened to be, you could not beat having your family name being part of a real ancient town in Scotland. We cannot finish without the mention of the famous city of Dallas in America.

Well yes, that is odd too. You see George Mifflin Dallas 1792-1864 was Vice-President of America, to the 11th President James K. Polk, and believed to have given his name to the now famous city of Dallas in Texas. This man's great, great, great-grandfather was born in the small town of Dallas in Scotland having a direct lineage to Sir William de Ripley 1165 given lands on Dallas Scotland by King William the Lion.

Interesting, do you not think?

www.ingramcontent.com/pod-product-compliance
Lightning Source LLC
Chambersburg PA
CBHW021038090426
42738CB00006B/141